Le Chat qui désirait la lune

Pour recevoir notre catalogue
et son bon de commande
à chaque nouvelle parution,
écrire aux :

Éditions Corps 16
3 rue Lhomond 75005 Paris
Tél. 01 44 32 05 90
Fax 01 44 32 05 91

Vous pouvez également consulter
et vous procurer nos ouvrages
à l'adresse ci-dessus, du lundi au
vendredi de 9 h à 18 h.

ISBN 2-84057-428-4

JULIA DEULEY

Le Chat qui désirait la lune

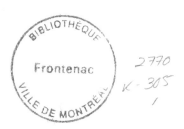

Nouvelles

latitudes
CORPS 16

à Sébastien et à Benoît

Il y a plus de choses sur la terre
et dans le ciel,
Horatio, que n'en rêve votre philosophie.

Hamlet
SHAKESPEARE

Voici mon secret. Il est très simple :
on ne voit bien qu'avec le cœur.
L'essentiel est invisible pour les yeux.

Le Petit Prince
ANTOINE DE SAINT-EXUPÉRY

Le Chat qui désirait la lune

Le compagnon félin de Montaigne portait, dit-on, sur son collier, l'inscription suivante : « Monsieur de Montaigne habite chez moi. » Je peux en dire autant à propos du chat qui m'accorda la faveur de partager mon existence.

Bien que je ne sois à ses yeux qu'une femelle bipède, c'est-à-dire d'une engeance peu fiable, passablement schizophrène et assez subalterne, j'ai le privilège de parler couramment le dialecte des chats, ce qui nous permet d'entretenir des relations courtoises et d'aborder tous les sujets, des plus futiles aux plus philosophiques. Ceci à mon plus grand bénéfice, car – le fait n'est pas discutable – les chats sont autrement plus subtils, plus libres, plus sages que nous autres pauvres humains, empêtrés dans nos contradictions, ficelés dans nos préjugés, et bétonnés dans notre arrogance.

J'ai rencontré ce chat en allant flâner au marché. Il déambulait tranquillement sur la place, toisant avec dédain la foule des commerçants, des badauds et ménagères. Je fus attirée par son superbe pelage noir, son allure fière et impassible, ses moustaches impériales, ses prunelles d'or liquide.

Nos regards se sont croisés, il m'a suivie. Il était partout chez lui.

Bizarrement, je me sentais son obligée. Dès nos premières conversations, il m'a tout de suite prévenue : « Si vous souhaitez goûter ma compagnie pendant une partie de la journée, sachez, ma chère, que mes nuits m'appartiennent. Vous ne devez sous aucun prétexte chercher à savoir ce que je fais ni où je vais du coucher au lever du soleil. »

En effet, chaque soir, il s'éclipsait mystérieusement. C'est bien plus tard qu'il s'est progressivement laissé aller aux confidences.

Nous avions institué un rituel immuable. Chaque matin, je lissais, peignais, brossais longuement sa magnifique fourrure. C'était une opération délicate qu'il savourait en ronronnant lascivement. Je ne l'avais jamais questionné sur ses virées nocturnes. Et c'est spontanément dans un de ces moments d'abandon matinal consacré à la cérémonie du brossage qu'il a commencé son récit.

« Puisque vous savez si bien me caresser, dit-il en miaulant voluptueusement, et puisque vous savez notre langage, c'est que vous avez eu quelque félin de haute lignée parmi vos ascendants, ou dans vos existences précédentes. Je puis donc vous raconter mon histoire. »

Étant de caractère espiègle et un rien persifleuse, je ne résistai pas au plaisir de le taquiner un peu.

« Vous êtes sûr que ma modeste oreille humaine, si pâle et disgracieuse comparée à votre pavillon fin et pointu, soit digne d'entendre vos discours ? »

Il fouetta l'air de sa queue et me fixa sans commentaire, avec un mélange d'agacement et de commisération.

« Vos babillages sont aussi caustiques et acidulés que ceux de certaines chattes que j'ai fréquentées. C'est l'effet, je suppose, de la nature féminine. Mais peu importe. Voyez-vous, ma chère, j'ai connu bien des tribulations et bien des aventures, car je suis un chat très intrépide et d'une curiosité sans bornes. J'ai visité bien des pays fabuleux, j'ai côtoyé des créatures fascinantes ou redoutables. J'ai prospecté des mondes dont les humains ne soupçonnent guère l'existence, décrypté bien des énigmes et découvert souvent la face cachée des choses. Les astronautes et les savants bipèdes affirment que la Lune est une grosse boule désertique et glacée, tournoyant sans fin dans l'abîme. Évidemment ils se trompent. Les poètes, qui sont déjà plus perspicaces, y ont vu tour à tour l'horloge des âmes égarées, le porte-manteau des enfers, la serrure verrouillant la porte de l'au-delà, le volant permettant de conduire l'attelage des dieux, l'hameçon scintillant où viennent s'accrocher les nébuleuses frétillantes, la marmite où mijote la friture des vents, ou la langue tirée par les démons dans les ténèbres. En fait, la Lune est une grande, une somptueuse chatte nocturne, qui somnole d'un œil, lovée dans son panier d'étoiles. Pendant d'interminables saisons, sur les gouttières, en haut des cheminées et à la cime des arbres, j'ai miaulé ma passion et chanté mon désir. Un soir, alors que j'étais pâmé dans la contemplation de ses courbes exquises, la Lune s'est lentement penchée vers moi en frisant ses moustaches de brise, et m'a murmuré : "Petit frère de chair, si tu veux me séduire et me posséder, tu dois explorer mes provinces. Mon territoire c'est celui des mythes, des contes et des légendes. Les hommes qui comprennent tout de travers les ont à peu près tous défigurés. Ta tâche, si tu tiens à me plaire, sera de visiter chaque nuit un conte, afin d'en rétablir le véritable sens." Voilà donc où je m'absente à la tombée du jour. Dans les domaines de la Lune, qui finira par m'accorder ses faveurs. »

Après cette confidence, nous avons, le chat et moi, conclu un accord : chaque matin, tandis que je lisserais et démêlerais sa fourrure, il me rapporterait ses aventures de la nuit, que je devrais transcrire fidèlement. Telle est l'origine de ces pages, dictées par le chat qui désirait la Lune.

Orphée

Il était une fois un poète, le plus grand et le plus sublime des poètes. Il s'appelait Orphée. Ses vers avaient la légèreté d'un bruissement d'ailes dans le feuillage, et la profondeur du ciel étoilé. Son chant était si mélodieux, si émouvant, qu'il subjuguait aussi bien les créatures vivantes que les anges, les spectres, les démons ou les goules. Il ne pouvait se déplacer sans attirer une foule d'admirateurs dont l'enthousiasme confinait à l'hystérie.

Honoré, adulé, Orphée n'avait qu'une passion humaine, c'était Eurydice.

Le couple était inséparable. Eurydice était d'une beauté pure et diaphane, avec des formes tout en grâce et en fragilité. Orphée l'aurait suivie au bout de l'univers.

Un soir, alors que les amants fêtaient en tête à tête le dernier triomphe de la vedette qui venait d'électriser des milliers de spectateurs, la jeune femme abusa de produits euphorisants. Elle fut foudroyée par une syncope. En dépit de ses efforts désespérés, Orphée fut incapable de la ranimer. L'esprit de sa bien-aimée flottait déjà à la dérive, vers le royaume des ombres – le pays d'où l'on ne revient pas.

Révolté contre un sort aussi cruel, Orphée refusa l'évidence et défia résolument les puissances de la mort.

Il descendrait au cœur de l'infernal séjour et convaincrait les forces ténébreuses de lui rendre son Eurydice.

Il lui fallait un guide.

Comme tous les chats, je connaissais les routes secrètes reliant les deux mondes, et je lui proposai de me suivre. Il faut dire que moi-même, je n'étais pas insensible à l'ineffable beauté de ses chants.

Il m'emboîta le pas sans hésiter. Je l'invitai fermement à jouer de la guitare et à psalmodier ses vers tout au long du parcours sans jamais s'arrêter.

Alors commença la descente vertigineuse pour pénétrer dans le tunnel de la lumière noire.

Tout commençait dans le métro, à la station sans nom. C'était un quai immense, très sombre et très vétuste, où convergeaient les âmes des trépassés en une masse hébétée, informe et glauque.

De longues rames hoquetantes et grinçantes s'arrêtaient régulièrement, où s'entassaient les défunts en partance. Un contrôleur blafard et décharné avec des yeux de braise sous une casquette mitée, prélevait directement le prix du transport : un souvenir pur et généreux. Les voyageurs insolvables étaient refoulés, condamnés à errer aux abords de la station, ou même expulsés vers la surface, sous forme de spectres.

La musique d'Orphée déjoua les réticences du contrôleur, qui nous laissa monter. Notre rame s'enfonça rapidement dans un espace obscur, une zone interdite au vivant. À l'extérieur, on devinait des silhouettes vagues et menaçantes qui tournoyaient en un hideux ballet et pressaient parfois leurs faces monstrueuses aux parois des wagons.

À l'autre bout du tunnel, sur un quai aux cloisons scintillantes et liquides, s'ouvrait un gigantesque sas où campait le gardien des abîmes.

C'était un être colossal aux formes changeantes surmonté de trois têtes livides. La première avait les yeux grands ouverts et sa bouche disait « oui ». La deuxième avait les paupières closes et sa bouche disait « non ». La troisième avait un œil ouvert, un œil fermé. Ses lèvres proféraient « peut-être ».

Pour passer, les âmes devaient offrir en pâture à cette créature vorace leur part d'enfance. Toutes celles qui avaient perdu la leur en cours de route étaient impitoyablement dévorées.

La voix et la guitare de mon compagnon surent amadouer ce prédateur d'outre-vie.

Nous étions maintenant dans une région crépusculaire, hantée de grands oiseaux multicolores au bec crochu et acéré, qui virevoltaient frénétiquement au-dessus de la foule. Ces volatiles plongeaient brusquement pour lacérer, fouiller, picorer les crânes qu'ils vidaient de leur mémoire. Ces souvenirs étaient ensuite éparpillés aux quatre vents de l'éternité, dans l'incessant ouragan des existences futures en gestation.

Les mélodies du poète éloignèrent ces féroces rapaces.

Ayant perdu toute référence et toute identité, les ombres ne pouvaient plus dès lors que rêver.

Il nous fallut traverser les sept cercles du domaine funèbre.

Dans le premier cercle, étaient parqués tous ceux dont l'avidité avait gouverné les actions. Ils étaient rassemblés en files interminables dans des salles d'attente, sous un éclairage morne et cru. Ils attendaient ainsi sans fin ni pause, fiévreusement, sans savoir ce qu'ils attendaient et leur tour ne venait jamais. Des voix impersonnelles et nasillardes résonnaient dans d'invisibles haut-parleurs, mais l'attente se prolongeait indéfiniment. Nul ne pouvait quitter ce lieu, chacun était muré dans son mutisme.

Le deuxième cercle concernait les lâches et les pleutres, ceux qui s'étaient laissé dominer par la peur. Ces ombres-là erraient le long d'autoroutes béantes que sillonnaient des bolides lancés à toute allure et en tous sens. Chacun risquait à tout instant de se faire télescoper ou broyer par ces engins aveugles et frénétiques. Nul n'osait esquisser le moindre geste. Tous étaient pétrifiés de terreur.

Le troisième cercle rassemblait les vaniteux. C'était un espace étrange, une vaste soupente où s'amoncelait un bric-à-brac de débris divers, un capharnaüm d'accessoires brisés, de mécanismes rouillés, de meubles éventrés, de parures en loques, d'objets hétéroclites qui tombaient en poussière dès qu'on s'en approchait. Ceux qui hantaient ces lieux étaient maculés de déchets et de souillures dont ils essayaient en vain de se débarrasser, en se grattant, frottant et s'arrachant des lambeaux de chair.

Le quatrième cercle était une succession de banlieues, déshéritées, un long défilé de trottoirs gangrenés, de façades enfumées, fissurées et lépreuses, de terrains vagues et de décharges. Des chiens squelettiques rôdaient en rasant les murs et en jappant plaintivement. Des gosses pâles et tristes collaient leurs minois fanés aux vitres sales, et dans cette grisaille crépusculaire s'élevaient des criailleries de mégères avinées. C'était le cercle maudit des cœurs secs, sans compassion, sans indulgence ni bienveillance.

Au cinquième cercle, se rattachaient les possessifs et les jaloux. On était dans un supermarché aux proportions cyclopéennes. Des milliers de clients harassés s'affairaient à pousser des Caddie chargés à ras bord. Il était presque impossible de circuler dans ce dédale de rayons surpeuplés. Tous étaient obsédés par la recherche de produits introuvables, dont ils ignoraient d'ailleurs la nature. Des haut-parleurs diffusaient régulièrement des appels proférés d'un ton métallique : « Aujourd'hui promotion exceptionnelle au rayon charcuterie ! » « On demande une vendeuse au poste 26 ! » Ici les caisses étaient inaccessibles et les issues bloquées.

Le sixième cercle regroupait les fanatiques de toutes espèces. Il s'agissait d'un gratte-ciel, une tour dont le sommet se perdait dans les hauteurs. Le bâtiment était occupé par des bureaux administratifs où des employés renvoyaient mécaniquement les visiteurs de guichet en guichet, de section en section et d'étage en étage, à l'infini. Il manquait toujours une information, un papier, un cachet, une signature. Les solliciteurs étaient systématiquement éconduits, repoussés d'antichambre en vestibule et en secrétariat.

Le septième et dernier cercle était celui des

tortionnaires, des bourreaux, des pédophiles violeurs et des tueurs d'animaux. C'était une piste de danse aux reflets chatoyants dans un auditorium où s'égrenait une petite musique vacillante et aigre, une litanie de fausses notes répétitives accompagnée de voix fluettes et grinçantes fredonnant à contretemps des comptines débiles. Sur la piste les danseurs se déhanchaient et se contorsionnaient, s'épuisant vainement à composer un rythme cohérent. Ce septième cercle était comme un immense disque rayé.

Mais Eurydice était encore bien loin.

Au-delà s'étendait un espace concentrationnaire, hérissé de barbelés et hanté de miradors. On y parquait les gens de la haute finance, spéculateurs, trafiquants en tous genres, marchands de mort, d'abêtissements et d'illusions.

Sur les corps de ces malheureux poussaient et mûrissaient des centaines de têtes, des grappes fourmillantes de visages et de crânes qui enflaient puis explosaient comme des bulles, tandis que surgissaient de nouveaux appendices. Le torse, les bras, les jambes, le bassin, tout était infesté par cette prolifération grimaçante. Et des milliers de bouches béantes se tordaient en lançant des hurlements muets.

J'entraînai vivement Orphée vers d'autres horizons, plus ténébreux encore.

Nous étions maintenant dans une salle d'audience, un immense prétoire. Une innombrable foule de prévenus y attendait de comparaître. Chaque accusé se présentait devant un juge, un avocat et un procureur qui n'étaient autres que lui-même dans des costumes différents. À l'issue des plaidoiries et des réquisitions, l'âme était réexpédiée sur terre, en vue d'une autre incarnation, d'un autre destin.

Plus tard, nous avons embarqué à bord d'un vaisseau vide, sans marin ni capitaine, qui fendait un océan de lait où flottaient à la dérive des noyés aux yeux blancs et glacés. De temps à autre, ces corps heurtaient notre coque avec des bruits mous et des clapotis sourds. Nous traversions le détroit des suicidés.

Nous avons dû longer ensuite les usines et les laboratoires tentaculaires où étaient distillés et confectionnés les cauchemars et fantasmes dont on saupoudrait le sommeil des mortels. Des machines aux rouages fracassants touillaient des cuves géantes au contenu sulfureux où grondaient, gargouillaient et se tortillaient des séquences de terreur.

Il y avait aussi la grande forêt d'ouragans où les démons tutélaires nidifiaient et pondaient leur progéniture qu'ils nourrissaient des larmes et des sanglots de l'Histoire.

Nous approchions du but de notre quête.

Orphée n'avait cessé de chanter, amadouant ainsi les sombres puissances qui occupaient ces parages. Mais nous allions devoir affronter le Seigneur des métamorphoses dont dépendait le sort d'Eurydice, le seul habilité à exaucer mon compagnon.

En perpétuelle rotation sur lui-même, il avait des milliers de bras qui s'agitaient en tous sens et des gueules fumantes aux crocs ensanglantés. Il trônait sur un odieux podium jonché de corps déchiquetés. C'était aussi le maître de la danse et son rythme échevelé mettait en mouvement le Temps, les atomes, les étoiles et les points cardinaux. Lui aussi fut subjugué par la musique d'Orphée.

« Que désires-tu poète, toi qui oses pénétrer là où nul mortel ne s'est jamais aventuré ?

– Rends-moi mon Eurydice, trop tôt enlevée par un sort inique !

– Ce qui advient advient, et ce n'est pas à toi d'en juger. Cependant ô poète, j'accéderai exceptionnellement à ta demande. Mais à une condition. Eurydice va te suivre vers la surface. Mais pendant tout le chemin vers la vie, tu ne dois sous aucun prétexte te retourner pour essayer de la voir. Si tu enfreins cette règle, alors tu la perdras cette fois pour de bon. »

Nous fîmes route en sens inverse. À présent, l'ombre légère et presque imperceptible encore d'Eurydice nous suivait pas à pas, s'étoffant et prenant de la consistance à mesure que nous avancions. Ses contours se distinguaient de plus en plus nettement. Mais Orphée avait promis de ne pas se retourner.

Évidemment, il se retourna. Et Eurydice disparut aussitôt à jamais.

« Te voilà bien avancé ! m'écriai-je. Nous avons fait tout ce périple pour rien. On t'avait pourtant bien prévenu de ne pas te retourner ! Regarder en arrière, c'est se rendre prisonnier du passé, s'enfermer dans ses souvenirs, se vouer au néant. Car le passé est définitivement mort. C'est empêcher la vie de suivre son cours, de se renouveler. Ainsi tu as toi-même tué Eurydice pour la seconde fois !

– Hélas ! gémit Orphée, je n'avais pas le choix ! Mon Eurydice est tout pour moi. Une force irrésistible m'a poussé à la revoir. Pauvre de moi ! Je n'ai plus à présent aucune raison de vivre !

– Orphée, tu confonds tout. Ce que tu appelles amour n'est que de la passion aveugle. Ce n'est pas Eurydice qui t'importe, c'est l'image que tu en as. Sans quoi, tu te serais bien gardé de te retourner afin de lui offrir une deuxième chance. Ce que tu cherches vraiment c'est le malheur et le désespoir, voilà ta source d'inspiration intarissable. Avec Eurydice, vous auriez fini par mener l'existence d'un couple heureux et banal, petites joies, petites peines. La routine, l'ennui… »

Grâce à la disparition d'Eurydice, Orphée sut traduire les affres de la souffrance amoureuse. Sa musique et ses vers atteignirent les paroxysmes de l'émotion. Il était désespéré – et comblé.

Ses œuvres connurent un succès inégalé, qui ne faiblit guère avec l'âge. Il mourut vieux, riche et célèbre – pleurant toujours, et toujours inspiré.

Le récit du chat me laissa perplexe.

« J'ai toujours entendu dire, objectai-je, qu'à son retour des enfers, Orphée s'était fait mettre en pièces par la meute de ses admiratrices jalouses et hystériques…

– Ça, c'est la version officielle. Les hommes ont besoin pour leurs héros, de pathétique et de grandiose. En fait, Orphée était un assez pauvre type. Il n'aimait pas vraiment Eurydice. Il était juste obsédé par son image. Mais c'était un grand poète, ce qui mérite, je l'avoue, un ronronnement d'estime… »

Le chat s'installa sur mes genoux et s'y endormit pesamment, grognant chaque fois que je manifestais une quelconque velléité de me lever.

Ce jour-là, je fus en retard à tous mes rendez-vous.

Le Tueur de dragons

Il était une fois, dans une contrée lointaine, un vieux dragon – un des derniers de son espèce – qui, comme tous ses congénères, semait le trouble et la terreur dans tout le voisinage.

Or ce dragon était pourtant la plus débonnaire et la plus pacifique des créatures. Il n'eût pour rien au monde agressé hommes ou bêtes, et ses menus se composaient exclusivement de feuillages, ou en hiver, d'écorces et de racines.

Quelques expéditions avaient été organisées pour occire le monstre, mais le dragon, qui était futé, possédait quelques cachettes inviolables.

Un jour, un pauvre hère, moitié chevalier, moitié saltimbanque, avide d'aventure et cherchant fortune, traversa la région. Ayant eu vent de l'alléchante récompense offerte au courageux mortel qui réussirait à capturer la bête, il se mit à traquer le dragon.

La chance lui sourit; et un matin il se trouva nez à nez avec son adversaire. Il s'apprêtait à dégainer son épée, mais le dragon, qui mâchonnait paisiblement de jeunes pousses et des pommiers en fleurs, le salua courtoisement et lui tint ce langage :

« Me tuer, Messire, vous rapporterait certes un peu d'or et quelque considération, mais j'ai beaucoup mieux à vous proposer. Associons-nous vous et moi. Nous ferons aisément croire à tous ces paysans apeurés et naïfs que vous m'avez terrassé. Je jouerai les dragons morts et vous exhiberez fièrement ma dépouille. On vous donnera des trésors. Ainsi nous irons de pays en pays, et cette comédie vous procurera honneur, prestige, richesse… »

L'homme accepta l'offre avec enthousiasme.

Le plan fut mis à exécution et se déroula conformément aux vœux des deux compères. Le dragon avait un remarquable talent de comédien. Quand son complice était censé lui avoir assené le coup de grâce, il ouvrait une gueule béante, tirait une langue pathétique, révulsait à merveille ses énormes yeux glauques et se tenait raide comme un tronc abattu.

De province en province, le chevalier remportait un franc succès. Sa renommée, comme tueur de dragons, lui attirait la sympathie et l'admiration des foules. Les princes puisaient à pleines mains dans leurs trésors pour s'assurer ses services.

Après des années de connivences lucratives, l'homme et son ami dragon atteignirent un royaume gouverné par un cruel sorcier qui exerçait sur ses sujets et vassaux une tyrannie farouche, d'autant que sa redoutable magie lui permettait de percer à jour les secrets les mieux gardés.

Le thaumaturge ne fut pas dupe des vantardises du pseudo-héros, et il éventa sans peine la supercherie des duettistes qui était pourtant maintenant très au point.

« Extermine le dragon, dit-il au chevalier, et je te donnerai un coffre plein de pierres précieuses. Mais tu devras l'affronter en combat singulier et lui trancher la tête. Je la suspendrai comme trophée au-dessus de ma cheminée. Si tu échoues, c'est ta tête que je ferai couper et empailler pour la mettre à sa place. »

Quand sonna l'heure du combat, le dragon se coucha sur le flanc. De grosses larmes humectaient mollement ses écailles. Il susurra à l'oreille de son ami : « Écoute, camarade, je suis vieux, ceux de mon espèce ont depuis longtemps presque tous disparu. Tu as été mon seul vrai compagnon, ma joie et ma consolation en ce bas monde. Ensemble, nous nous sommes bien amusés, nous avons eu des moments formidables, et notre numéro était parfait. Alors n'hésite pas. N'aie aucun scrupule, aucun remords. Tu dois absolument me trancher la tête. Autrement, cet affreux sorcier nous fera périr tous les deux. Un jour, si tu as des enfants, tu leur conteras ce que fut l'amitié d'un dragon… »

L'homme était en pleurs. Il ne pouvait se résoudre à brandir l'épée pour accomplir le geste fatal.

« Vas-y, insista le dragon, fais vite mon ami, et ne t'inquiète de rien… »

Le magicien assistait à la scène en ricanant.

Mais ce démon ne connaissait de l'existence que sa face obscure – la peur, le mensonge, la félonie, la cupidité, la haine. Il ne soupçonnait pas ce que pouvait être un acte pur et désintéressé, un élan de sacrifice et d'abnégation.

Le sublime dévouement du dragon fit voler en éclats tous ses pouvoirs et fracassa son esprit pervers. Il se recroquevilla et s'affaissa jusqu'à n'être plus qu'un petit tas informe et poussiéreux, d'insignifiants chiffons dont les enfants se firent des poupées.

Libérés du joug implacable de leur oppresseur, les habitants du village acclamèrent les deux compères et les récompensèrent largement.

Quant à eux, ils repartirent ensemble pour de nouvelles aventures.

« Me feriez-vous encore la tête ? »

Le chat me tournait délibérément le dos et agitait la queue avec un agacement ostentatoire.

« Écoutez, convenez-en, nos relations ne sont guère équitables. Je suis prodigue pour ma part des confidences les plus intimes. Alors que vous ne dites jamais rien vous concernant !

– C'est que ma vie a beaucoup moins d'intérêt que la vôtre !

– Fadaises et balivernes ! La vérité, c'est que vous êtes frileuse et cachottière. Même si votre existence est passablement terne et insipide, les petits problèmes humains me font toujours rire et me procurent des moments de franche gaieté. Alors, soyez donc un peu moins égoïste… »

Rencontre avec la Mort

La Mort déambulait dans une rue commerçante et bruyante, sous les traits d'une petite vieille vacillante et fluette, trottinant à petits pas comptés pour faire du lèche-vitrine. De temps à autre, elle décochait un regard bref mais appuyé à tel ou tel quidam qui compterait bientôt parmi sa clientèle.

Ses gestes doux, sa démarche hésitante, ses vêtements de grand-mère coquette et surannée, dissimulaient fort bien la faux sinistre et l'aiguillon fatal.

Soudain surgit une bande de chenapans qui se mirent à la taquiner et à la chahuter, histoire de se donner de l'importance aux yeux des autres potaches de leur âge. La vieille dame fut un peu secouée, un peu décoiffée et copieusement persiflée.

Un passant chevaleresque s'en mêla, volant au secours de l'aïeule. Il dispersa sans ménagement les godelureaux qui s'égaillèrent comme une volée de moineaux.

Pour le remercier, la Mort invita son sauveur dans le meilleur salon de thé de la ville et lui offrit quelques friandises raffinées. Puis elle dévoila sa véritable identité.

« Ne crains rien, lui dit-elle, ce n'est pas pour toi que je suis ici aujourd'hui. Et pour te marquer ma gratitude, je t'autorise à me poser la question de ton choix concernant notre prochaine rencontre – qui sera bien sûr la dernière. Je peux assouvir toutes tes curiosités sauf à propos toutefois de l'après-vie car je n'en sais pas plus à ce sujet que toi-même. Ma mission se borne à opérer le passage.

– Bien, acquiesça le jeune homme en frissonnant un peu. Dans ce cas, je voudrais savoir quand, où et comment je vais mourir…

– Ça fait trois questions et tu n'as droit qu'à une seule. Alors je ne te dirai ni quand, ni où, mais dans quelle circonstance. Ce sera pendant l'office, en assistant à la grand-messe… »

Le jeune homme s'efforça d'obtenir quelques précisions, mais la Mort demeura intraitable. Elle prit courtoisement congé et disparut.

Après cet entretien étrange, le mortel se promit d'éviter à tout jamais la fréquentation de la messe et même la proximité des églises. Guère ennemi de la religion, il n'avait jamais été très pratiquant, et cette précaution ne lui coûtait pas outre mesure.

Les années passèrent. Il se maria, eut des enfants, exerça un métier plutôt lucratif, eut une vie ordinaire.

Son refus obstiné de pénétrer dans un lieu saint étonnait quelquefois ses proches, mais on attribuait cette répugnance à quelque lubie contractée dans l'enfance. Il n'était pas question pour lui d'assister aux mariages et aux enterrements, sauf s'ils étaient strictement civils. Même la simple présence d'un prêtre le mettait mal à l'aise.

Ses enfants grandirent, fondèrent à leur tour des foyers, il jouissait d'une santé robuste. Aucun accident physique ou moral, aucune épreuve grave n'était venu assombrir sa destinée. Parfois, il finissait par croire qu'il avait dû rêver cette rencontre avec la Mort, ou alors que la vieille dame d'autrefois s'était gentiment moquée de lui.

Lorsqu'il prit sa retraite, il s'établit dans une jolie fermette bien restaurée à la campagne. Il prit l'habitude de se promener dans les sous-bois des environs. Il se plaisait en compagnie des fleurs, des arbres, des animaux, dont il apprenait peu à peu les habitudes, le langage, les rituels.

Au début de l'été, à la nuit de la Saint-Jean, sa balade quotidienne le conduisit dans une vaste clairière où s'étaient rassemblées toutes les créatures de la forêt afin de célébrer le jour le plus long de l'année.

Un pur chant de grâce, d'amour et de gratitude s'éleva vers le ciel étoilé pour remercier le divin Seigneur et louer son œuvre admirable.

C'était une vraie messe, la grand-messe de la vie et de la création triomphante.

L'homme fut aussitôt frappé d'apoplexie, et succomba sur-le-champ.

La vieille dame n'avait pas menti.

Mon ami ronronnait bruyamment, presque agressivement, comme un feu de broussailles crépitant et ronflant. Son gosier parfois devenait une onde folle, un filet d'eau furieuse bouillonnant au creux d'une vallée encaissée. C'était comme un étrange tricot qui ourlait les minutes. Le très soyeux et murmurant fourreau du silence.

Ce ronflement ne faiblit guère tout au long de la journée.

Peter Pan

Depuis déjà un certain temps, tout se détériorait, se détraquait insidieusement au pays des rêves, dans l'île enchantée de Peter Pan et des enfants perdus.

Au commencement une lancinante et inexplicable mélancolie avait peu à peu affecté le capitaine Crochet et ses féroces pirates, la princesse Lily la tigresse et sa tribu d'Indiens, les sirènes de la crique enchantée, tout le petit peuple du pays imaginaire, elfes, gnomes, lutins, farfadets et fantômes, Wendy, ses frères et les autres compagnons de Peter Pan, même le crocodile glouton qui avait jadis dégusté la main gauche du hideux Crochet avant d'avaler un bruyant réveille-matin dont le tic-tac épouvantait et obsédait le capitaine, même ce saurien vorace, habituellement joyeux drille, et assez boute-en-train, semblait avoir perdu sa bonne humeur et végétait entre deux eaux, tournant en rond, sans appétit, sans but et sans ressort.

Quant à la fée Clochette, ses pétillements et scintillements devenaient rares et ternes, elle perdait le goût des cabrioles moqueuses et des pirouettes irisées.

Finis les grandioses défis entre l'agile Peter et le cruel capitaine. Finis les combats rocambolesques, les envolées lyriques, les manigances, félonies, revirements et rebondissements multiples.

Un voile opaque, une brume délétère pesait progressivement sur l'île magique.

Peter Pan avait beau s'efforcer de distraire son petit monde en multipliant les facéties, les espiègleries, cascades et bravades, chacun le sentait bien, le cœur n'y était plus vraiment.

Dans la tribu de Lily la tigresse, les Indiens oubliaient la cérémonie rituelle et n'invoquaient même plus le Grand Esprit. Le feu était négligé et les totems délaissés. Les sirènes avaient cessé de chanter et de minauder. Celles qui passaient habituellement le plus clair de leur temps à se faire belles et désirables, semblaient avoir oublié leur vocation d'éternelles séductrices.

Pour leur part, les flibustiers n'entretenaient même plus leur navire, les canons rouillaient lentement sur leur affût, le pont, la coque, les voiles et les cordages restaient sans soin ni surveillance. L'équipage macérait dans une somnolence alcoolisée. Et le tic-tac du réveille-matin trahissant le va-et-vient du crocodile ne résonnait plus dans les parages. La nuit, la voûte céleste commençait à se plisser, à gondoler, à se percer bizarrement par endroits, en longues déchirures par où les étoiles suintaient et saignaient. Tout pâlissait et se décolorait.

Derrière ce ciel lacéré et souillé, d'immenses et monstrueuses machines, camions-grues, bulldozers, se frayaient un chemin destructeur. Cet univers tout entier allait bientôt s'envoler en éclats, broyé par cette inexorable meute mécanique.

L'effroi et le découragement étaient au paroxysme.

Peter Pan, Lily la tigresse, le capitaine Crochet, le crocodile avaleur de pendules décidèrent une trêve.

Ils se réunirent pour se concerter, en vue de définir une parade. Mais comment endiguer ce processus infernal ?

« Moi, suggéra le crocodile, je mange bien des réveille-matin, j'arriverai certainement à dévorer ces grosses machines !

– Allons, allons, persifla le capitaine Crochet, tu n'es qu'une vilaine grande mâchoire avec une minuscule cervelle pas plus grosse que celle d'un moustique ! Le ciel est en train de nous tomber dessus, et rien ne l'arrêtera ! Toute la puissance de feu de notre fier vaisseau restera sans effet !

– Peut-être qu'on pourrait organiser une belle cérémonie magique pour provoquer l'intervention du Grand Esprit ? » proposa Lily la tigresse.

Mais c'était sans véritable conviction.

Peter Pan se tourna vers Wendy et la questionna du regard. Cette petite n'avait-elle pas toujours des idées lumineuses ?

« Voilà, dit-elle après un temps de réflexion. Je pense pouvoir expliquer ce qui nous arrive. Les gens de cette époque et surtout leurs enfants ne s'intéressent plus à nous et ne croient plus en nous. Il n'y en a plus que pour les Playstation, internet, les personnages et les histoires des jeux vidéo. Le monde merveilleux du rêve et de la véritable enfance ne fait plus recette. Il suffirait qu'un seul poète nous consacre quelques pages et donne envie de croire en nous pour détourner l'actuelle menace. Tant que les enfants continueront à nous faire vivre dans leurs songes les plus intimes, nous ne courrons aucun danger… »

Peter partit aussitôt prospecter le monde réel à la recherche d'un poète.

Mais les rares poètes encore vivants étaient beaucoup trop vieux, épuisés, amnésiques, à peine capables de tenir un stylo. L'affaire semblait désespérée.

C'est alors que je fis sa rencontre, une nuit où il s'amusait à poursuivre son ombre, le long d'une gouttière. Et c'est à moi qu'échut finalement la responsabilité de maintenir intact le fil de la croyance dont dépendait l'île des enfants perdus.

Et c'est maintenant à vous de jouer ma chère, puisque c'est vous qui tenez la plume. N'oubliez pas : Peter Pan, la fée Clochette, Wendy, Lily la tigresse, le capitaine Crochet, le vieux crocodile avaleur de réveille-matin doivent pouvoir compter sur vous…

Le matou avait une mine boudeuse, avec une nuance de réprobation dans le regard.

« Quelque chose ne va pas ? Auriez-vous des reproches à me formuler ?

– Il y a une grave lacune dans nos relations. Je ne vous ai jamais vu dormir. Contempler le sommeil d'un proche, c'est lui pardonner d'avoir vu le jour, et c'est aussi accepter sa mort. C'est pourquoi dormir ensemble est un acte si important et si intime. On touche ici au fond de l'âme, à l'absolu. Beaucoup d'individus partagent facilement leurs émotions et leurs plaisirs mais répugnent à partager leur sommeil.

– Est-ce de ma faute si vous vous absentez chaque nuit ?

– Il faudrait vous coucher plus tôt dans la journée… »

Le Croquis en mal d'amour

Il était une fois un dessinateur de renom, un des plus doués de sa génération, créateur de bandes dessinées très populaires, publiées à la une de plusieurs grands quotidiens.

Un jour, l'artiste conçut un petit personnage dont il tomba bizarrement amoureux. Il mit dans sa composition tant de passion, de précision, de verve et de vérité, que le croquis, comme animé soudain d'une vie et d'une substance balbutiantes, s'arracha aux contraintes de sa condition, brisa ses chaînes d'encre et s'évada de sa prison de papier.

Il se tenait, encore vacillant et tremblant, mais fièrement et non sans panache, campé devant son créateur un peu interloqué. Malgré tout ce n'était qu'un dessin, doté certes d'une conscience et d'une certaine autonomie, mais gravement handicapé par ses origines et sa nature première.

« Je veux, dit-il, s'adressant à l'artiste, devenir un être humain normal ! Tu es responsable de mon existence ! Alors tu dois m'aider ! Après tout, tu as une dette envers moi. Dis-moi ce que je dois faire pour devenir un être humain à part entière et en finir avec cet état intermédiaire somme toute inconfortable et peu satisfaisant ? »

Le dessinateur était perplexe mais il eut un brusque éclair d'inspiration et dit : « J'ai la solution. Tu dois te faire aimer d'un amour pur et véritable. Va, parcours le monde et cherche cet amour. Quand tu l'auras trouvé, la métamorphose aura lieu sur-le-champ. En attendant, ton apparence est assez convaincante pour tromper même un œil averti. Et grâce à ta condition particulière, tu n'auras à souffrir ni de la faim, ni du froid, ni de la fatigue… »

Le cœur vaillant et débordant d'espoir, notre personnage se lança dans sa quête, découvrant de pays en pays, de rencontre en rencontre, mille traits, ignorés de lui, concernant l'espèce humaine, ses innombrables contradictions, défaillances, inepties, complexités inextricables.

Un soir, dans un petit bar d'une ville portuaire, il fit la connaissance d'une très belle fille, une rousse flamboyante, pulpeuse et capiteuse à souhait. En l'abordant, il remarqua dans ses yeux fauves une soudaine lueur, violente et douce. Cette étincelle gourmande était-elle le premier symptôme de ce que l'on appelle amour ?

Grâce à sa légèreté presque diaphane, il dansait à merveille. Ils tournoyèrent ainsi ensemble, de plus en plus chaudement enlacés, toute la nuit. Puis elle s'offrit à lui, dans le premier hôtel, résolument et fougueusement. Et tout au long d'une étreinte qui n'en finissait pas, elle ne cessa de répéter avec une sorte d'euphorie angoissée, comme une litanie : « Aime-moi ! Aime-moi ! Aime-moi ! »

Assurément, là n'était pas le pur et véritable amour. D'ailleurs aucun changement ne s'opéra en lui.

Sa déconvenue était profonde, mais il n'était pas question de renoncer. Il fallait juste persévérer.

Et il reprit le cours de ses tribulations.

Après des mois d'errance, il rencontra dans une gare un voyageur qui paraissait comme lui rechercher l'aventure, traquant de continent en continent quelques chimères intimes, quelques secrets mirages. Voici enfin, songea-t-il, un compagnon à ma mesure, peut-être un authentique ami…

Et en effet, ils furent très vite inséparables, partageant le gîte, le couvert, les bonnes fortunes comme les vicissitudes. Leur complicité paraissait admirable et totale. Ce que l'un désirait, l'autre le désirait aussi – mêmes jeux, mêmes plaisirs, mêmes craintes.

L'ami, qui pilotait à merveille, proposa un jour à notre héros une virée dans un petit avion de location. L'appareil en plein vol subit une brusque panne. La chute était inéluctable. Il n'y avait à bord qu'un unique parachute. L'ami s'en empara fébrilement et sauta dans le vide, sans un regard pour son compagnon.

Notre héros flotta au gré des courants aériens et atterrit en douceur. Sa déception était amère et son chagrin immense.

Existait-il un homme capable d'aimer ?

Au cours de ses pérégrinations, il n'avait côtoyé que des couples divorcés, amants désunis, amitiés bafouées et trahies par peur ou ambition, enfants reniant leurs parents et les abandonnant dans des mouroirs par lassitude ou par cupidité.

Blessé, découragé, il rentra chez son créateur.

« L'amour véritable et pur n'est qu'un leurre, un cruel trompe-l'œil, lui dit-il. Jamais je ne deviendrai un homme à part entière. »

L'artiste était de plus en plus perplexe. Puis une inspiration lui vint.

« Va tout au bout du monde, au bord de l'univers, là où le ciel et la terre sont à tout jamais scellés dans un baiser vertigineux par l'horizon. Tu y trouveras ce que tu cherches… »

Le personnage entreprit ce long voyage et finit par atteindre les confins du monde. C'était le domaine du dieu Soleil, qui régnait ici sur son trône incandescent.

« Approche, approche, s'écria-t-il, petit bonhomme d'encre et de papier. Moi qui éclaire indistinctement le bon et le méchant, je donne la vie et la consume pour qu'elle puisse renaître encore et encore. Voilà ma vérité. Ce qu'on appelle amour. »

Aussitôt le dessin s'enflamma et fut réduit en cendres.

À sa place surgit un homme de chair et de sang. Le vœu du croquis était enfin exaucé.

« Hé, hé, ma chère, il y a depuis quelque temps dans cette maison comme un arrière-goût de laisser-aller. Vous êtes moins assidue à ma toilette quotidienne, moins appliquée dans vos caresses et dans vos soins accoutumés. Il va falloir vous ressaisir !

– Non mais quel toupet ! Votre ingratitude est aussi noire que votre fourrure ! Jour après jour, je transcris fidèlement vos récits que je n'apprécie pas toujours, soit dit en passant. Pour vous, je me prive de mes anciennes distractions, je réduis mes sorties, et comme vous ne supportez pas la présence d'intrus, j'ai renoncé à inviter ici mes plus proches amis ! Vraiment ! Que ne faut-il pas entendre !

– C’est vous, ma chère, qui avez tenu à ma présence féline. Je ne suis pas un animal de compagnie, vous devriez le savoir ! Nous autres chats, ne demandons jamais rien à personne. Alors n’attendez ni courbette, ni merci. Notre amitié est une grâce, de l’ordre du magique et du surnaturel. Réfléchissez bien à ceci : dans toute cette affaire, qui de nous deux y trouve le plus son compte ? »

J’en demeurai sans voix, et quelque peu troublée je l’avoue.

La Petite Marchande de fleurs

Il était une fois, au cœur d'une grande métropole, une petite fille pauvre, si pauvre et misérable qu'elle dormait sous des combles, sans électricité, chauffage ni eau courante.

Abandonnée dès le plus jeune âge, elle n'avait pas connu ses parents, ne possédait aucune famille, et vendait, pour subsister, des fleurs artificielles aux terrasses des cafés, pour le compte d'un marchand, brute avide qui lui laissait à peine de quoi ne pas tomber d'inanition.

Ses seuls amis étaient les chiens perdus et affamés comme elle et les chats de gouttière qui la nuit se glissaient dans son taudis pour la réchauffer et la réconforter en ronronnant dans son cou.

Cette année-là, l'hiver fut particulièrement rude.

La fillette grelottait, usant ses dernières forces à proposer d'une voix enrouée ses tristes bouquets de papier fané aux passants distraits, endurcis et stressés.

Le soir de Noël, le froid avait enseveli la ville sous une chape de givre, et une bise glacée sifflait rageusement sur les toitures. Mais les façades s'ornaient de joyeuses guirlandes. Les avenues étaient brillamment éclairées. Les boutiques étincelantes proposaient leurs étalages de friandises, foie gras, chapelets de boudin blanc, saumon fumé, dindes rôties ruisselantes de sauce, pyramides de chocolats et confiseries diverses.

Dans les grands magasins tout scintillants de paillettes et boules dorées, des panoplies de jouets attendaient le bon vouloir de la riche clientèle. La pauvre vendeuse de fleurs, dont les grands yeux limpides semblaient dévorer la petite figure pâle et chiffonnée, longeait toutes ces vitrines comme un pays enchanté dont la frontière lui restait à jamais interdite. Il lui fallait à tout prix réussir à placer quelques bouquets car elle se sentait de plus en plus faible.

Les passants, bien emmitouflés, hâtaient le pas, surexcités par la perspective du réveillon prometteur et bien arrosé en famille ou entourés d'amis. C'était une foule compacte, pétillante, bariolée, où chacun anticipait déjà sur la fête imminente. À tous les coins de rue, déambulaient des pères Noël publicitaires, harnachés de panneaux aux slogans racoleurs.

La fillette s'efforçait d'attirer l'attention, proposant ses bouquets d'une voix chétive, à peine audible. Mais les passants l'ignoraient ou la repoussaient sans ménagement.

« S'il fallait donner à tous les laissés-pour-compte, on n'en finirait pas ! » s'exclama une élégante rombière qui s'apprêtait à grimper dans un luxueux coupé.

Les heures passèrent.

La petite vendeuse était bredouille. Tremblant de froid et de faim, elle se traîna jusqu'à une impasse, un peu à l'écart des artères principales. Elle s'y affaissa lentement, sentant la vie lui échapper peu à peu. Pour elle, tout était clair : elle était en train de mourir.

Curieusement, elle n'éprouvait aucune crainte, elle se sentait au contraire envahie peu à peu par un sentiment très doux, très pur, un vaste espace de paix et de plénitude.

Sur la petite dépouille affalée au bord du trottoir gelé, se penchait une chaude et immense lumière ailée. C'était l'âme d'une étoile venue chercher sa petite sœur terrestre. Chaque fois que disparaît un enfant pauvre et mal aimé, un astre descend vers lui, enlace tendrement son esprit et l'emporte dans la voûte céleste où il devient à son tour une resplendissante étoile.

Le chat me fixa longuement puis éclata de rire en faisant mine de griffer l'air, dans ma direction. Il fit ensuite plusieurs bonds sur place sans cesser de ricaner.

« Qu'est-ce qui vous prend ! lui dis-je. Encore une de vos crises de folie ?

– Je suis fou ! Les murs sont fous ! Le ciel est fou ! Et alors, ça vous gêne ? Tenez, allez plutôt me chercher une étoile de neige, une corne d'abondance, une larme de crocodile… car comme le dit le proverbe : quand le chat n'est pas là, les souris dansent.

– Je ne vois pas le rapport.

– Il n'y en a pas.

– Vous avez vraiment un grain…

– Un grain de malice, un grain de désespoir, un grain de rêve. Vous voyez, ça fait trois grains. »

Il se remit à faire des bonds, puis s'abîma dans une profonde contemplation. Ce jour-là, il n'y eut rien à en tirer de plus.

Les Jardins de l'ondine

Il était une fois un jeune homme d'une beauté si attirante et si parfaite qu'il était lui-même subjugué par son image chaque fois qu'il se regardait dans un miroir.

Toutes les femmes étaient à ses pieds. Nul ne pouvait lui résister. Mais tant de succès le laissait indifférent. Une seule chose le fascinait, jusqu'à l'obsession : sa propre image dans la glace.

Éperdument amoureux de ce reflet insaisissable, ce désir impossible à combler le plongeait peu à peu dans une amère mélancolie.

Un jour, alors qu'il errait dans la campagne en agitant de noires pensées, ses pas le conduisirent dans une clairière, au bord d'un vaste étang aux eaux limpides.

Il s'étendit dans les hautes herbes qui longeaient la berge et se pencha sur la surface moirée de l'onde.

Son image lui semblait plus proche, plus désirable que jamais. C'était comme s'il allait pouvoir enfin l'épouser et s'y fondre. Ses lèvres de chair s'unirent à ses lèvres liquides. Il se laissa doucement glisser dans l'eau. Immergeant peu à peu ses paupières, son front, sa chevelure, son visage tout entier.

Or, l'étang était le domaine d'une puissante ondine, qui, tout au fond, régnait dans son palais aquatique sur une nombreuse population d'esprits inféodés à sa magie.

Le jeune homme fut invinciblement attiré sous les flots, vers le séjour de la nymphe.

Il se sentit couler, mais au lieu de se noyer, il parvenait étrangement à respirer sous l'eau, sans la moindre difficulté. Il avançait au ralenti dans cet univers glauque, au milieu de formes vagues et lascives, qui le frôlaient et le palpaient langoureusement.

L'ondine avait une nature voluptueuse, une sensualité dévorante. Elle était tombée sous le charme du jeune homme et l'avait entraîné vers son repaire. Elle connaissait bien plus de tours et d'exquises caresses, voire de suaves diableries que les simples mortels pour troubler et affoler les émotions viriles, mais elle eut beau déployer ses sortilèges féminins les plus raffinés, tendre ses pièges érotiques les plus sophistiqués, le jeune homme restait obstinément insensible.

Seule sa propre image continuait de le fasciner.

Elle essaya bien de l'enivrer en lui offrant du sirop de Lune rousse et de la liqueur d'étoiles filantes, qui est le champagne des ondines. Toutes ses manigances et même les plus subtiles ruses demeurèrent inutiles.

La nymphe, qui était capricieuse et volage, finit par se lasser. Mais piquée dans son amour-propre, elle résolut de se venger. Autour de son palais, s'étendaient les jardins de l'ondine, un vaste labyrinthe floral aquatique. Le jeune homme s'égara au milieu des bosquets et massifs irisés qui ondulaient comme des chevelures molles.

À chaque étape de ce dédale mouvant, de grandes fleurs fluides et blêmes exhalaient des séquences du passé, principalement de l'enfance et de l'adolescence.

Il se retrouva successivement à l'école primaire, dans la cour de récréation, en famille les jours de fête, à l'université, avec ses camarades de fin d'étude. Mais tous ces revenants lui ressemblaient à l'identique. Chaque séquence n'était peuplée que de ses doubles – sosies parfaits qui se diluaient et dérobaient à son approche.

Il était prisonnier d'un tourbillon répétitif où il s'exténua peu à peu.

Il se réveilla au bord de l'étang, croyant avoir dormi et rêvé.

Il se releva péniblement, et rentra chez lui.

Mais le paysage avait bizarrement changé. Plus rien n'était pareil. Il ne reconnaissait ni les maisons, ni les rues, ni les boutiques. Les gens portaient des vêtements différents et ne conduisaient plus les mêmes véhicules. Des décennies venaient en fait de s'écouler. Un siècle ou presque.

L'homme tenait à peine debout. Il se sentait d'une faiblesse extrême. Ses os craquaient, sa carcasse grinçait. C'était un vieillard.

Il réussit à se traîner jusqu'à l'étang. L'eau était noire, aveugle, paupière visqueuse et morte.

L'homme comprit que sa belle jeunesse était à jamais captive de l'ondine.

Le gros chat s'installa sur mes genoux, en frottant son museau contre mes joues et mon nez en ronronnant. Il mordilla délicatement mon menton au passage et fit sa pelote sur mes cuisses mais en prenant bien soin de ne pas trop sortir ses griffes.

Ce fut une journée de tendresse débordante, où il multiplia les marques d'affection exaltée.

Le Petit Poucet

Une chatte, qui demeurait dans une maison cossue et bourgeoise, eut une portée de sept chatons.

Le couple de retraités qui l'hébergeait n'eut pas le courage d'éliminer les nouveau-nés. Mais dès qu'ils furent sevrés, ils les conduisirent au loin pour les perdre dans la campagne.

Les sept frères et sœurs furent donc abandonnés en pleine forêt. Il y avait parmi eux un chaton d'une taille minuscule, qu'on surnommait Petit Poucet. Il était également particulièrement vif, malin, perspicace et futé.

Il avait su parfaitement repérer le chemin suivi par le couple, et il n'eut aucun mal à guider toute la tribu vers la maison natale.

Cette fois, les humains enfermèrent les chatons dans un sac, qu'ils placèrent dans le coffre de leur voiture, et ils n'hésitèrent pas à parcourir des kilomètres pour aller les perdre dans une région inconnue. Là, Petit Poucet était impuissant, et la tribu, coupée de ses lieux familiers, était livrée à une errance désespérée.

Prenant néanmoins rapidement la direction des opérations, Petit Poucet se percha sur la plus haute branche d'un arbre centenaire qui dominait les environs. C'est ainsi qu'il aperçut une belle demeure, au milieu d'un grand parc, où la petite colonie pouvait trouver refuge et même peut-être de quoi reprendre des forces.

L'endroit paraissait accueillant. C'était une gentilhommière, pleine de meubles anciens, d'argenterie luxueuse et de lourdes tentures.

Un groupe d'enfants alertes et joyeux jouait en s'esclaffant dans le parc, boucles au vent. Dès qu'ils virent les chatons, ils poussèrent des cris d'émerveillement.

Petit Poucet et les siens furent triomphalement plébiscités et aussitôt adoptés.

La mère des marmots, quelque peu réticente, émit de timides objections et réserves, mais elle fut débordée par l'enthousiasme de sa progéniture.

Plus tard dans la soirée, le maître de céans fit son apparition.

C'était un grand chercheur, qui travaillait toute la journée dans son laboratoire, attenant à la maison.

Ce savant, qui était un fou de la pire espèce, pratiquait toutes sortes d'expériences inhumaines, de la mutilation à la vivisection, sur d'innocentes créatures capturées par ses soins et livrées à son désir fanatique.

De petite taille, entièrement chauve et corpulent, il était affligé d'une intense myopie, ce qui l'obligeait à porter d'énormes verres à triple foyer. Mais ses petits yeux glauques et clignotants semblaient s'effaroucher à la lumière du jour.

Dès qu'il vit les chatons, il se frotta les mains et prit sa femme à part.

« Ceux-là il me les faut, murmura-t-il. Dès qu'ils seront endormis, je leur ferai une piqûre paralysante.

– Les enfants auront beaucoup de peine.

– Mais ils n'en sauront rien, j'agirai pendant leur sommeil. On leur dira qu'ils se sont sauvés. »

Petit Poucet avait tout entendu. Quand vint l'heure d'aller au lit, les enfants installèrent leurs nouveaux amis tout près d'eux, sur leur couette. Le savant fou vint les border en prenant soin de bien repérer l'emplacement des chatons.

Peu après Petit Poucet réveilla discrètement ses frères et sœurs. Il disposa ensuite des jouets en peluche à l'endroit qu'ils étaient censés occuper. Puis la tribu attendit silencieusement pelotonnée dans un coin de la chambre.

Le savant ne tarda guère à revenir, sur la pointe des pieds, en brandissant une seringue dont il injecta le contenu dans les peluches qu'il enfourna dans un grand sac. Il se hâta aussitôt avec son butin vers son laboratoire.

Petit Poucet et les siens s'y faufilèrent également. Ils commencèrent par libérer les malheureux captifs encore valides, puis renversant les éprouvettes mélangeant les solutions, provoquant un peu partout des courts-circuits et dégageant des gaz pestilentiels, ils finirent par déchaîner un incident qui ravagea tout le local.

Le chercheur affolé, n'y voyant goutte, courait dans tous les sens inutilement. Il fut happé par les flammes.

Après le deuil d'usage, la veuve et les enfants reprirent le cours normal de leur existence.

Cette fois, ils recueillirent définitivement les sept chatons qui n'avaient plus rien à craindre.

Ce matin, dès la fin du récit, le matou se précipita dans ma chambre et se faufila sous ma couette. Malgré mes plus vives protestations, il refusa obstinément d'en sortir. Je l'invitais en vain à faire sa toilette et à se sustenter. Il demeura ainsi bien calfeutré pendant des heures.

À la tombée du jour, il était de nouveau introuvable.

L’Esprit de Noël

Monsieur Quentin dirigeait les services informatiques d’une société de grande surface. Quoique encore jeune, il était presque chauve, avait un teint grisâtre, et affichait un air sévère et compassé qui le vieillissait prématurément.

C’était un homme sans histoires, un peu terne, tout lisse et bien carré. Il avait un caractère pragmatique, rationnel, peu porté à la fantaisie, et il se glorifiait de son solide réalisme. Son existence était bien réglée, ses comptes bien tenus : pas de dépense inutile, et guère de caprice. Tout superflu était rigoureusement prohibé. Peu d’amis, des loisirs mesurés, des distractions saines et un régime équilibré. Ses rencontres féminines étaient plutôt rares, de brèves liaisons sans lendemain, plus pour l’hygiène que pour le plaisir.

Bref, c’était un cadre apprécié de ses supérieurs, qui menait une vie régulière et rangée, insensible au tumulte et aux passions du monde. Il ignorait l’ennui parce qu’il refusait l’exaltation. Il évoluait au milieu de parfums insipides et de couleurs délavées.

Un soir de Noël, après une journée de travail bien remplie, il rentra chez lui – un spacieux et confortable studio, doté de toutes les techniques et prestations les plus modernes. Son intention était de passer un réveillon tranquille et solitaire, devant son écran de télévision et quelques friandises achetées chez le traiteur du coin.

Il prit un long bain chaud, se mit à l'aise, et s'installa devant son poste de télévision. Pourquoi dépenser des fortunes en folles soirées, avec l'assurance de lendemains lourds et barbouillés ? Un ou deux verres de champagne suffiraient largement.

Il pianota sur sa télécommande, à la recherche d'une émission conforme à son humeur et à ses goûts. Mais l'écran restait obstinément brouillé, neigeux et chaotique.

Or, peu à peu s'y ébaucha une forme blanchâtre et vaporeuse dont le visage aux contours indéfinis, semblait tantôt celui d'un vieillard, tantôt celui d'un petit enfant.

Quentin passa en vain de chaîne en chaîne. La même silhouette était partout présente, et de plus en plus insistante.

« Qu'est-ce que c'est que cette plaisanterie ? Une émission pirate ou quoi ?… »

À travers la barrière cathodique, la créature paraissait le fixer avec d'immenses yeux de braise.

« Je suis venue pour toi Quentin, dit l'ombre. Spécialement pour toi !

– Non mais je rêve ! C'est une farce idiote ! Si je tenais celui…

– Ceci n'a rien d'une blague. Regarde plutôt ! »

Le spectre allongea un bras immatériel et fluorescent qui sortit de l'écran et vint effleurer l'incrédule.

« Mais, bredouilla l'homme, qu'est-ce que ça signifie ? Est-ce que je vais mourir ?

– Non. Je suis l'Esprit de Noël, l'Esprit de tous les Noëls. Et je suis là pour te montrer quelque chose… »

L'homme fut saisi par les cheveux, et littéralement happé par un tourbillon, à l'intérieur du poste de télévision.

Porté par le fantôme, il se retrouva en plein ciel, au milieu des nuages menaçants poussés par de grands vents glacés. Les horizons défilaient rapidement, dévoilant des paysages de plus en plus sauvages et sombres. Ils survolèrent un bourg, coquettement décoré et joyeusement illuminé pour fêter la naissance du Sauveur.

Quentin pouvait voir distinctement l'intérieur des maisons. Des ribambelles d'enfants surexcités disposaient fébrilement leurs souliers, sabots et bas de laine devant les cheminées. Aux cuisines, des dindes bien grasses et bien farcies rissolaient lentement sur des broches, à côté des chapons, et des oies luisantes et ruisselantes de sauce. Santa Klaus n'allait pas tarder à se montrer dans son traîneau, avec ses rennes et sa hotte géante.

Dans l'église du village, on s'apprêtait à célébrer la messe de minuit.

Les cœurs étaient à l'unisson et débordaient d'allégresse. C'était le seul jour de l'année où, en serviteur d'une grande âme, d'une pure lumière apparue dans ce monde, chacun devenait meilleur, se montrait plus généreux et plus ouvert.

L'Esprit dit à Quentin : « Voici le Noël des temps anciens, lorsque au cœur des nuits les plus noires veillait toujours une étincelle d'espoir. »

L'homme ressentit un malaise indéfinissable.

Le spectre entraîna son compagnon dans une nouvelle course vertigineuse.

Cette fois, ils surplombaient une campagne morne et déshéritée.

Dans une petite ferme battue par les intempéries, une famille de modestes paysans était fébrilement rassemblée autour d'un âtre aux flammes vacillantes. Les enfants portaient des vêtements troués. Une maigre soupe mijotait dans une marmite rouillée. Un chien rachitique rongeait laborieusement un os dans son coin. Mais les galoches étaient soigneusement rangées devant la cheminée. Chacun recevrait un hochet, une babiole, et ce serait pour tous le même émerveillement.

« Voici, dit le fantôme, le Noël des enfants pauvres. Ce soir-là, une simple poupée de chiffon en fait les rois de la terre… »

Quentin se sentait de plus en plus déstabilisé.

Au terme d'un voyage à dos d'ouragan, ils atteignirent les abords d'une somptueuse villa brillamment éclairée.

Dans la pièce principale était dressée une vaste table chargée de mets rares et raffinés servis dans une vaisselle luxueuse. Un couple en tenue de soirée s'empiffrait en silence.

L'homme et la femme, d'âge mûr, étaient tous les deux d'une obésité considérable. Ils avaient un regard éteint, des bajoues flasques et une moue désabusée. Tout autour, s'amoncelait une profusion de paquets cadeaux, portant les labels de marques renommées.

« Voici le domaine des Noëls morts, dit le spectre. On ne sait plus ni donner ni recevoir. On ne sait que consommer. Voilà ton univers et ton destin. La mort de Noël. C'est la mort de l'âme. »

Quentin se réveilla en sursaut devant son poste. Sur le petit écran se déroulait une de ces émissions de variétés avec beaucoup de paillettes et de plumes dont les spectateurs sont si friands ces soirs-là.

L'homme se leva, prit son pardessus et quitta son appartement. Quelque chose en lui avait définitivement basculé. Il allait partir loin, très loin là où l'on savait encore donner et recevoir.

Il avait rendez-vous avec la vie.

Après son habituelle séance de brossage et de caresses matinales, je demandai au chat : « Où en êtes-vous avec la Lune ? Parviendrez-vous bientôt à vos fins ?

– La route est encore longue, et mes tribulations sont loin d'être à leur terme…

– Je comprends mal. Avec toute votre ruse, toute votre sagacité féline, vous ne trouvez aucun stratagème pour écourter ces épreuves ?

– Là n'est pas la question. Les puissances de l'ombre n'obéissent guère à votre logique. La Nuit n'observe pas les mêmes règles du jeu. Pensez un peu aux lois qui gouvernent vos rêves. Vous aurez une petite idée, un indice de ce que j'essaie de vous faire comprendre… »

L'Homme qui n'avait plus d'ombre

Il était une fois un intrépide et séduisant jeune homme éperdument épris de liberté. Tout semblait lui réussir – rencontres, amours, fortune. Bref, la vie lui souriait et lui ouvrait tout grand les bras.

Or, cet heureux mortel éprouvait pourtant une étrange contrariété qui tournait peu à peu à l'obsession : il ne supportait plus son ombre.

Ce double inconsistant servilement attaché à ses pas, mimant ses moindres gestes, rampant sur les trottoirs et sur les murs, tenait à ses yeux à la fois du chien et de l'espion. Il en était exaspéré. En plein jour, il avait l'impression que cet obscur et inséparable partenaire le tenait rivé au sol, pesait sur son existence même et son destin.

La nuit, c'était bien pire : son ombre s'allongeait et s'étirait, devenait élastique. Il en était alors le pantin, la docile marionnette manipulée par ces longs doigts ténébreux.

Cette ombre avait par ailleurs des pouvoirs redoutables. Elle était tantôt gigantesque et tantôt minuscule, s'escamotait pour réapparaître aussitôt, plus menaçante et plus pesante que jamais.

Comment se débarrasser d'un compagnon aussi indésirable ?

Le jeune homme connaissait un chiffonnier un peu sorcier, grand amateur de vieilles hardes et babioles diverses qu'il allait vendre sur les marchés de province. Ce grigou avait plus d'un tour dans son sac à malice : il connaissait des sortilèges et des philtres qui sentaient davantage le soufre que l'aubépine. On le soupçonnait de dissimuler des cornes sous sa casquette et de serrer des pieds fourchus dans ses bottines. Il avait l'œil torve, la dent gâtée, l'haleine fétide, l'index crochu, la démarche reptilienne et sournoise, mais sa science pouvait être utile ; vu la nature de sa requête, le jeune homme ne pouvait se montrer trop regardant.

« L'affaire, mon garçon, n'est pas simple, dit le marchand, mais si tu es prêt à y mettre le prix, je crois pouvoir te satisfaire. »

La discussion fut rude car le bonhomme était rapace et cupide, mais le solliciteur, qui n'était pas dans le besoin, finit par céder. Il paya la somme exigée. Le sorcier prit alors une petite paire de ciseaux magiques avec laquelle il incisa très habilement l'ombre incriminée, la sépara prestement du jeune homme et la rangea dans une penderie, en l'accrochant à un rayon de lune qui servait de cintre, au milieu d'un bric-à-brac hétéroclite – ailes de fées noyées de chagrin, rêves jamais rêvés, lambeaux de crépuscule arrachés à la foudre, ou promesses d'amoureux égarées dans la brume.

« Voilà qui complétera ma collection. Tu peux partir tranquille, ton ombre n'est pas près de m'échapper. »

Commença alors une période de chance et de prospérité sans précédent.

Allégé, affranchi de cette ombre entêtante, le jeune homme triomphait de tout ce qu'il entreprenait. Il mit sur pied des sociétés florissantes, réalisa des spéculations boursières mirobolantes, acheta des clubs sportifs qui remportèrent les coupes les plus prestigieuses. On ne voyait plus que lui dans les médias, et les paparazzi ne lui laissaient guère de répit. Il acquit les plus belles propriétés dans les sites les plus enchanteurs. Sa table était d'un raffinement sans égal, et les femmes les plus convoitées se donnaient à lui fougueusement. Quelque chose pourtant s'était bizarrement détérioré. Dans cette situation brillante et dominante où ses moindres désirs étaient exaucés, il lui semblait que rien n'avait plus de goût. Les femmes les plus lascives paraissaient insipides. La vie avait perdu son sel, et la beauté sa sève. Les jours se succédaient dans une monotonie lancinante. C'était un mal pernicieux qui le rongeait et le plongeait dans les affres d'une mélancolie fatale.

Il essaya de retrouver le colporteur qui avait acheté son ombre. Mais le vieux démon avait déménagé depuis longtemps, et toutes les recherches demeurèrent vaines.

Alors, grâce à ses nombreuses relations, il entra en contact avec le maître des lutins et des trolls, le seigneur Abracadabranovitch.

Ce dernier vivait au fond d'une forêt encore inconnue des humains, au beau milieu d'un lac, dans un gracieux palais musical dont les murs étaient des éclats de rire, des soupirs d'extase, des murmures d'enfants, et des chants de rossignols. La grossière intrusion de ce mortel sema un peu la panique parmi les elfes et les gnomes, mais le superbe Abracadabranovitch, juché sur un trône de clameurs, toisa ironiquement le visiteur et le questionna sur l'objet de sa présence. Le jeune homme raconta son histoire, exposa sa déconvenue et son état pitoyable.

« Seigneur, je te supplie d'intervenir, toi seul as les pouvoirs nécessaires… »

Abracadabranovitch ne s'était pas mêlé depuis des lustres des affaires humaines, car les mortels, avec leur présomptueuse technique, étaient devenus si infatués, si arrogants qu'ils jugeaient leur science bien supérieure à l'ancienne magie et n'avaient plus recours à ses services. La plupart allaient même jusqu'à contester son existence. Il ne lui déplaisait donc pas de jouer un peu avec ce jeune fou.

« Sais-tu bien, petit homme imprudent, qu'en vendant ainsi ton ombre, tu as gravement offensé notre Mère Nature ? L'ombre est pour toute créature vivante et pour tous objets inanimés l'aiguille qui indique sans cesse la direction du mystère et de l'abîme. C'est la boussole des ténèbres et de l'indicible. Sans elle l'existence perd tout sens et toute motivation. Comme je suis bon prince, j'accéderai à ta demande, sans rien exiger en échange. Ton ombre d'origine, je ne peux te la restituer. Elle appartient à ce sorcier de malheur. Mais dès que tu auras quitté cette forêt, mon domaine, la première ombre disponible s'accrochera à tes pas… »

Le jeune homme se confondit en remerciements, et prit congé sans remarquer les ricanements étouffés d'Abracadabranovitch et de ses sujets.

Dans la campagne, il croisa un vieil épouvantail sur le point de s'affaisser sous les assauts du vent. L'ombre du mannequin moribond, profitant de l'aubaine, s'attacha immédiatement à la silhouette du passant.

Et ce dernier, cloué sur place par son nouveau double, fut aussitôt changé lui-même en épouvantail.

Il n'effraya d'ailleurs que quelques midinettes superstitieuses et les dernières bigotes des bourgs environnants. Bientôt, tous les oiseaux du coin en firent leur perchoir de prédilection, ce qui fut pour moi l'occasion de quelques succulents festins.

Le matou avait l'air particulièrement satisfait de son récit.

Assis en équilibre sur une minuscule étagère, il prenait des poses avantageuses, plissant les yeux, moustaches fièrement troussées, queue nonchalamment ondulante. Je crus même surprendre un clin d'œil à mon intention, aussi rapide qu'inattendu.

« Mais oui, dit-il, allant au-devant de mes questions, nous autres chats nous avons un pacte avec les ombres. Nous sommes les gardiens de la nuit, les ambassadeurs du Mystère. Il n'y a d'ailleurs que les bipèdes humains qui soient assez stupides et prétentieux pour oser défier ce grand ordre immuable… »

Ce matin-là, il s'attarda longuement à sa toilette quotidienne. Ensuite, il somnola en ronronnant à mes côtés une bonne partie de la journée.

La Femme du pêcheur

Il était une fois un pauvre diable qui menait une existence misérable dans une vieille cabane insalubre en lisière de forêt.

Pour survivre, il n'avait que l'aide publique, des petits travaux occasionnels et quelques expédients de fortune – cueillette de champignons et chasse aux escargots qu'il allait vendre à la sauvette sur les marchés des environs. Il lui arrivait aussi de pêcher, pour améliorer l'ordinaire, car sa pitance quotidienne était maigre et peu variée.

D'un naturel timide, rêveur, doux et compatissant, il partageait son triste sort avec une femme acariâtre, virago et mégère qui le menait à la baguette, le houspillait à tout propos et le traitait matin et soir de crétin, fainéant, bon-à-rien, et de bien d'autres noms d'oiseaux.

D'humeur toujours égale et d'une patience d'ange, il se contentait de hocher la tête en souriant, ce qui avait le don d'exacerber les crises de son irascible épouse, dont le caractère s'aigrissait de plus en plus avec l'âge.

Bref, les jurons, reproches cinglants et sifflements de rage allaient bon train dans ce curieux ménage. Mais dans ce contexte plutôt déshérité, le petit homme ne se sentait pas pour autant malheureux. Sa petite vie inconfortable et marginale lui suffisait apparemment et semblait même lui convenir assez.

Non loin de la masure, il y avait un étang où prospérait un peuple de grenouilles dodues et bavardes.

Un jour, notre héros se mit en tête d'aller pêcher quelques-unes de ces créatures à la chair savoureuse : avec les épices appropriées, il s'offrirait une succulente et croustillante friture.

Installé au bord de l'étang, il ne fut pas long à repérer une rainette qu'il ramena promptement au bout de sa ligne. Il s'apprêtait à la jeter au fond de son sac, lorsque à son grand étonnement, il entendit le batracien l'apostropher en ces termes : « Petit homme, tu as intérêt à me relâcher au plus vite, car je suis la reine des grenouilles, et qui plus est une fée puissante qui pourrait bien te changer en vulgaire moustique et en méchant caillou. Alors laisse-moi partir si tu ne veux pas aller au-devant des pires ennuis… »

Le pêcheur obéit sans se faire prier. Puis il prit ses jambes à son cou pour aller, émerveillé, conter son aventure à sa pimbêche de femme.

« Cesse de me prendre pour une imbécile, grogna l'aimable personne, ou alors tu dors debout ! Et tu ne sais même plus faire la différence entre le rêve et la réalité. »

L'homme protesta énergiquement de sa bonne foi. « Arrête donc de me casser les oreilles avec tes jérémiades ! Écoute, si tu as vraiment rencontré une fée, tu aurais dû lui demander d'exaucer un vœu en échange de sa liberté. D'ailleurs, puisque tu es si sûr de toi, pourquoi n'y retournes-tu pas à l'instant même ? Et dis à ta grenouille magique que je veux une belle et grande maison, avec tout le confort, le mobilier haut de gamme et les gadgets dernier cri ! »

Le pêcheur aussitôt s'exécuta.

L'étang dissimulait son vaste œil glauque sous les mille paupières de ses lourds nénuphars. Tout autour, les brises colportaient des énigmes futiles et les feuillages susurraient des élégies acidulées.

La reine des grenouilles se présenta au premier appel.

« C'est ma femme, expliqua le solliciteur. Elle dit que je suis stupide et que j'aurais dû exiger une faveur. Elle veut une grande maison avec tout l'équipement le plus sophistiqué…

– Ta femme n'a rien à demander. Comme tu as été un honnête gaillard, tu peux rentrer chez toi sans crainte. Ta requête est d'ores et déjà satisfaite. »

C'est à ce moment de l'histoire que je crus bon d'intervenir. Ce pêcheur m'inspirait une certaine sympathie.

« Tu aurais tort, lui dis-je, de croire ce batracien sur parole… »

Je me tournai ensuite vers la magicienne, toutes griffes dehors, queue frémissante, poils hérissés, menaçant : « Je te conseille de tenir tes engagements, car toute reine des grenouilles sois-tu, il me suffira d'un coup de patte pour t'attraper et te croquer sans autre forme de procès… »

Je raccompagnai mon nouvel ami, qui, à la place de sa cabane crasseuse, découvrit une somptueuse demeure où son épouse l'attendait avec une pose avantageuse et un petit sourire arrogant. Dès qu'elle m'aperçut, elle eut un haut-le-cœur : « Tu n'as tout de même pas la prétention de faire entrer cette sale bête dans notre nouvelle maison ? Ceci n'est pas un taudis. Les sans-abri n'ont qu'à chercher des bonnes poires ailleurs !

– Ce chat est mon ami et je ne le chasserai pas ! »

Au bout de quelques jours, la sulfureuse matrone se mit à piaffer et à tempêter : « Ta fée s'est payé ta tête, cette bicoque est une plaisanterie ! Ce qu'il me faut, c'est un luxueux hôtel particulier, avec un parc, des domestiques, des limousines, une piscine, un tennis et bien sûr, un revenu digne de moi ! Retourne donc à l'étang pour obtenir ce qui m'est dû ! »

Le bonhomme, toujours conciliant, obtempéra.

Un silence pesant étreignait la clairière, et sur l'eau se formaient de lentes ondes qui roulaient et rampaient comme des reptiles vers les berges. La vie semblait murée derrière les arbres aux troncs massifs et aux branches sourcilleuses.

Le pêcheur exposa son affaire.

« Le souhait de ta femme est dès maintenant réalisé ! » annonça la magicienne. J'estimai judicieux de placer mon grain de sel : « Fais bien attention, car si tu ne tiens pas ta promesse, tes cuisses mignonnes et ton ventre replet seront pour moi un hors-d'œuvre très convenable... »

La coquette maison s'ornait d'une pancarte :

« À VENDRE » où figurait aussi la nouvelle adresse de la propriétaire. C'était dans la banlieue résidentielle d'une vaste métropole, une magnifique villa, entourée de hauts murs, bien protégée par des systèmes d'alarme ultra-perfectionnés. Toute une armée de gardiens, jardiniers, femmes de chambre, cuisiniers et valets s'affairaient à l'entretien des lieux.

« Ah bon, te voilà donc ! ulula la maîtresse de céans avec des airs de grande dame offusquée. Si tu tiens à garder cet animal pouilleux et plein de puces, va donc l'enfermer dans une de ces remises. Qu'il serve au moins à détruire les souris !

– Ce chat est mon ami et il ne me quittera pas ! »

Les semaines suivantes, Madame écuma les bijouteries de renom, les magasins de haute couture et les grands antiquaires de la place. Elle en fit tant qu'elle eut bientôt l'air d'un sapin de Noël ambulant. Coiffeurs dans le vent, kiné, chirurgiens esthétiques, restaurants quatre étoiles, psy, voyantes, conseillers en gestion, rien n'était trop beau ni trop dispendieux. On ne fréquentait plus que les célébrités mondaines, la crème du show business et le gratin de la jet set.

Nous étions, l'homme et moi, installés dans un modeste pavillon, un peu à l'écart au fond du parc, où nous coulions des jours paisibles, sans chichis ni ostentation.

Un matin, la mijaurée, toute pomponnée, liftée de frais, enrubannée, surgit, croulant sous les colliers, bagues et bracelets. Pointant sur mon compère un doigt crochu et potelé, elle aboya : « Allez, ouste ! Cours voir ta stupide grenouille ! dis-lui que je veux être la femme la plus puissante de toute la terre. Et ne t'avise pas de reparaître avant la réalisation de ce vœu, car tel est mon destin. Mon chauffeur te conduira jusqu'aux abords de la forêt. »

L'étang était d'une couleur crépusculaire et irisé de lueurs bleues. La surface était gondolée de bulles et de cloques géantes et visqueuses qui mûrissaient et crevaient en dégageant des fumées âcres et une brume fétide. Tout autour, les ramures haletantes semblaient se tordre les bras d'angoisse.

La fée nous attendait, trônant sur un magnifique nénuphar.

« Ma femme s'est jurée de devenir la première dame de la planète. Pourrais-tu nous aider cette fois encore ?

– Rassure-toi, murmura la créature, la chose est déjà faite.

– Prends garde à toi, enchanteresse. Si tu trompes mon collègue ici présent, tu ne vaudras guère plus entre mes griffes que le plus débile des mulots, car un chat n'a que faire des sortilèges. »

L'épouse du pêcheur s'était établie dans une gigantesque tour de verre. Entourée d'un régiment de secrétaires, de gardes du corps, elle possédait des jets privés, des îles dans le Pacifique, des terrains, des hôtels, un immense parc immobilier sur les cinq continents, des casinos, quelques grandes compagnies aériennes, des chaînes de journaux et de télévision, des sociétés informatiques, des réseaux satellites, des groupements financiers et boursiers, de nombreuses mafias locales et bien sûr, des comptes vertigineux dans tous les paradis fiscaux. D'un simple battement de cils, elle pouvait provoquer à distance la chute d'un gouvernement ou la ruine d'un État.

Aucune loi d'importance ne pouvait être décrétée sans son aval occulte. Tous aides, investissements, interventions étaient tributaires de son consentement. Et elle restait évidemment dans l'ombre, où son pouvoir absolu n'avait aucune rivalité à craindre, aucune campagne de presse à redouter. Elle n'avait ni ennemi ni opposant politique puisque ses adversaires potentiels ignoraient jusqu'à son existence.

Les mois passèrent. Nous nous étions choisi une douillette retraite dans une accueillante chaumière loin de la gesticulation et du tohu-bohu des grandes cités. Nous avions presque oublié la femme qui dominait secrètement le monde, bien plus puissante que ne le furent jamais les plus illustres conquérants et les pires tyrans, lorsque cette harpie insatiable se présenta un soir à l'improviste !

« Je suis lasse, glapit-elle, de tous ces petits jeux mesquins. Qu'est-ce que cette planète dérisoire à côté des milliards d'étoiles, de nébuleuses, de galaxies qui naissent et se résorbent dans le vide éternel ? Qu'est-ce que cette pitoyable condition humaine si fragile, si fugace, face aux torrents d'énergie incandescente ruisselant dans l'espace ?

Ce qu'il me faut, c'est l'univers tout entier, la position suprême, la place de Dieu ! Si tu ne veux pas encourir ma colère, retourne voir ton espèce de crapaud thaumaturge et fais-lui part de ma volonté ! J'ai pour toi un hélicoptère prêt à décoller ! »

L'étang était tout boursouflé de vagues noires et d'écume violette. De violents tourbillons éventraient la surface et laissaient deviner des abîmes hurlants et sans fond. Des vents funèbres carillonnaient sinistrement dans les parages.

« Quoi encore aujourd'hui ? coassa la fée grenouille.

– C'est ma femme. Elle veut être Dieu, bredouilla le pêcheur.

– Eh bien, eh bien ! ricana l'amphibie. Vas-y, c'est déjà fait ! »

Je me précipitai : « Là, tu exagères un peu ! De tels souhaits sont hors de ta juridiction… »

Mais la magicienne avait disparu.

Quand nous sommes rentrés, la femme du pêcheur était de retour dans la misérable cabane du début. Elle avait tout perdu et était complètement retombée en enfance.

L'homme reprit le cours serein de son existence, mais délivré des incessantes scènes conjugales, il baignait désormais dans une pure félicité. Quant à son épouse, elle avait atteint cet état de paix intérieure commun aux saints, aux sages, aux nourrissons et à Celui qui n'a de nom dans aucune langue.

Le chat me dévisageait d'un œil goguenard. Puis il affecta de se désintéresser de mon cas pour se lécher la patte et se frotter vigoureusement l'oreille.

« Votre version du conte est immorale, protestai-je. Dans l'original, la femme du pêcheur voit son avidité sévèrement châtiée, puisqu'elle tombe de haut et finit ses jours dans le malheur.

– Balivernes, ma chère ! Bien au contraire, la fée accède à ses désirs. Voyez-vous, les humains ont la naïveté de croire que Dieu est tout en haut. Ce serait là une position bien inconfortable. La seule place éternellement parfaite et immobile est à l'intérieur, au plus profond, en bas, tout en bas.

– Je sais bien que vous raffolez des paradoxes, des énigmes et des propos abscons, mais vous en faites un peu trop.

– Décidément vous n'entendez pas grand-chose à la métaphysique.

– Ni vous aux femmes ! »

Cette journée fut une longue bouderie mutuelle. Et c'est à peine s'il daigna humer son assiette de croquettes. Je transcrivis néanmoins son récit à contrecœur.

Le soir, comme d'habitude, il s'absenta.

Le Chat botté

Dans la tour d'une de ces cités qui gangrènent les abords des grandes métropoles, vivait un vieux travailleur émigré avec ses quatre fils. Leur local était exigu et insalubre, le voisinage cacophonique, malodorant, infesté de vauriens de toute espèce. Bref, l'existence n'était guère un lit de roses.

Ce brave homme mourut prématurément, des séquelles du stress et de la pollution. Son héritage se composait d'une antique voiture en phase terminale qui échut à l'aîné, de quelques ustensiles ménagers dont s'empara le deuxième et de quelques nippes rapiécées que s'appropria le troisième. Quant au cadet, il lui resta les dettes et un vieux chat édenté qui avait eu son heure de gloire mais qui avait largement fait son temps.

Pour le jeune homme, les dettes, c'était déjà beaucoup. Le matou, c'était trop. La mort dans l'âme – car il avait bon cœur – il allait devoir s'en séparer.

Il devenait urgent de m'en mêler.

« Grand-père, dis-je à mon homologue, les humains manquent singulièrement d'imagination et de subtilité. C'est à toi de faire la fortune de ce jeune homme, d'assurer son avenir et le tien par la même occasion.

– Hélas, répondit-il, nous ne sommes plus au siècle de Charles Perrault et des frères Grimm. Il n'y a plus d'ogre de nos jours, plus de Chat botté, plus de roi, plus de trésor miraculeux. Aujourd'hui les princesses épousent des moniteurs de ski, des gigolos internationaux, de grands patrons du marketing ou des stars du rock.

– Laisse-moi faire, grand-père, tu n'auras pas à le regretter. »

Ce matou, qui jadis n'avait pas son pareil pour la chasse aux rats, était las et détaché des intérêts de ce monde. Il accepta ma proposition avec autant de courtoisie que de scepticisme.

Je rejoignis le jeune homme qui errait en broyant du noir dans les rues de la cité. L'avenir lui paraissait plombé, l'issue courue d'avance.

Il finirait soit sans-abri, laissé-pour-compte, soit dealer, gibier de potence voué au pénitencier.

De telles perspectives avaient de quoi décourager. Bien que le langage humain m'ait toujours semblé superficiel et disgracieux, je suis capable de le pratiquer couramment. J'abordai donc ce petit en termes fort civils.

« Tiens, dit-il, un chat qui parle ! J'ai dû trop fumer ! ou alors l'adversité me rend cinglé !... » Je le rassurai aussitôt : « Suis scrupuleusement mes conseils : tu ne seras pas déçu... »

Je l'entraînai dans les beaux quartiers, là où se faisait et se défaisait puissance, fortune, gloire, célébrité.

L'homme du moment contrôlait un vaste réseau médiatique comprenant des sociétés de production et de diffusion dont dépendaient la carrière et la renommée de nombreux artistes. Ses bureaux personnels occupaient les étages supérieurs d'une construction étincelante, d'où il dominait la ville et ses environs.

Le personnage était considérable à tout point de vue. Il pesait bien ses trois cents livres, dévorait à lui seul rôtis, chapons et gigots entiers. Son appétit était vorace, impatient, sans limite. Il en était à sa huitième ou neuvième femme sans compter une ribambelle de maîtresses, principales, secondaires ou de simple passage.

Avec ses concurrents et ses rivaux, qui fleurissaient à son approche comme de la mauvaise herbe, il était d'une cruauté brutale, impitoyable. Toute velléité d'opposition était promptement abordée, terrassée, éradiquée. Les malheureux finissaient à la rue, en prison ou à la morgue.

Son imposante masse étant difficile à déplacer,

il passait le plus clair de son temps dans son immense bureau, attablé devant une multitude d'écrans, de claviers et de télécommandes. Ses doigts courts et boudinés sautillaient, frétillaient, bourdonnaient sur les touches qu'il butinait à longueur de journée comme d'étranges fleurs desséchées où il prélevait tout un pollen électronique d'images virtuelles et de chiffres. Ce sybarite goulu menait avec une tyrannie faussement débonnaire et un paternalisme vaguement salace toute une volière de secrétaires et d'assistantes. Mais ce que la plupart ignoraient, c'est que ce satrape du show-biz était aussi un très puissant sorcier, possédant plus d'un tour pendable et plus d'un sortilège sulfureux dans son sac à malice.

Je conduisis mon protégé vers ses studios où piétinait et piaffait une foule de figurants, candidats et solliciteurs qui espéraient un bout de rôle, un entretien, une audition.

J'invitai mon jeune ami à m'attendre discrètement, et je me faufilai jusqu'au bureau directorial.

Mon intrusion parut divertir l'important personnage. Mais dans ses petits yeux, je distinguai nettement une étincelle d'amusement sadique. « Toi, ricana-t-il, tu ne manques pas de toupet ! Sais-tu que ton impertinence pourrait te coûter cher ? Il me suffirait d'un battement de cils pour te réduire en amuse-gueule.

– Je n'en doute pas, ô colosse indomptable, mais je suis comme tous les chats d'une curiosité insatiable et maladive. Aussi voulais-je voir si toutes les merveilles qu'on m'a contées à votre sujet étaient conformes à la réalité. Par exemple, on m'a dit que vous étiez doué de pouvoirs extraordinaires.

– Là, je t'arrête tout de suite ! Je connais mes classiques, l'histoire de ce stupide sorcier qui se change en souris pour épater le Chat botté… Ne compte pas sur moi pour tomber dans des pièges aussi puérils…

– Je n'aurais pas l'impudence de sous-estimer votre haute sagacité. Mais est-il exact que vous fassiez la pluie et le beau temps dans le domaine du spectacle et du show-biz ? Que sur un signe de votre part n'importe qui peut devenir célèbre du jour au lendemain ?

– Sur ce point, petit drôle à moustaches, on ne t'a pas induit en erreur.

– Donc, si je choisissais au hasard le premier venu parmi la foule de ceux qui attendent votre bon vouloir, vous pourriez en faire une star ?

– Rien de plus facile. »

Je lui désignai alors mon jeune ami qu'on pouvait apercevoir parmi les autres sur un écran géant. Le bibendum alluma des consoles, manipula des télécommandes, pianota sur divers claviers. « Voilà, dit-il, ce quidam est maintenant une star internationale avec une dizaine de comptes en banque pléthoriques…

– Seigneur des illusions et de l'escamotage, je suis vraiment curieux de savoir à quel sommet vertigineux accède votre magie.

– Ton insolence, petit piège à puces, est insondable. Observe et admire ! »

La salle parut alors s'élargir et s'allonger démesurément. Nous étions dans un gigantesque vaisseau interstellaire, une cabine aux proportions gigantesques où clignotaient des milliers de cadrans lumineux.

Le maître des lieux était devenu lui-même une créature phosphorescente et protéiforme, dotée d'une multitude de tentacules et d'antennes.

La minute suivante, nous étions dans une jungle gorgée de moiteurs suffocantes. La clarté du jour s'y frayait un difficile chemin et à travers l'épaisse muraille végétale, on devinait d'inquiétants frémissements et feulements. Le sorcier apparut sous les traits d'un monstrueux anaconda, un prédateur auquel rien ne pouvait résister.

Le décor se transforma encore. Nous étions cette fois dans un fleuve. Dans un flux translucide flottaient mollement des organismes aux contours étranges. Le magicien s'était changé en onde vénéneuse et corrosive qui répandait la mort sur son passage.

À présent, nous étions de retour dans le bureau.

« Alors, qu'en dis-tu ? sourit le producteur avec suffisance.

– Étonnant, vraiment étonnant ! Mais il ne s'agit là que de tours d'illusionniste – exceptionnels j'en conviens. Ô prince des maléfices, j'ai bien plus difficile à vous proposer. Vous avez là plusieurs cassettes vidéo. Pourriez-vous par exemple vous introduire dans l'un de ces films et vous mêler aux personnages de l'histoire ? Je serais curieux de voir ça.

– Aucun problème… »

Il déclencha son magnétoscope et disparut pour se matérialiser aussitôt dans les images du film sélectionné.

D'un rapide coup de patte, j'éteignis l'appareil, récupérai la cassette et lacérai la bande. Puis je rejoignis mon jeune protégé. Son avenir et celui du vieux chat étaient désormais assurés.

Cette version du Chat botté m'avait laissée songeuse. Je lui fis part de mon trouble

« J'ai parfois du mal à vous suivre. Vous n'avez que dédain pour l'espèce humaine. Et pourtant vous vous acharnez à vouloir intervenir dans nos petites affaires qui ne devraient guère vous concerner…

– Décidément, les mammifères bipèdes ne comprennent rien à rien ! » grommela le matou noir.

Puis il me tourna délibérément le dos et affecta de m'ignorer. L'air vaguement offusqué, il alla se percher en haut d'une armoire, en refusant de m'adresser la parole ou même de pousser la condescendance jusqu'à me regarder.

Ce jour-là j'essayai en vain de l'amadouer sur tous les tons, des plus suaves aux plus incisifs.

À la nuit tombée, il s'était évidemment éclipsé.

Le Chat perdu

Un homme et un chat vivaient en parfaite harmonie. Le matou tenait lieu à son compagnon humain d'ami intime, de frère, de confident, voire de maître à penser. Tous deux étaient inséparables. Ils partageaient la même couche, mangeaient dans la même assiette, lisaient les mêmes livres allaient ensemble au marché ou en promenade.

L'homme n'était pas riche mais il disposait d'un petit héritage dont le revenu lui permettait d'assurer l'indispensable, et d'ailleurs il se contentait de peu. Le rare superflu était réservé au félin.

Or, un jour, le chat disparut.

L'homme le chercha partout, fébrilement, et en vain. Ses appels angoissés restèrent sans effet. Il placarda des petites annonces avec promesse de récompense généreuse, dans toute la ville, et fit du porte-à-porte.

Mais les gens raillaient son insistance et haussaient les épaules.

L'animal était introuvable.

Persuadé que le matou avait dû quitter la région, l'homme décida de tout abandonner pour essayer de le rejoindre.

Sa quête, désespérée, le conduisit de cité en cité, de pays en pays, au-delà des plus hautes montagnes et même des plus vastes océans.

Il lui semblait parfois qu'il était sur le point d'aboutir, mais le chat lui échappait toujours. Il allait d'échec en échec, de déception en déception.

Les mois et les années passèrent.

L'homme ne renonçait pas. Il avait accompli plusieurs fois le tour du monde, sillonné les contrées les plus étranges et les plus inhospitalières.

Parvenu au seuil de la vieillesse, il retourna chez lui.

En pénétrant dans sa demeure, il jeta machinalement un coup d'œil au miroir de l'entrée. Le chat était perché sur son épaule.

Pendant tout ce temps, toute cette interminable quête, il n'avait jamais quitté son épaule – trop évident et trop présent pour être vu.

« Ma chère, dit le conteur, j'exige désormais des menus plus variés. Je trouve que vous manquez un peu d'imagination culinaire. Par exemple, je voudrais des olives, des chips, de la ciboulette et du foie de morue. Des calamars feront aussi l'affaire, ainsi que ces petites graines gluantes et succulentes que vous appelez caviar. Mais bien entendu, je désire le meilleur, pas un de ces ersatz insipides et bon marché complètement dénué d'intérêt.

– Je veux bien essayer de vous faire plaisir. Mais ne croyez quand même pas que votre position particulière vous donne tous les droits !

– Allons, soyez raisonnable, et venez donc plutôt me câliner comme il se doit. »

Il passa le reste du jour à s'étirer dans tous les sens et à bâiller, mâchoire béante.

La Jeune Fille et le dragon

Un hideux dragon terrorisait les habitants d'une contrée lointaine.

Le monstre avait un aspect vraiment abominable, avec des ailes fourchues et dentelées, une peau fumante hérissée d'une forêt de crocs écumants, des écailles cornues, un crâne plat jonché de piquants et de pustules.

Dans la région, chacun fuyait épouvanté à son approche. Tous espéraient qu'un homme, un jour, aurait la force et le courage de l'affronter et de l'éliminer.

Or, cette bête à l'apparence féroce était en fait un beau et gentil prince qu'un sorcier difforme et envieux avait métamorphosé en le frappant d'un sortilège puissant et particulièrement vicieux. Car outre son aspect répugnant, le malheureux dragon était condamné à exprimer le contraire de ce qu'il ressentait. Plus il était sous l'emprise de la peur, plus il avait l'air redoutable et impitoyable. S'il éprouvait une joie quelconque, il paraissait atteint d'une incurable mélancolie.

De temps à autre, quelques valeureux chevaliers, armés jusqu'aux dents, proposaient à la population de combattre le fléau et d'exterminer le monstre.

Dès que le pauvre dragon apercevait l'un de ces intrépides champions, si fier et menaçant, bien décidé à l'anéantir, l'angoisse l'étreignait et la terreur le submergeait, car c'était un cœur sensible, une nature douce et impressionnable.

L'étrange malédiction lui donnait alors une allure si atroce et insoutenable, lui inspirait des rictus si grimaçants, des rugissements si tonitruants que les plus braves prenaient leurs jambes à leur cou sans demander leur reste.

Aussi le dragon passait-il le plus clair de son temps à trembler intérieurement tout en semant l'effroi, ce qui ne manquait pas bien sûr, de le désoler. Mais plus il se morfondait, plus il devenait objet d'horreur et d'exécration.

Un jour, après avoir copieusement brouté les pâturages alentour – car il était végétarien – il faisait paisiblement la sieste en dorant le bout de son museau écailleux et cornu au soleil.

Une belle voyageuse passait dans les parages. C'était une jeune fille curieuse et entreprenante, qui avait dédaigné les mises en garde effarouchées des habitants du coin, persuadés que cette téméraire allait promptement se faire dévorer.

Le dragon entrouvrit un œil et fut immédiatement subjugué par la visiteuse. Pour tout dire, il en tomba follement amoureux. C'était pour lui comme un éblouissement qui éclairait son être d'une félicité intense.

La méchante magie dont il avait été victime agit hélas inexorablement. Et il manifesta tous les signes de la plus affreuse détresse.

La voyageuse fut intriguée, puis peu à peu émue par le torrent de larmes qui jaillissait de ses prunelles fauves et par les sanglots qui secouaient son immense carcasse reptilienne. Elle lui caressa le mufle trempé de pleurs.

« Eh bien, dragon, pourquoi donc as-tu tant de peine ? On m'avait pourtant dit que tu étais cruel et intraitable… »

Le sorcier qui avait jadis envoûté le prince n'avait guère prévu qu'une âme pure pourrait éprouver de la compassion pour le monstre.

Le sortilège fut instantanément annulé. Et le prince épousa la belle voyageuse.

Après la toilette et les câlineries d'usage, le chat se mit à poursuivre une grosse mouche fébrile et bruyante qui bourdonnait rageusement contre les vitres du salon. Il épiait son vol désordonné, remuant assez comiquement l'arrière-train, puis bondissait, saisissant l'insecte d'un savant et fulgurant coup de patte, l'estourbissant un peu pour le relâcher ensuite et continuer ce petit jeu ambigu.

« Vous retombez en enfance, lui dis-je. On dirait un chaton écervelé.

– Fournissez-moi donc des proies dignes de ce nom ! La chasse me manque. Donnez-moi des mulots, des souris, des pies ou des moineaux !

– Et quoi encore ! Je ne vais pas transformer cette maison en charnier pour satisfaire vos caprices. Nous ne sommes pas ici sur un terrain de safari !

– Alors, laissez-moi m'amuser avec les mouches, et vaquez à vos occupations habituelles. »

Je renonçais à le convaincre – je connaissais trop bien sa mauvaise foi – et m'absorbai dans d'autres tâches.

Béatrice

La petite princesse Béatrice vivait heureuse, dans un joli palais, au milieu d'un peuple prospère et jovial.

Le roi et la reine, ses parents, étaient des souverains débonnaires et bienveillants, toujours prompts à secourir un sujet en détresse. Aucune gâterie n'était trop belle pour leur enfant chérie, et chaque mois ils inventaient une fête nouvelle en son honneur.

Ainsi la jeune Béatrice grandissait dans la soie et la douceur, choyée par ses proches et vénérée par le peuple.

À sa naissance, toutes les fées des environs s'étaient penchées avec empressement pour lui assurer beauté, santé, fortune, amour, et pour parer son caractère de toutes les plus hautes et nobles vertus.

Or, une très vénéneuse et sadique sorcière avait surgi après le départ des bonnes marraines. « Voici mon cadeau personnel ! » coassa-t-elle, avec un grand rire sardonique. Il s'agissait d'une magnifique tapisserie représentant un parc luxuriant rempli de fleurs géantes et multicolores.

La méchante magicienne fixa l'ouvrage au-dessus du lit de la princesse en précisant qu'il serait vain d'essayer de l'arracher ou de le déchirer.

« Le jour de ses quinze ans, conclut-elle, cette tapisserie causera inéluctablement sa perte ! »

Et elle s'en fut repue de haine, sifflant de rage et claudiquant car elle avait un sabot fourchu en guise de pied droit.

Le roi et la reine étaient consternés. Chacun dans le château se désolait.

Heureusement une petite fée retardataire débarqua inopinément. Elle était toute petite, très boulotte, affreusement distraite, passablement farfelue, et affligée d'un fort bégaiement.

On lui exposa la situation. Pouvait-elle contrecarrer les menaces de la sorcière ? Elle fouilla dans les nombreuses poches de ses jupes et jupons dont elle sortit successivement un piège à gnome, un élixir à effacer les mauvais souvenirs, un entonnoir pour engraisser les elfes anorexiques, un purgatif pour dragons boulimiques, quelques plumes d'anges tombées du nid, et un rossignol magique pour changer l'aube en crépuscule, plus quelques accessoires d'un usage incertain.

« Ah voi... voi... voilà ! dit-elle enfin. De la pou... pou... pou... poudre d'éveil ! »

Le roi demanda fort poliment quelques explications, mais elle bégayait tant que ses propos se noyèrent dans d'inintelligibles onomatopées. Il fallut bien s'en contenter.

Quinze années passèrent.

Le jour fatidique arriva.

La tapisserie s'anima d'une vie ondulante et grouillante. Entre les fleurs, derrière les buissons et parmi les taillis, des museaux reptiliens et des mufles hideux aux babines fumantes et aux crocs acérés commencèrent à se dévoiler, grossissant peu à peu, prenant mouvement, volume et consistance. Des pattes griffues tâtèrent le terrain, des tentacules rageuses fouettèrent l'espace, des yeux de braise et de métal liquide scrutèrent les environs, des langues visqueuses et noires s'entortillèrent autour des tiges.

Ces monstres n'allaient pas tarder à déserter la tapisserie pour envahir la chambre, dévaster le palais et ravager toute la contrée.

Chacun tremblait de terreur. Les bons monarques étaient atterrés.

La reine dit soudain : « J'ai une idée ! Voici qui pourra peut-être nous sauver !... »

Elle brandit une fiole contenant des flocons de rêves – cadeaux de sa marraine, une vieille fée qu'elle n'avait pas vue depuis son enfance. Elle en saupoudra les monstres qui s'assoupirent, mais leur sommeil était léger, tout hérissé de cauchemars voraces, et il fallut recommencer encore et encore.

Au bout de quelques heures la fiole était vide. Et l'affreuse progression reprit inexorablement. Le pays tout entier allait être saccagé, et ses habitants dévorés.

La princesse alors se souvint de cette poudre d'éveil que lui avait donnée jadis la drôle de petite fée retardataire. Nul ne savait à quoi elle pouvait servir au juste. Mais elle prit le flacon et en respira le contenu.

Béatrice fut réveillée par une appétissante odeur de croissants frais et de chocolat chaud. « Allons, debout, grosse paresseuse, lui dit sa mère. Aujourd'hui c'est le grand jour, tu as quinze ans ! Dépêche-toi un peu ! Il y a plein de bonnes choses qui t'attendent… »

À la fin du récit, le matou se mit à miauler plaintivement, comme un chaton perdu. Il me regardait fixement, droit dans les yeux, avec une expression de muette interrogation, puis miaulait à nouveau d'une petite voix presque éplorée.

« Seriez-vous malade ? Auriez-vous des soucis ? du chagrin ? »

Il continua ses plaintes pendant une bonne partie

de la journée. Puis il choisit de m'ignorer et s'endormit comme si de rien n'était, m'abandonnant à ma perplexité.

Avec lui, je n'étais pas au bout de mes surprises.

Le Petit Chaperon rouge

Il y avait, à une époque certaine qui pourrait aussi bien être la nôtre, un loup très détestable, féroce et abominable qui faisait honte à son espèce, laquelle est noble et nécessaire.

Cet animal hideux, qui arborait une mèche toute raide et une ridicule petite moustache, s'appelait Adolf. Il régnait en maître cruel et inflexible sur une contrée sombre et froide, où il commandait une horde vorace de prédateurs tous empressés à le servir, pour partager quelques minutes de son pouvoir dément.

Cette meute malfaisante et teigneuse ravageait les terres voisines et parquait dans des abattoirs certaines catégories de la population dont la chair lui semblait particulièrement goûteuse et succulente. Festins, orgies et bacchanales sanguinaires se succédaient à un rythme hallucinant, car Adolf et ses partenaires n'étaient jamais rassasiés.

Le loup se prélassait dans ses nombreuses tanières, dont il venait de dévorer les précédents occupants. Un jour, s'y présenta une étrange petite fille, avec un beau panier rempli de friandises. Elle était frêle, fluette, gracieuse. Des yeux immenses éclairaient ses traits purs et des tresses toutes frisées encadraient son visage. Elle portait un manteau rouge où était brodée une magnifique étoile de fils d'or.

Aux yeux d'Adolf, la petite était la proie la plus appétissante qu'il eût jamais eue à sa merci.

Pour mieux tromper ses victimes, ce loup impitoyable aimait jouer les papas gâteaux, ami des gens et des bêtes. Plus d'une créature inoffensive s'y était laissé prendre, malgré les preuves manifestes de la barbarie d'Adolf.

La petite fille fut conduite dans son repaire.

« Je viens, dit-elle au monstre, rendre visite à un lointain cousin. Êtes-vous celui que je cherche ?

– Assurément mon enfant, je suis bien celui-là. Et j'attendais ta venue… »

Il s'agissait bien sûr de l'ancien propriétaire qu'Adolf avait dégusté en brochettes.

« Eh bien cousin, pourquoi êtes-vous si grand et si velu ?

– C'est pour être le plus fort mon enfant.

– Et pourquoi avez-vous de si grandes oreilles ?

– Pour avoir l'ouïe la plus fine !

– Et des yeux aussi brillants ?

– Pour avoir la vue la plus perçante !

– Et un aussi long nez ?

– Pour avoir l'odorat le plus performant !

– Et pourquoi, cousin, des mains aussi crochues ?

– Mais parce que j'appartiens à la race des seigneurs, mon enfant !

– Et pourquoi donc, cousin, d'aussi puissantes mâchoires ?

– Mais pour mieux te manger mon enfant ! »

Le loup, qui bavait déjà de concupiscence, se jeta sur l'enfant et la croqua aussitôt, savourant chaque bouchée.

Seulement, Adolf ignorait un détail, cette petite fille en rouge n'était pas une enfant ordinaire. C'était un djinn chargé par les dieux, excédés, d'une mission particulière. En s'offrant délibérément à l'appétit du loup, elle l'infecta d'un mal incurable qui se propagea et contamina rapidement tous les fidèles suppôts d'Adolf.

La terre en fut ainsi débarrassée.

Mais le monde n'est pas pour autant à l'abri des monstres de cette espèce.

Ce matin, le chat me parut quelque peu mélancolique. Il dédaigna ses croquettes et bouda même la quotidienne séance de brossage.

« Pourquoi cette humeur sombre et une telle tristesse ? lui demandai-je.

– C’est la Lune. Cette nuit, elle sera pleine, si belle, si douce, irrésistible. Elle me laisse toujours languir. Quand donc se donnera-t-elle à moi ? Quand répondra-t-elle à mes avances ?

– Allons, un peu de patience. Je crois que vous avez encore pas mal de chemin à parcourir… »

Le Dieu sans tête

Le Seigneur Shiva, souverain des sphères, créateur du ciel et de la terre, était embarrassé.

Il se sentait irrité contre lui-même, ce qui le rendait de fort méchante humeur.

Il réunit le ban et l'arrière-ban de ses ministres et conseillers, tous esprits subtils et d'une haute sagacité.

« Voilà, proféra-t-il d'une voix dont l'écho tonitruant remplissait les plus vertigineux espaces et se répercutait d'infini en infini. Je ne suis guère satisfait de l'univers que j'ai produit. Il y manque quelque chose, quelque chose d'essentiel, mais je ne saurais dire quoi. Vous, mes fidèles serviteurs, j'attends à ce sujet vos suggestions et vos propositions.

– Seigneur, protestèrent les plus timorés, ta science est infaillible et tes pouvoirs illimités ! Comment pourrait-il y avoir le moindre défaut, la plus petite carence dans ta divine création ?

– Je n'ai que faire de vos flagorneries. Ce qu'il me faut c'est un avis lucide, une opinion éclairée.

– Seigneur, intervinrent quelques anges supérieurs, laisse-nous quelque temps pour réfléchir à la question.

– Qu'il en soit ainsi », consentit Shiva.

Deux ou trois éternités passèrent. Et le Seigneur suprême convoqua à nouveau son conseil.

« Eh bien, ô ministres loyaux et zélés, quels sont les fruits de vos méditations ? J'attends vos recommandations. »

Les esprits s'exprimèrent tour à tour et le débat fut vif. Les arguments et objections fusaient de toutes parts avec un luxe inouï de considérations théologiques et de développements métaphysiques d'une complexité transcendante.

Mais Shiva n'était pas convaincu.

Après un long silence passablement oppressant, un modeste djinn qui occupait un rang subalterne dans la céleste monarchie émit dans un timide murmure : « Seigneur Shiva, si j'ose me le permettre, je me risque à croire que tu n'as pas été assez présent dans l'univers. Ton œuvre était certes admirable, mais tu en étais toi-même trop éloigné… »

Le maître écarquilla son troisième œil immense, plus profond que la nuit, plus lumineux que mille soleils, en guise d'assentiment.

« Je vais y réfléchir, dit-il. Je vous ferai sous peu connaître mes conclusions… »

Au bout de deux ou trois grandes ères galactiques, le temps qu'explosent et meurent plusieurs myriades d'étoiles, mais pour Shiva l'affaire de quelques heures, l'omniprésent souverain des sphères, prince des métamorphoses, maître du ballet cosmique, de la chorégraphie des nébuleuses et des atomes, s'adressa en ces termes à la très vénérable assemblée : « Ô nobles et très sages conseillers, voici ce que j'ai décidé. Dans le précédent univers, je n'étais pas présent parmi mes créatures. Et c'est cette grave lacune dont j'ai trop tard mesuré tous les inconvénients. La prochaine fois je m'engage à procéder différemment.

– Mais à quel signe pourra-t-on reconnaître et déceler ta présence ?

– Là où je me manifesterai, je serai Celui-qui-n'a-pas-de-tête. Et je serai le seul, l'unique à n'avoir pas de visage. Chaque fois, je serai le seul à n'avoir rien au-dessus des épaules et du cou, au milieu des innombrables créatures équipées d'une tête et d'un visage. Et ce Rien sera conscience, connaissance, et Amour. »

Le gros chat noir était songeur.

« Je me demande, lui dis-je, où vous avez été pêcher ce conte à dormir debout, avec ces allusions ésotériques et ces références vaguement hindoues…

– Comme toujours, vous et vos semblables, vous pensez, discutez, ergotez. Essayez plutôt d'être, et de voir la simple évidence !

– Décidément, vous vous complaisez dans l'hermétisme et vous vous délectez de rêveries absconses. »

Il sourit, comme seuls savent sourire les chats, en plissant les yeux et retroussant les moustaches. Puis il s'installa sur le canapé du salon, dans une pose énigmatique et hiératique, ce qui était une manière de me signifier que mes questions l'importunaient, et que toute insistance de ma part serait du dernier mauvais goût.

J'avais ce jour-là de nombreux rendez-vous. Quand je rentrai, en fin d'après-midi, il n'avait pas bougé d'un millimètre et affichait la même expression ironique. Mais le mystère n'était-il pas sa seconde nature, presque sa carte de visite ? Voire son état civil…

Le Divorce

Il était une fois un petit fonctionnaire modèle qui affichait en toute circonstance une rigueur morale exemplaire. Il était d'une honnêteté pointilleuse, travailleur infatigable, toujours ponctuel, d'une politesse irréprochable, empêtré dans les principes et dans les convenances, très soigné de sa personne. Avec ça, modeste, attentionné, bon père, bon époux, respectueux des usages, payant scrupuleusement ses impôts et ses charges, et parfaitement à jour dans ses cotisations.

Bref, un petit homme tout lisse, bien briqué, bien net, sans la plus petite bosse, ni la moindre aspérité.

Mais ce joli représentant des vertus cardinales était secrètement chatouillé par des tentations répétitives et lancinantes – un jupon retroussé par le vent dans la rue, quelques menus larcins, une soudaine envie de médisance, ou quelques bonnes vieilles gifles distribuées sans raison. Rien de vraiment méchant, mais de brusques pulsions, des caprices inexplicables qui restaient à l'état de pures velléités insoupçonnables même aux yeux du psychologue le plus averti.

Ces égarements et dérapages intimes étaient pour le bonhomme un véritable tourment. Il en chercha fiévreusement la cause, et finit par se persuader que son ombre était la seule responsable de ses manquements réitérés. Son union avec ce sosie obscur, muet, et assurément malfaisant, n'avait que trop duré. Il lui avait été imposé dès la naissance, et le suivait depuis lors pas à pas, lui inspirant des pensées, des états d'âme subversifs, inacceptables.

Il engagea résolument une procédure de divorce. Le silence persistant de l'ombre valant un consentement, l'administration qui ne tient compte que des chiffres et des formulaires, accomplit sa besogne et expédia les formalités sans se pencher outre mesure sur cette étrange requête, et le divorce fut prononcé.

L'ombre partit de son côté vivre sa vie d'ombre. Quant à l'excellent homme, il ne fut plus jamais perturbé par de mauvaises pensées parasites. Il mena jusqu'au bout une existence irréprochable, dans le strict respect des lois et des commandements, et dans l'estime générale.

Pendant ce temps, l'ombre avait fait son chemin. Ayant l'âme perverse et l'esprit retors et possédant des talents d'illusionniste peu courants, elle réunit et dirigea en despote absolu le gang le plus sanguinaire des annales criminelles. N'étant plus bridée par les vertueux scrupules de son ancien partenaire, l'ombre s'en donnait à cœur joie, s'embusquant le jour et agissant la nuit où elle était comme un poisson dans l'eau.

Tout finit par s'user. Après des années de forfaits impunis, l'ombre s'étiola et mourut.

Au même instant, l'homme exhalait son dernier soupir au milieu d'une famille éplorée.

Le trépas ressouda aussitôt les deux entités, et c'est un seul fantôme qui se présenta devant le juge des enfers.

Le verdict fut sans appel : « En répudiant ton ombre, tu l'as laissée libre de ravager le monde à sa guise. Cette part de ténèbres, tu en avais la charge et la garde. Tant pis pour toi ! »

Le défunt fut précipité au cœur du gouffre le plus gluant et le plus oppressant.

Ce matin-là, le chat se montra inhabituellement espiègle, turbulent, voire insupportable. Il se lança d'abord dans une poursuite effrénée de sa propre queue, tournant sur lui-même comme une toupie folle. Puis il se jeta sur les rideaux qu'il lacéra du sol au plafond. Il sauta ensuite sur une table en renversant et dispersant les pièces d'un échiquier. Je m'efforçai de l'attraper pour lui infliger une bonne leçon. Mais il était beaucoup plus souple et bien plus vif que moi. Il se faufila sous mon lit en ricanant. Il crut bon même de me narguer : « Allez, allez, vous pouvez toujours courir… »

Il resta couché toute la journée dans son refuge. Au coucher du soleil, il avait disparu.

La Mort amoureuse

La Mort avait rendez-vous avec un vieux philosophe dont la dernière heure allait bientôt sonner.

Cet homme étant d'une haute sagesse et d'un profond savoir, la Mort se présenta un peu en avance, car, curieuse de tout, elle souhaitait parfaire ses connaissances et sa compréhension des choses en partageant pendant quelques jours le quotidien du vieillard.

Ce dernier guettait sa venue depuis déjà un bon moment. Sa sérénité ne fut donc nullement troublée.

Elle lui apparut sous les traits d'une pimpante et savoureuse jeune fille, sans doute pour adoucir le pénible passage.

« Je t'attendais, lui dit-il. Et je ne vois aucun inconvénient à passer en ta compagnie les derniers jours de mon existence. Mais comment dois-je te présenter aux miens ? Faut-il leur avouer la vérité qui risquerait de les chagriner prématurément ? Je ne veux pas d'un concert de lamentations avant de quitter cette terre...

– Dis-leur que je suis une lointaine parente venue ici faire un séjour à l'improviste... »

Cette soudaine intrusion ne choquait guère le voisinage car la Mort sut se montrer discrète, souriante et légère.

Le philosophe avait un fils, jeune homme original et un peu fou, qui charmait tous les cœurs car il était poète. Il advint que la Mort, côtoyant de fort près ce séducteur au timbre mélodieux et aux belles envolées métaphoriques, en tomba passionnément amoureuse.

Elle avait revêtu les traits les plus harmonieux et les plus suaves, propres à troubler n'importe quel représentant de l'espèce masculine. Le poète se sentit donc naturellement fondre devant la beauté de cette sémillante personne.

Un flirt s'engagea aussitôt, suivi de quelques séances érotiques assez torrides.

Mais la Mort voulait davantage.

Il y avait chez le jeune homme comme une distance, une retenue qui l'empêchait de se donner complètement au moment crucial. Et la Mort amoureuse n'aspirait qu'à cette grande fusion. Les petits jeux charnels n'étaient pour elle que des enfantillages de surface, des simulacres dénués d'intérêt, uniquement destinés à fourvoyer les mortels pour les inciter à se reproduire. Le véritable amour était d'une tout autre nature.

Devant cette étrange et persistante dérobade, elle finit par dévoiler à son amant sa véritable identité, et la raison de sa présence.

« Si tu te donnes à moi entièrement, lui dit-elle, tu partageras mon pouvoir qui est prodigieux, illimité, bien au-delà de tes plus délirants fantasmes. Sache que je puis être au même instant à des milliards d'endroits différents à chaque point où une créature de chair doit passer de vie à trépas. Tu ne soupçonnes pas l'extatique jubilation qui marque chacune de mes interventions. Tout ceci, je te l'offre. Il suffit que tu t'ouvres pleinement et sans arrière-pensée.

– J'apprécie à sa juste mesure tant de sollicitude mais je ne me sens pas libre d'accepter ta proposition. Mon cœur est pris ailleurs… »

La Mort, furieuse, se jura de découvrir qui était cette impudente rivale, et de l'éliminer promptement. Mais en dépit de ses moyens, qui étaient immenses, toutes ses investigations se soldèrent par un échec. L'heureuse élue demeurait mystérieuse, introuvable.

Excédée, elle questionna son amant :

« Dis-moi le nom de cette péronnelle qui te fait languir au point d'ignorer mes avances et qui m'est une offense permanente ! Ne sais-tu pas que l'anéantir serait pour moi un jeu d'enfant ?

– Je ne crois pas, répondit le jeune homme, car celle à qui j'appartiens s'appelle Poésie… »

Le soir même, la Mort acheva sa mission auprès du philosophe et quitta la maison sans regret.

Le matou minaudait et miaulait avec des mines faussement effarouchées.

« Si j'étais un tout petit chaton, est-ce que vous me donneriez le sein comme dans la chanson ?

– Permettez-moi de vous dire que votre humour est discutable. La chanson est délicieuse, mais elle n'a rien de réaliste.

– Qu'en savez-vous ? Avez-vous déjà tenté l'expérience ?

– Mais enfin…

– Il n'y a pas de mais, ni de enfin qui tiennent ! Voilà encore vos préjugés, votre conformisme !

– Quel caractère !

– Je suis un chat. N'essayez donc pas de me faire prendre des vessies pour des lanternes ! Restez à l'étroit dans votre réalisme, et laissez-moi musarder au milieu des chimères ! »

L'Enfant du temps

Sa mère était une femme étrange, loin des sentiers battus et du conformisme ambiant. Elle était très belle, très douce, avec une espèce de mélancolie que rien, jamais, ne pouvait altérer.

Physiquement, la petite lui ressemblait d'une manière troublante, presque parfaite. Elle était fille unique et n'avait jamais connu son père. Lorsqu'elle avait commencé à la questionner sur ce sujet, sa mère lui avait simplement dit, avec un sourire triste : « Un jour, bien assez tôt, tu sauras tout… » Bien sûr, cette réponse énigmatique n'avait fait qu'attiser sa curiosité.

Moralement, elle avait souvent l'impression, d'être en tout point à l'opposé de sa mère. Autant elle était espiègle, enjouée, capricieuse, distraite, dispersée, souvent imprévisible, autant sa mère était calme, stricte, concentrée.

Femme intellectuellement brillante et d'une vaste culture, elle l'avait tenue à l'écart de toute école, assurant elle-même son instruction, et la petite avait grandi sans camarade de jeux, à l'exception de quelques rares voisins ou de rencontres fortuites lors de sorties et promenades.

La mère et la fille se prénommaient toutes les deux Sarah : il y avait donc Sarah I et Sarah II.

À cause de cet isolement systématique et de cette répugnance obstinée à vivre comme tout le monde, Sarah II détestait parfois Sarah I, avec de brusques bouffées de colère et de révolte.

Chaque soir, Sarah I obligeait sa fille à lire les principaux journaux du jour et à retenir par cœur certains gros titres ainsi que les résultats des courses ou du loto. Aux yeux de l'adolescente, cette manie confinait au délire, d'autant que sa mère imposait cette discipline absurde avec une rigueur extrême.

À l'âge où toutes les jeunes filles avaient leur premier flirt, Sarah II vivait confinée, presque recluse, avec sa mère pour seule compagnie.

Sarah I exerçait un métier peu ordinaire : elle était voyante. Non pas une de ces diseuses de bonne aventure pour amateur de frissons et créatures crédules, mais une authentique sibylle, douée de facultés exceptionnelles qui lui valaient une renommée internationale. Parmi ses habituels consultants, elle avait des stars, des chefs d'entreprise, des hommes politiques, voire des chefs d'État. Ses performances lui avaient valu d'amasser une fortune, car ses prévisions étaient toujours d'une incroyable exactitude.

À dix-huit ans, Sarah II fit accidentellement la connaissance d'un jeune homme dont le charme et l'intelligence la subjuguèrent aussitôt. Lui-même, partageant pleinement cette attirance, fut également conquis.

Assez bizarrement, Sarah I, qui était généralement si réticente et si sévère sur le chapitre des sorties et des fréquentations de sa fille, semblait cette fois l'encourager, voire la pousser dans les bras de son soupirant. Elle refusa toutefois qu'il lui soit présenté, prétextant divers impératifs ou rendez-vous professionnels, et laissant volontiers les jeunes gens en tête à tête.

L'amoureux de Sarah II était chercheur. Il avait obtenu les plus hautes distinctions universitaires, et il était promis à un bel avenir.

La nuit où elle se donna à lui, à la fois tendrement et fougueusement, il lui parla de ses travaux et lui confia un grand secret. Il venait de mettre au point une technique révolutionnaire lui permettant de se déplacer dans le temps. Le matin même, il avait réussi à expédier une souris dans le passé – un saut de cinq minutes en arrière. L'animal était d'ailleurs apparu dans le laboratoire avant qu'il ne finisse l'expérience, et pendant cinq minutes, les deux exemplaires d'une même souris avaient cohabité dans un même espace.

Jusqu'à présent, sa méthode ne permettait qu'un

mouvement à sens unique vers le passé. Aucune projection dans l'avenir n'était encore possible.

Puis le jeune homme avoua son grand projet: il était bien décidé à opérer lui-même un bond dans le passé d'une vingtaine d'années. Sarah II n'hésita guère, elle serait du voyage. Il était impensable à ses yeux d'envisager une séparation.

Il l'aimait. Il accepta.

Pour elle ce serait étonnant de pouvoir rencontrer sa mère jeune – et surtout de connaître enfin ce père absent et mystérieux. Ils allaient tout abandonner derrière eux, brûler tous leurs vaisseaux. Mais l'aventure était exaltante, surhumaine.

Ils effectuèrent un saut de dix-neuf années dans le passé, arrivant un peu moins d'un an avant la naissance même de Sarah, près de la ville où elle avait vécu toute son enfance.

La jeune femme avait traversé la barrière du temps sans le moindre dommage. Mais son compagnon avait subi un choc fatal. Une fausse manœuvre ou un mauvais calcul l'avait tué.

Sarah, impuissante, était désespérée, elle dut s'éloigner de sa dépouille.

Elle chercha tout d'abord à contacter sa mère. Elle savait bien qu'elle venait de perdre à tout jamais sa joie de vivre mais il fallait bien se raccrocher à quelque chose.

Sa mère était introuvable, inconnue à des lieues à la ronde.

Elle se résigna donc à faire le travail qu'on lui proposait pour subsister – serveuse, vendeuse, hôtesse d'accueil. Elle était toujours aussi jolie, mais sa profonde tristesse décourageait d'avance tout prétendant éventuel.

Elle s'aperçut qu'elle était enceinte – ultime cadeau de son amour perdu.

Par ailleurs, connaissant parfaitement les événements majeurs des vingt prochaines années, elle avait ouvert un cabinet de voyance où elle fit rapidement fortune.

Au bout de neuf mois, elle accoucha d'une petite fille qu'elle prénomma naturellement Sarah.

Maintenant, elle savait. Elle savait qui elle était vraiment et qui était son père. Sarah II était devenue Sarah I, l'Enfant du temps.

Sa propre mère et sa propre fille pour l'éternité.

« Ma chère, que diriez-vous de devenir chatte pour pouvoir approfondir notre intimité ? Peut-être même au passage m'offrir une ou deux portées…

– Vous avez vraiment de drôles d'idées !

– Ne vous y trompez pas, ce serait pour vous une promotion et un honneur ! Il y a bien peu de femelles bipèdes à qui un chat proposerait une telle faveur. Votre destin humain est si peu enviable ! Nous sommes tellement plus libres, plus sages et plus poètes !

– Je vous promets d'y réfléchir…

– Voilà bien le mental calamiteux et embrouillé des bipèdes ! Question simple, réponse cafouilleuse… »

La Reine des fées

La reine des fées dansait et virevoltait joyeusement, bondissant de cascade en cascade, voletant de brise en brise, glissant sur les arpèges de la lumière matinale et s'ébrouant dans la rosée.

Le printemps revenait avec son enivrant cortège de senteurs douces, de frissons juvéniles et de petites malices. L'air était à nouveau chargé d'une promesse de vie exaltante, légère et sensuelle. Les feuillages s'humectaient d'épices, de sèves et d'essences, le vent charriait une fièvre d'accouplement, la terre elle-même redevenait le théâtre des lentes stratégies amoureuses.

Pour la reine des fées c'était toujours une période privilégiée.

Elle jetait alors son dévolu sur les plus séduisants mortels du voisinage et collectionnait les amants qu'elle statufiait ensuite à l'issue de leur prestation érotique. Elle possédait ainsi au fond d'une caverne secrète toute une population d'anciens soupirants pétrifiés pour l'éternité.

Ce printemps-là, elle se sentait particulièrement jeune et performante, affamée de friandises charnelles.

Elle envoya les nymphes et les ondines, ses suivantes, à la recherche des plus jolis godelureaux et savoureux jeunes hommes de la région. Il ne fut guère difficile de les attirer dans ses nombreux pièges hypnotiques, puis de les soumettre à ses alléchants stratagèmes.

Elle ne fut pas déçue et connut une belle succession de nuits scintillantes.

Le prince des elfes, des lutins et des faunes, son époux, excédé par les frasques de sa dulcinée, décida de lui jouer un bon tour.

Tandis qu'elle se prélassait dans une sieste réparatrice, après des ébats acrobatiques prolongés, il saupoudra ses paupières closes d'un pollen magique : à son réveil, elle tomberait follement amoureuse de la première créature aperçue.

Quand la reine des fées ouvrit les yeux, son regard s'attarda sur un énorme crapaud qui se dorait au soleil. Elle se sentit irrésistiblement attirée par ce bellâtre aux pustules si excitantes, aux membres si harmonieusement squameux et glaireux. Une telle harmonie de couleurs et de formes lui parut un enchantement. Pour tout dire, c'était l'être vivant le plus accompli et le plus parfait qu'elle eût jamais rencontré.

Elle mit en œuvre toutes les ressources de sa séduction la plus lascive pour entraîner le crapaud dans sa couche nuptiale.

En dépit d'un esprit obtus et d'une sensibilité plutôt limitée, le batracien ne se fit pas prier longtemps. La reine des fées n'en finissait plus de se pâmer devant les charmes de son partenaire, s'extasiant bruyamment au spectacle de ses yeux globuleux et de ses pattes palmées.

Devant ce couple extrêmement farfelu, il y eut un grand rassemblement de gnomes, de trolls, de djinns et de génies subtils qui s'esclaffèrent, s'époumonèrent et s'étouffèrent de rire. Un tel vacarme attira les autres espèces, notamment les grenouilles et les crapauds qui voyant l'un des leurs adulé par la fée comme une divinité solaire furent eux aussi secoués d'un tonitruant et rauque fou rire.

Et c'est depuis ce temps que ces animaux coassent.

Lorsque le prince des elfes leva le sortilège, son épouse fut si honteuse et si mortifiée qu'elle jura de se rendre invisible aux créatures mortelles pendant au moins mille ans.

Et c'est aussi depuis ce temps que les hommes ont cessé de fréquenter les fées.

Bien entendu les chats, qui sont dotés d'un organe visuel très spécial, font exception à la règle et continuent de voir distinctement ce que vous autres bipèdes ne percevez plus qu'en rêve.

Le chat s'était posé sur mes genoux, les paupières mi-closes.

« Tenez, murmura-t-il, chantez-moi une berceuse !

– Et quoi encore !

– Oui une de ces jolies comptines dont raffolent vos petits bipèdes… »

Avec lui, je n'avais jamais le dernier mot. Alors, ce matin-là, je fredonnai toutes les bribes de chansons enfantines qui me revenaient en mémoire, tandis qu'il ronronnait paisiblement, entrouvrant parfois un œil pour réclamer : « Encore une… encore… »

L'Ogre et le saint

Il y avait un ogre, brute sanguinaire et colossale aux énormes mâchoires plantées de crocs féroces, aux bras immenses terminés par des griffes avides semblables à des fourches et aux lourds pieds difformes conçus pour écraser les obstacles et pour broyer ses proies récalcitrantes.

Ce monstre obèse aux petits yeux fiévreux et au double menton maculé de fétides résidus culinaires, écumait la région pour kidnapper les enfants égarés dont il dévorait la tendre chair avec délectation. Son grand plaisir était de suçoter les os pendant des heures avant de s'abîmer dans une sieste épaisse au fond de son repaire, une profonde caverne, si sale et répugnante que même les putois et les hyènes s'y seraient évanouis de dégoût.

Des centaines d'enfants avaient ainsi disparu, car sa boulimie était sans limite.

Toutes les familles du coin étaient en deuil, toutes les mères pleuraient la perte d'un rejeton escamoté au cours d'une randonnée, d'une partie de pêche ou d'une simple course dans la campagne voisine.

Un jour un étrange petit garçon, doux, souriant et paisible, s'aventura jusqu'à la tanière du monstre. Sans s'offusquer de la laideur et de la pestilence des lieux, il demanda poliment l'autorisation de se reposer un peu sur place.

L'autre gloussa, frotta ses mains crochues et saisit le marmot qu'il dépeça rapidement pour le croquer en quelques bouchées juteuses.

Or cet enfant était un grand saint, doté de pouvoirs angéliques puissants.

Sitôt dans l'estomac de l'ogre, il rappela à la vie toutes ses petites victimes.

L'affreux géant, les entrailles tordues d'insupportables crampes, fut contraint d'évacuer tout ce petit monde, et de lui rendre la liberté.

« Dorénavant, lui dit le saint, tu seras obligé de nourrir tous les enfants pauvres de la région, ainsi que les chiens abandonnés et les vieux chats malades. Faute de quoi, je te condamne à ne pouvoir plus rien avaler, pas même une racine ou un brin d'herbe, et à périr d'inanition après des semaines d'agonie ! »

L'ogre se le tint pour dit, et devint même avec l'âge la providence de tous les petits malheureux, de tous les animaux éclopés ou maltraités de la contrée.

Le matou affichait ce matin-là une expression de colossale autosatisfaction. Il avait les prunelles dilatées, irisées de pétillements sauvages. Son pelage était particulièrement lustré. Il pointait orgueilleusement son panache et se déplaçait avec une lenteur magistrale – l'onction et la componction d'un prélat s'apprêtant à bénir la foule agenouillée des fidèles.

J'ignorais ce qui pouvait bien lui inspirer une telle suffisance. Mais je me gardai bien de toute inquisition, car je connaissais son quant-à-soi sourcilleux et son extrême susceptibilité.

Le Souper du diable

Le diable qui venait de s'installer en ville et qui menait grand train organisa un soir une fête brillante à laquelle furent conviées toutes les notabilités de la région.

Il y avait là le maire, le préfet, le député, le chef de la police, le président du tribunal, le bâtonnier, deux ou trois industriels de renom, un chirurgien célèbre, un banquier, sans oublier le principal chroniqueur du journal local, ainsi que leurs épouses respectives.

Il y avait même l'archevêque du diocèse voisin. Le diable, qui savait vivre, fit servir à ses hôtes un somptueux festin dans une luxueuse vaisselle. Il ne manquait ni caviar, ni homard, ni champagne, ni vin capiteux des meilleurs crus. Les conversations allaient bon train. C'était un subtil dosage d'étalage culturel, de mondanités branchées, de grivoiseries acidulées, de rumeurs assassines. Chacun y allait de son histoire insolite, de son ragot légèrement salace, et de son allusion féroce.

Le tout bien saupoudré de quelques traits d'esprit bon chic bon genre.

Les dames papotaient : chiffons, coiffures, croisières, mérites respectifs des domestiques immigrés d'Afrique ou d'Asie, exploits et bavures des psychanalystes et gynécologues du coin.

Ces messieurs avançaient des points de vues chiffrés et définitifs concernant la délinquance juvénile, le chômage, la pollution, l'éducation et la croissance. Les politiques, bien sûr, recevaient au passage quelques vilaines égratignures dont monsieur le député, beau joueur, ne prenait pas ombrage.

Tous et toutes bramaient à l'unisson, avec une sincérité vertueuse, pour s'indigner du sort des enfants maltraités, des minorités persécutées et des atteintes aux droits de l'homme. La ritournelle humanitaire était toujours assurée de remporter un grand succès.

L'archevêque, un joyeux drille avec un joli coup de fourchette, et le chef de la police, un gnome sombre à la mine perpétuellement courroucée, échangeaient en aparté des confidences instructives sur leurs ulcères et leurs hémorroïdes. C'était une soirée parfaite, bien fréquentée, bien animée. L'accueil était admirable. On servit le café, les infusions, les digestifs et les cigares provenant directement de La Havane.

Au douzième coup de minuit, le diable se leva en brandissant son verre pour s'adresser à ses convives.

« Mes chers amis, je vais maintenant vous proposer un jeu qui est d'ailleurs, je dois l'avouer, le but de cette fête. Depuis quelques secondes, cette maison est hermétiquement isolée du reste de l'univers. Nul ne peut en sortir…

– Qu'est-ce que ça signifie ? s'étrangla le préfet, serait-ce une prise d'otages ?

– Monsieur, ulula le président du tribunal, vous allez au-devant des pires ennuis !

– Allons, crut bon d'ajouter le banquier, si c'est une plaisanterie, elle est d'un goût douteux !

– Constatez par vous-mêmes », ricana le démon.

Le journaliste se précipita vers la porte d'entrée qu'il ouvrit sans ménagement. Elle donnait sur un brouillard opaque, méphitique, impénétrable. L'homme y aventura la main. Une espèce de résistance vaguement élastique s'opposait à tout mouvement vers l'extérieur. Il prospecta d'autres issues avec le même résultat.

« Enfin, écuma-t-il, qu'attendez-vous de nous, et d'abord, qui êtes-vous ?

– Je suis le tentateur, l'archange déchu, l'innommable, le Très Malin et très putride, celui auquel même vos hommes d'Église ne croient plus guère et que vous appelez le diable. »

L'archevêque esquissa un signe de croix et marmonna quelques exorcismes approximatifs.

« Cessez donc ces enfantillages, susurra le diable, vous n'arriverez à rien de cette manière. Écoutez attentivement, c'est simple. Vous tous ici rassemblés, vos âmes me sont plus ou moins acquises. Dans vingt-quatre heures, vous m'appartiendrez tout à fait. À moins que l'un d'entre vous n'accepte de se sacrifier pour les autres. !

– Dans ce cas, dit l'un des chefs d'entreprise, qui avait le pragmatisme et la logique d'un polytechnicien, il serait naturel que le plus vieux d'entre nous se dévoue ! »

Il s'agissait en l'occurrence du bâtonnier qui ne l'entendait pas du tout de cette oreille. Il protesta vertement : « Voilà qui serait inique et absurde ! tirons au sort !

– Vous m'avez mal compris, intervint le prince des ténèbres. Le sacrifice doit être volontaire et spontané ! »

Pendant l'heure, s'établit un silence pesant. Chacun restait prostré, à sa place. Nul n'osait regarder son voisin dans les yeux.

Affalé dans un fauteuil cossu, Satan feuilletait négligemment quelques revues de mode, s'attardant avec complaisance sur la silhouette des top models.

La plupart des convives, apeurés, finirent par sombrer dans une somnolence chaotique.

Au petit matin, les hommes étaient hirsutes, bouffis, ils avaient l'œil chassieux, le menton râpeux, la langue pâteuse. Les femmes avaient l'air de clowns tristes, avec leur maquillage défait, leurs boucles en bataille et leur robe fripée.

Ce fut une ruée générale pour un brin de toilette et un petit déjeuner improvisé avec les reliefs de la veille.

Les masques s'effritaient.

On se disputait sans pudeur les morceaux de pain rassis et de gâteaux desséchés. On injuriait ceux qui tardaient à libérer les sanitaires. La mauvaise humeur, la colère, le stress étaient unanimes. C'était comme un grondement sourd qui prenait peu à peu de l'ampleur.

Le diable quant à lui consultait ironiquement sa montre.

« N'oubliez pas, le temps vous est compté... »

Il souriait. L'ambiance était de plus en plus chargée, explosive. Le journaliste mit de l'huile sur le feu.

« On n'en serait pas là, dit-il, si les autorités avaient fait correctement leur travail en enquêtant sur le propriétaire de cette maison !

– Mêlez-vous de vos chiens écrasés, fulmina le préfet.

– À votre place, je me tairais. Tout le monde sait que votre femme vous cocufie avec le député !

– Ceci est intolérable ! s'égosilla le président du tribunal.

– Vous, l'obsédé, continuez donc à faire la sortie des lycées, nous n'avons nul besoin de vos conseils ! »

Le banquier commençait à s'agiter sur sa chaise.

« Avec tous vos millions détournés et placés dans des paradis fiscaux, vous pourriez peut-être négocier une solution acceptable ! suggéra le député.

– Et vous, avec tous les pots-de-vin que je vous ai versés, qu'attendez-vous pour intervenir ? »

Les insultes et les plus graves accusations pleuvaient de toute part. On en vint aux gifles. Les femmes étaient les plus déchaînées. Toutes les vieilles rancœurs, les vieilles jalousies, les haines recuites remontaient à la surface comme des bulles nauséabondes.

L'ange déchu buvait du petit lait. La journée s'écoula.

« Allons, mes amis, voici l'heure, dit le diable, quel est celui parmi vous qui est prêt à s'immoler pour les autres ? »

À cet instant un vieux matou que le hasard avait conduit la veille dans ces lieux, sortit de sa cachette. C'était un chat particulièrement futé, intrépide et savant, qui connaissait les Écritures, les clefs de l'invisible et les arcanes du Mystère bien mieux que la plupart des théologiens.

« Moi, s'écria-t-il en hérissant les moustaches et en pointant les oreilles, je suis prêt à me sacrifier sur-le-champ ! »

Il connaissait les ruses du Malin et les limites de son pouvoir.

Satan fronça les sourcils et sa bouche se tordit en un rictus de dépit.

Le félin se coucha sur le flanc.

« Voilà, dit-il, je suis prêt à mourir… »

Le diable était berné. Son sortilège s'effaça, et il plia rapidement bagage.

Par la suite, les invités de cette étrange soirée se sentirent obligés de choyer et gâter le matou sa vie durant.

Il avait bien calculé son coup et mené judicieusement son affaire.

Ce matin-là le chat scruta méticuleusement tous les angles et recoins de la maison, suivant d'une prunelle soupçonneuse la progression et les mouvements d'invisibles visiteurs à califourchon sur les reflets et les courants d'air. Bondissant de fauteuil en bureau, de console en étagère, il se figeait dans une position d'affût. Ses moustaches frémissaient, ses babines tremblotaient, son panache ondulait et vibrait.

« Qu'est-ce que vous pouvez bien guetter avec une telle fébrilité ? lui demandai-je intriguée.

– N’insistez pas, vous ne pourriez pas compren-dre. Vos sens sont tellement limités !

– J’ai plutôt l’impression que vous êtes en train de vous payer ma tête !

– Ce n’est pas à vous d’en décider. De toute façon, le mystère est partout… »

Le Miroir magique

Un vieil homme à l'agonie appela son fils à son chevet pour lui transmettre ses ultimes recommandations :

« Je n'ai à te léguer qu'un seul objet, précieux entre tous, qui est ce miroir magique. Je n'ai pas de fortune, mais cet unique bien te sera plus utile que tous les trésors de la terre… »

Il lui désigna un vieux trumeau d'apparence modeste, sans fioritures, et au verre légèrement dépoli.

« Ce miroir reflète la vérité. Il te montrera toujours tel que tu es et qui tu es vraiment… »

Puis le vieil homme mourut.

Après avoir enterré sa dépouille et honoré sa mémoire comme il convient, non sans verser des larmes abondantes, car le défunt avait été un excellent père, le jeune homme examina son héritage de plus près. Il n'y vit qu'une image banale, celle d'un garçon aux traits tirés par l'affliction et à la mine dubitative.

L'existence reprit son cours. L'orphelin était un gaillard sain et robuste dans la fleur de l'âge, et il regardait avec une concupiscence extrême le moindre jupon passant dans les parages.

Sa boulimie sensuelle et sa lubricité étaient telles qu'il s'enfiévrait à la vue de toute silhouette féminine – sveltes nymphettes, midinettes chichiteuses, sportives bien charpentées, femmes d'affaires au tailleur strict, donzelles des faubourgs, mondaines replâtrées, bigotes effarouchées, ou même grand-mères à dentelles et mitaines. Il les lui fallait toutes, et pour atteindre son but, il était prêt à tous les subterfuges, à toutes les machinations, voire à toutes les bassesses.

Comme il n'avait pas trop vilaine figure, la plupart lui cédaient assez spontanément.

Bien sûr, il ne laissait derrière lui qu'un champ de cœurs en ruines et d'espoirs brisés.

Un jour, passant près du miroir magique, il y jeta un regard machinal. L'image qu'il y découvrit était celle d'une étrange créature tenant à la fois de l'homme, du bouc et du goret, avec un groin avide et des petits yeux brûlants. Le miroir ne pouvait mentir. Il lui montrait sa véritable nature.

Horrifié, il se jura de se consacrer désormais à d'autres centres d'intérêt. Il était temps pour lui de s'affirmer sur le plan professionnel et social, de faire fortune.

Il avait des diplômes, des projets, et ne manquait pas de persuasion. Il fonda des sociétés, accumula des bénéfices, prospéra en bourse. L'argent attire l'argent. Il lui en fallut toujours plus. Il devint un spéculateur obsessionnel, un financier impitoyable, sourd aux problèmes de ses semblables, aveugle à la souffrance, insensible aux misères du monde.

Un soir, après une journée riche en profits de toutes sortes, il jeta un coup d'œil au miroir. Il y vit l'image d'un reptile géant qui étouffait dans ses anneaux monstrueux des milliers de proies pantelantes. Des pièces d'or étincelaient entre ses crocs fumants.

Épouvanté, il décida de se vouer dorénavant aux causes les plus nobles et de ne plus travailler qu'au triomphe de la justice.

Il se lança de toutes ses forces dans la politique. Il fut parlementaire, chef de parti, ministre. Sa brillante ascension paraissait devoir surmonter un à un tous les obstacles. Les allées du pouvoir s'ouvraient toutes grandes devant lui. Un pouvoir de plus en plus solitaire et absolu. Où il en vint à oublier complètement ses généreuses intentions initiales.

Son action tournait à la tyrannie.

Un matin, presque par accident, il croisa le miroir. Il s'y vit cette fois sous les traits d'un hideux vieillard à mille têtes soufflant le monde comme une bougie de son haleine pourrissante.

Fuyant honneur et gloire, il se retira pour méditer dans le plus strict dépouillement au cœur d'une forêt profonde où il séjourna de longues années.

Il était à présent un vieil homme, il avait obtenu la paix de l'esprit et la sagesse.

Un jour enfin, il osa consulter le miroir, le seul objet qu'il avait emporté dans son exil volontaire.

La glace était lumineuse, transparente et vide. Pour la première fois, il voyait ce qu'il était vraiment. Le fin fond de son être.

Ce jour-là, je fus accaparée par des impératifs touchant au quotidien de la maison.

« Allons ma chère, levez donc un peu le nez de vos petites affaires. Tenez, aujourd'hui, si vous savez affûter convenablement votre regard, vous pourrez voir neiger des anges. Il en dégringole de tous les côtés, dans tous les sens. Ils s'accouplent sur le balcon, dans vos géraniums, dans les rayons de la bibliothèque, les penderies, et même dans vos pantoufles. Ils pondent des milliers d'œufs diaphanes dans votre trousse de toilette et votre verre à dents. Faites attention en vous maquillant à ne pas en écraser par mégarde… »

La Musique

Dans des temps très anciens, au commencement des âges, les quatre Parrains de la nature, Esprit de la Terre, de l'Eau, de l'Air et du Feu se concertèrent en vue d'offrir aux espèces vivantes les instruments nécessaires à la célébration de l'univers.

La Terre convoqua ses génies et ses djinns.

Trois d'entre eux furent sélectionnés.

Le premier surgit d'une caverne profonde. C'était un buffle énorme, impétueux et farouche. Ses innombrables pattes martelaient le sol, armées de mille sabots frémissants et fumants.

Ainsi furent créées les percussions.

Le deuxième, un titan à trois pieds doté d'un long dard sombre, arborait un large sourire éclatant. Ses dents étincelaient. Sa poitrine était gonflée d'hymnes tonitruants et d'harmonies subtiles. Telle fut l'origine du piano.

La Terre arracha ensuite une portion d'arc-en-ciel et lâcha sa nymphe la plus agile, la plus gracieuse et capricieuse. Elle se mit à danser d'un pied vif et fantasque. La guitare était née.

L'Eau intervint alors.

Elle réunit quelques-unes de ses nymphes et naïades.

Il y eut la lorelei des noyades éperdues et des engloutissements sans fin dont les sanglots béants s'élevaient en colonnes liquides et en ondulations nacrées. Elle inspira la construction des orgues.

Apparut un cygne royal glissant fièrement au fil de grands lacs calmes. De ses ailes déployées ruisselaient des notes exquises, fragiles et cristallines. Ce cygne devint harpe.

Une étrange ondine se mit à tournoyer dans la brume. Elle était chaussée de larges gouttes de pluie qui crépitaient et soliloquaient à la surface des eaux dormantes, émettant un florilège de vibrations graves et lentes : la contrebasse vit le jour.

Ce fut à l'air de se manifester.

Il fit appel à un vieux démiurge fracassant et joufflu qui s'engouffra en ouragan dans les vallées et dans les gorges, s'égosilla aux flancs des montagnes, et claironna ses joies, ses rages et ses tristesses jusqu'aux étoiles. La trompette était née.

Surgit ensuite un elfe espiègle, mince et malicieux, habile à faire danser les papillons, les libellules et autres feux follets, aimant aussi à rêvasser et dériver dans les brises du soir, à l'heure où rentrent les troupeaux fourbus. La flûte était donnée au monde.

L'Air évoqua encore une créature fabuleuse, un être sauvage, fascinant et redoutable, félin ailé, grand fauve des nuits d'orage dont les miaulements lancinants provoquaient des transes d'amour et de mort, des halètements de plaisir et d'agonie, de purs frissons d'abîmes entrevus. C'était l'esprit du violon.

Des myriades de farfadets pétulants et farceurs déboulèrent avec mille pirouettes, pétillements et grincements. Ils déchaînèrent des houles chuintantes et pétaradantes, une espèce de cacophonie facétieuse et frisée. La cornemuse faisait son entrée dans l'histoire.

Restait la fée du vent des steppes, elle se tortillait et se contorsionnait à la manière d'une chenille fiévreuse et syncopée, avec des accents lascifs d'une pathétique nostalgie. La fée du vent des steppes confectionna ainsi l'accordéon.

C'était au tour du Feu d'apporter sa contribution.

« Moi, dit-il, je n'ai nul besoin de tous ces artifices. Ma musique signe le destin même de toute chose, car toute chose finit en cendres. Mon chant est sage, serein et immuable. Il me suffit d'en faire cadeau à la plus sage des créatures, le chat. Lorsqu'il exprimera sa plénitude, ma musique intime résonnera doucement dans sa gorge. Voilà comment les chats ronronnent… »

Mon ami félin se mit en rond dans un fauteuil, et dormit tout le jour. J'admirais cette puissance de sommeil, et enviais cette prodigieuse capacité de lâcher prise.

Le Puits de la vérité

Il y avait, à la sortie d'une vieille bourgade, un puits antique et vénérable qu'on appelait « le puits de la vérité ».

L'eau de ce puits possédait des vertus exceptionnelles et miraculeuses. Mais beaucoup prétendaient que ce précieux liquide était en fait d'origine diabolique et rendait fous ceux qui avaient le malheur d'y goûter. Si bien que finalement, nul n'osait consommer ce breuvage, ni même y tremper le bout du doigt. Comprenne qui pourra.

Depuis des lustres, les habitants du village discutaient à propos de cette eau, de sa provenance, de sa nature. C'étaient d'interminables et inutiles palabres. Des chercheurs, hommes de science, philosophes, universitaires venaient même parfois de fort loin et spéculaient sans fin sur l'exacte composition de cette eau, sur ses propriétés chimiques et ses effets possibles sur l'organisme, le système nerveux et le psychisme.

Mais même les plus curieux et les plus intrépides n'auraient pour rien au monde ingurgité une goutte de cet élixir. Comprenne qui pourra.

Un jour, un petit garçon tomba dans le puits et faillit s'y noyer. Sauvé *in extremis*, la Faculté se pencha aussitôt avidement sur son cas : grâce à cette étude *in vivo*, on percevrait enfin les secrets du puits de la vérité.

L'étude s'avéra décevante, malgré les moyens sophistiqués mis en œuvre. L'enfant était désespérément normal et banal. Comprenne qui pourra.

Le marmot, qui était fils de travailleur modeste, vivait dans une petite maison, non loin du fameux puits. Il continua tout naturellement à s'y désaltérer malgré la peur superstitieuse des habitants du coin.

Les années passèrent. Le garçon devint un jeune homme puis un adulte étrange, un esprit simple, toujours étonné, riant à tout propos, proférant volontiers des discours incohérents, des paroles incompréhensibles. On le disait idiot, ou fou, et on attribua sa démence à l'eau du puits de la vérité. Comprenne qui pourra.

Les garnements du village lui jetaient des pierres, certains parlaient de le faire interner. Tous se moquaient de lui, le houspillaient, le méprisaient.

Lui se contentait de hocher la tête en souriant et de vaquer à ses petites affaires, sans se soucier des regards venimeux et des gestes malintentionnés.

Bizarrement, les bêtes sauvages venaient manger dans sa main et les oiseaux se perchaient sur son épaule. Les loups lui léchaient les doigts, les serpents s'endormaient paisiblement à ses côtés, les frelons se posaient délicatement sur lui en prenant soin de ne jamais le piquer. Comprenne qui pourra.

Lorsqu'il mourut, à un âge fort avancé, sa dépouille baignait dans une radieuse lumière et dégageait un parfum suave de jardin en fleurs. Quelques malades ou éclopés de la région affirmèrent avoir été guéris rien qu'en touchant l'un ou l'autre objet lui ayant appartenu.

Bientôt le village s'honora d'avoir donné le jour à un grand saint. Les plus savants décrétèrent que cette grâce était due à l'eau du puits dont le bienheureux avait fait un si constant usage.

Ce fut dès lors une ruée avide. Tous voulurent recueillir et absorber leur part du précieux liquide et tous furent atteints de délire aigu et de convulsions. Et les bêtes, qui sur certains sujets en savent bien plus que les hommes, désertèrent la contrée. Comprenne qui pourra.

Après le récit du matou, je me mis à feuilleter une de ces revues féminines que j'avais l'habitude de consulter. Le chat soudain bondit et lacéra les pages du journal.

« Qu'est-ce qui vous prend ? Vous devenez fou ?

– Je suis fou ! Vous êtes folle ! Nous sommes tous fous ! Si vous voulez un jour devenir sage, il faudra que vous alliez encore bien plus loin dans la folie ! »

L'animal fila dans la pièce voisine, et disparut inexplicablement. En dépit de tous mes efforts, il me fut impossible de le retrouver ce jour-là.

L'irritation et l'inquiétude m'oppressèrent jusqu'au lendemain.

Qui est là ?

Un homme, renommé pour sa vertu exceptionnelle et sa grande piété, s'en vint à mourir.

Délivré des fardeaux de l'existence terrestre, il se présenta devant le Seigneur suprême, créateur du ciel et de la terre.

« Qui est là ? Qui frappe à ma porte ? demanda le Souverain Juge, l'âme de l'univers visible et invisible.

– C'est moi, Seigneur, ton plus fidèle et dévoué serviteur.

– Alors, retourne sur tes pas. Tu resteras encore sept années supplémentaires dans la sphère matérielle, à parfaire ton avancement spirituel, puis tu reviendras ici même. »

Un peu désappointé, l'homme se conforma bien sûr au vœu du Très-Haut et reprit le cours de son existence charnelle. « Sans doute, songea-t-il, n'ai-je pas été assez compatissant et charitable envers mes semblables et toutes les créatures vivantes… »

Il consacra dès lors tout son temps, toutes ses forces au sort des plus déshérités, apaisant leurs tourments, soulageant leurs souffrances, aidant les miséreux et les handicapés. Chacun le considérait comme un modèle de bonté, de sainteté, d'abnégation. Les plus dévots allaient jusqu'à lui prêter toutes sortes de pouvoirs miraculeux.

Au bout de sept ans, il frappa de nouveau à la porte divine.

« Qui est là ? Décline ton identité ! proféra l'Indicible, d'une voix qui se répercutait de nébuleuse en nébuleuse.

– C'est moi, ô Bien-Aimé, ton plus inconditionnel adorateur !

– Alors, retourne sur tes pas, séjourne sept années de plus dans la zone terrestre. Tu ne connais pas encore les arcanes et les clefs du grand mystère. »

L'homme obéit à contrecœur. Il s'isola au sommet d'une haute montagne, avec pour seuls compagnons les ours sauvages, les aigles et les tigres des neiges. Pratiquant un jeûne assidu, il se livra aux rigueurs d'une ascèse radicale, s'exposant nu pendant des heures aux pires intempéries, dans une immobilité cataleptique, buvant l'eau des glaciers, se nourrissant d'herbes et d'écorces, méditant sans relâche sur les causes premières et sur les fins ultimes.

Sept ans ainsi s'écoulèrent. L'homme était devenu un voyant, un grand initié, un sage. Il pensait toucher enfin au but et sollicita le Sublime Omniscient qui avait conçu les univers et enfanté les anges.

« Qui est là ? Qui me demande ?

– C'est moi, ô Éternel, le plus ardent et le plus vigilant de tes disciples.

– Alors, retourne sur tes pas. Sept années dans le monde te seront nécessaires pour être vraiment prêt. »

L'homme, résigné, s'exécuta.

Cette fois, il vécut simplement, naturellement, donnant leur juste place aux distractions et aux plaisirs, aux petites joies de l'existence, voire aux futilités, sans jamais s'y enfermer ni se prendre au sérieux.

Lorsqu'il avait faim, il mangeait. Lorsqu'il avait sommeil, il dormait. Lorsqu'il avait envie de s'amuser, il s'amusait. Quand il se présenta aux portes du dernier séjour, la même voix retentit :

« Qui est là ?

– C'est Toi-même Seigneur !

– Alors, tu peux entrer. »

Ce jour-là, j'avais un emploi du temps particulièrement chargé. J'étais donc assez peu disponible, et m'absentai de bonne heure. Je ne retrouvai le matou que plus tard dans l'après-midi. Il m'accorda un bref regard glacial, et me tourna délibérément le dos. Il était à l'évidence de fort méchante humeur. Il m'en voulait de l'avoir abandonné.

« J'ai moi aussi quelques impératifs, lui dis-je. Il faudra bien vous faire une raison… »

Il dédaigna de me répondre et se mura dans un silence réprobateur jusqu'au coucher du soleil.

La Mandoline ensorcelée

Dans une contrée sauvage et reculée, très à l'écart des métropoles et des grandes routes, pour tout dire oubliée de la civilisation, vivait un jeune homme pauvre, passionné de musique et de rythme.

Son rêve était de devenir musicien ambulant, afin de faire danser la terre entière, et même le vent et les étoiles, au son de ses mélodies.

Son maître, qui lui avait appris le solfège et les bases de l'harmonie, était un vieux sorcier initié à la science des vibrations subtiles et des échos profonds. Il connaissait la rugissante symphonie des ouragans s'engouffrant dans les cavernes, la rhapsodie syncopée des bourrasques d'automne, le menuet feutré des flocons sur les toits, la sonatine acidulée des petites brises printanières, le scherzo malicieux des cascades bondissant et gloussant sur les cailloux, le cantique des glaciers à la dérive, ou encore les majestueux arpèges de l'écume sur le sable. Même la silencieuse chorale des anges et la valse ténébreuse des démons n'avaient pour lui aucun secret.

Le jeune homme insista tellement auprès de son maître, l'assaillant de ses prières avec une telle constance, que le vieux sorcier finit par accéder à sa requête. Il lui offrit une mandoline enchantée dont les accords provoquaient une irrésistible envie de se mettre à danser, virevolter, se trémousser et gigoter dans tous les sens.

L'apprenti musicien partit donc à l'aventure avec son précieux instrument. Dans chaque bourg et village, dès qu'il commençait à jouer, la population tout entière se jetait dans une sarabande endiablée – les pieds, les jambes, les bras s'agitaient comme sous l'emprise d'un marionnettiste. Et nul ne pouvait plus s'arrêter – sauf à s'effondrer d'épuisement. Certains allaient même jusqu'à mourir sur place.

L'homme à la mandoline devint célèbre. On se l'arrachait pour les fêtes, les foires, les carnavals. Son vœu le plus intense paraissait exaucé : le monde entier dansait à son approche.

Un soir, au bord d'un campement de fortune, le musicien aperçut une belle diseuse de bonne aventure qui ondulait et se balançait langoureusement sous la Lune au son de castagnettes qu'elle agitait avec grâce.

À l'instant même, il en tomba éperdument

amoureux. Et tout naturellement, pour la séduire, il se mit à jouer de la mandoline. La jeune fille dansa pendant des heures, légère, insaisissable, infatigable, un sourire énigmatique et vaguement moqueur au coin des lèvres.

Mais le garçon avait beau multiplier ses prouesses de virtuose, poussant son instrument à des sonorités inouïes, la merveilleuse bohémienne restait insensible à ses charmes.

Les jours suivants, il ne la quitta pas. Mais ses efforts demeurèrent vains. L'amoureux éconduit était désespéré.

Il perdit l'appétit, le sommeil, et même le goût de la musique. La mandoline ensorcelée lui apparut bientôt comme la cause première de ses souffrances.

Dans un accès de rage, il saisit un bâton pour détruire l'instrument. Mais ce dernier qui avait plus d'une vertu magique, l'interpella en ces termes : « Épargne-moi, et je t'aiderai à gagner les faveurs de ta dulcinée. Place-moi sous ton menton et caresse doucement les cordes avec ton bâton… »

Le jeune homme obéit. Sans le savoir, il venait de jouer les premières notes de violon.

Elles étaient si envoûtantes, si chaudes et si déchirantes que la belle gitane succomba aussitôt à leur appel. Emportée par les trilles et les pizzicati, elle se précipita dans les bras de son soupirant et y versa toutes les larmes de son corps.

Le couple eut une descendance nombreuse. Tous furent nomades, musiciens dans l'âme et voyants.

Ainsi naquit le peuple des tziganes.

Toute la journée, le chat miaula bizarrement, l'échine et les moustaches frémissantes. Son timbre avait une nuance triste, farouche et lancinante. Il déambula ainsi de pièce en pièce, jusqu'au soir, avec ce chant à la fois grave, strident, plaintif et pur.

Je ne pouvais m'empêcher de songer au violon.

Drakul

Voici l'histoire très véridique du vampire, le mort vivant, le maître de la nuit, le prédateur des ténèbres.

Au temps jadis, Drakul était un prince vaillant et chevaleresque. Le plus loyal des hommes, le plus charmant des compagnons, le plus brillant et courageux des chefs de guerre.

Il avait une épouse, la princesse Ivana, modèle de vertu et de beauté, qu'il chérissait et adorait de toutes ses forces. Elle était à la fois sa femme, sa sœur, sa fille, sa confidente, sa maîtresse. Rien n'était jamais trop doux, trop raffiné ni trop précieux pour elle. Pour elle, il se serait laissé tuer ou torturer.

Avec elle, il connaissait un bonheur parfait, une complète félicité.

Un jour, tandis qu'il menait une rude et victorieuse campagne contre les envahisseurs barbares qui menaçaient son royaume et ravageaient ses frontières, son épouse fut victime d'un sordide et sanglant guet-apens. Lors d'une promenade en forêt, elle fut attaquée par des sujets félons qui la violèrent, l'égorgèrent et massacrèrent ses suivantes.

Lorsque le prince Drakul apprit la mort de sa femme, le désespoir le submergea comme un typhon. Son être n'était plus qu'une plaie cuisante, un paroxysme de rage et de chagrin. Tout plaisir, toute joie, toute lumière furent bannis de son existence. Un rêve obsessionnel de vengeance le poussait à des expéditions de plus en plus sauvages et meurtrières, qui se terminaient en carnage. Il se repaissait de charniers.

Une soif amère et inextinguible de sang se mit peu à peu à le ronger de l'intérieur et finit par le dévorer tout à fait.

Il était devenu le vampire, virtuellement immortel mais éternellement insatisfait, régnant sur les puissances de l'ombre, les fantômes, les goules, les charognards, les hôtes grouillants de l'abîme et le peuple visqueux des cauchemars.

Drakul devint siècle après siècle la terreur de toutes les créatures du jour.

Mais cette insatiable avidité qui l'obligeait à saigner et immoler ses victimes était loin d'apaiser son immémorial tourment. Il avait beau disposer de pouvoirs redoutables, se changeant à volonté en bête féroce, loup, lynx, grand duc ou reptile venimeux, volant sur l'aile glacée du vent des steppes, chevauchant la foudre ou s'affublant de mille apparences trompeuses, son ancienne peine était présente inexorablement.

Et même repu, sa monstrueuse soif ne lui apportait ni paix ni réconfort. Son âme égarée subissait les supplices de l'enfer. Et les fleuves de sang prélevés aux humains ruisselaient par ses yeux en torrents de larmes brûlantes.

Il attendait tapi dans son château légendaire, une ruine encore imposante dont la silhouette sinistre semblait concentrer tous les maléfices de la terre.

Nous autres chats, comme chacun sait, sommes les gardiens du seuil, les portiers du mystère, les plénipotentiaires de la nuit auprès du jour, les délégués du rêve et de la transe dans le monde ordinaire.

En poursuivant un gros rat téméraire, je me faufilai dans le repaire du vampire.

Le prince Drakul m'y accueillit comme un hôte de marque. Bien sûr les rares voyageurs évitaient avec effroi ces lieux inhospitaliers, car les habitants des bourgs voisins déconseillaient énergiquement de se risquer dans les parages.

Pour ma part, je décidai de m'attarder un peu auprès du prince, d'autant que son château regorgeait de souris, mulots et autres petits rongeurs succulents.

Je connaissais l'unique remède à la misérable condition du monstre, et je guettais l'occasion propice pour essayer de l'aider.

Un soir, une jeune touriste intrépide et curieuse, passant outre à toutes les mises en garde, vint frapper à la porte. Je l'y avais insidieusement encouragée.

La visiteuse ressemblait étrangement à la défunte épouse de Drakul, la princesse Ivana. Le vampire, subjugué, apparut à l'étrangère sous les traits d'un jeune et séduisant aristocrate, doué d'un charme ambigu et d'une prestance romantique.

Il invita l'inconnue à visiter les lieux. En dépit du décor suranné, oppressant et quelque peu funèbre, qui eût épouvanté toute autre promeneuse, la jeune femme n'avait d'yeux que pour son guide : le caractère lugubre et désolé des corridors interminables et des vastes salons pétrifiés ne l'affectait nullement. Elle se sentait étrangement, irrésistiblement attirée par ce prince des ténèbres et de l'abîme. C'était un délicieux vertige : elle souhaitait ardemment passer sur l'autre rive de la vie, sur l'autre face du réel, afin de tout partager, dût-elle encourir supplice et damnation.

Drakul était penché sur elle, toute offerte. Une soif torturante meurtrissait ses entrailles, dévastait son esprit. Boire goulûment le précieux liquide chaud dégoulinant de cette gorge palpitante, et fouiller de ses crocs cette chair délicate ! Quelle fulgurante jouissance !

Mais un bizarre sentiment, remuant des souvenirs très enfouis, le retenait au seuil de cet assaut délectable.

À nouveau, il aimait, comme jadis, à l'époque d'Ivana. Et toute concupiscence, d'un seul coup, se dissipa.

L'inextinguible soif disparut. Drakul était guéri.

Le prince était à nouveau un homme. Il prit doucement la visiteuse par la main, et tous deux s'éloignèrent vers une destinée commune.

« Je pense qu'il serait temps de vous donner un bain.

– La plupart de mes congénères détestent ce genre d'exercice, vous le savez bien. Mais je vais vous surprendre. J'adore me prélasser dans l'eau bien tiède, à condition qu'elle soit à la température adéquate, et que vous procédiez de manière suave… »

Il exigea la baignoire, et trempa plusieurs fois le bout de la patte avec méfiance avant de se laisser immerger. Il fallut le savonner à petites touches. Il s'offrit à mes caresses et manipulations, les paupières closes, les moustaches en éventail, les babines béatement retroussées.

Ce fut une journée lumineuse et câline.

Les Cœurs à nu

Il y avait un royaume gouverné par un souverain d'une pudibonderie et d'un puritanisme extrêmes.

Ses sujets étaient contraints de se couvrir en toute saison du bout des orteils jusqu'au menton, sous peine de châtiments sévères – coups de fouet, pilori ou cachot.

Les miroirs étaient rigoureusement prohibés, pour éviter de se complaire dans le spectacle de ses propres formes. Chacun était tenu de se laver dans le noir et de dormir tout habillé.

Bien sûr, les nuits de noces ne se déroulaient que dans des chambres vouées aux plus hermétiques ténèbres.

Un tailleur de renom s'installa un jour et prospéra dans la capitale, au point de devenir l'unique pourvoyeur des habitants de la cité.

Or, ce grand couturier était un magicien vicieux doué de pouvoirs peu ordinaires. Les vêtements et parures qu'il vendait – fort cher – à ses clients n'étaient que vent et duperie, simulacres de pourpoints, faux-semblants de culottes, hauts-de-chausses fantômes.

Les acheteurs quittaient son échoppe nus comme des vers, mais persuadés d'être habillés de pied en cap. Et ils ne voyaient pas non plus la nudité de leurs voisins, collègues et concitoyens.

Le souverain et ses courtisans furent parmi les premiers à porter ces vêtements illusoires, taillés évidemment sur mesure, et fort coûteux pour le trésor public.

Un voyageur s'en vint à séjourner dans le pays.

C'était un cœur innocent, une âme transparente et pure. Évitant de juger ses semblables, il était prompt à s'émerveiller plutôt qu'à réprouver. Le sortilège du tailleur magicien ne pouvait avoir d'effet sur lui, car il concernait seulement les esprits tourmentés, comprimés par trop de pesantes censures et d'interdits torturants.

En abordant la capitale, l'étranger se retrouva donc au milieu d'une foule de citadins vaquant à leurs occupations dans le plus simple appareil. Loin de s'en offusquer, le spectacle lui parut charmant. Et il crut même y voir une sage coutume somme toute conforme au plan originel de Mère nature.

Respectueux des usages et des mœurs, il ôta prestement ses vêtements.

Le tintamarre fut immense et le scandale unanime. Qui était donc ce mécréant, ce criminel effronté qui osait exposer sa chair honteuse au grand jour ?

Il fut aussitôt interpellé, arrêté, bâillonné, ficelé, encagoulé de haut en bas et jeté dans le plus sombre cul-de-basse-fosse du château.

Son procès fut rapidement instruit. La cause était entendue, le crime incontestable, indéfendable et inexpiable.

Il fut conduit, enchaîné, devant le roi, juge suprême. On ne lui laissa guère le loisir de s'expliquer. Il fut condamné au châtiment ultime, et le bourreau fut convoqué sur-le-champ pour lui trancher la tête.

Comme à tout homme promis au supplice, on lui demanda s'il avait une dernière volonté à formuler. « Je souhaite, répondit-il, qu'on apporte un miroir… »

La requête était quasiment subversive, puisqu'on avait banni les miroirs du royaume. Mais la dernière volonté d'un condamné à mort était sacrée.

Dans les combles du palais, on réussit à dénicher une glace antique, poussiéreuse, qui loin de la lumière du jour agonisait doucement.

Le voyageur brandit l'objet qu'il présenta au souverain et à la cour.

Le maléfice du sorcier ne s'appliquait guère à l'espace des miroirs. Et tous réalisèrent brutalement qu'ils étaient nus. Passée la première stupeur, ils furent comme éblouis par l'harmonie miraculeuse de ces formes qu'ils avaient si longtemps rageusement occultées.

Ils regagnèrent ainsi leur innocence et cessèrent de subir le joug du couturier maléfique.

Le roi décréta que désormais chacun pourrait librement exhiber son corps.

Le prisonnier fut évidemment gracié, congratulé, fêté de toute part. Et le sorcier dut s'exiler dans l'heure.

Le matou se grattait énergiquement le cou et la base du crâne avec sa patte arrière.

« Je crois bien, me dit-il, que deux ou trois vieilles puces ont élu domicile dans ma fourrure. Ayez donc l'obligeance de m'en débarrasser.

– Je vais vous appliquer un produit spécial très efficace.

– Pas question de supporter une de vos cochonneries de crème ou de poudre ! Il faut que vous débusquiez ces petites garces vous-même, et que vous les exterminiez une à une. Allons, j'attends… »

Je savais qu'avec lui toute discussion serait inutile. Il ne me restait plus qu'à m'exécuter.

La Créature d'outre-ciel

Elle était arrivée sur terre dans son vaisseau cristallin, presque diaphane et transparent, orné de fines structures aux courbes délicates et fragiles.

La créature elle-même était de forme indéfinissable, presque invisible, toute en terminaisons hypersensibles et en exquises vibrations. Son intelligence, vaste et lumineuse, ignorait la démarche rationnelle et le cheminement logique. Elle procédait par sympathie, par fusion, osmose, don de soi, élan d'amour et grande vague de communion universelle.

Son spationef avait été gravement endommagé en pénétrant dans l'atmosphère terrestre. Elle se savait donc condamnée à demeurer sur cette planète inconnue. Mais elle ne se sentait jamais étrangère en présence de vie et de conscience : il lui suffisait de s'ouvrir aux autres espèces pour les accueillir dans une douce et chaude effusion, bien au-delà des différences, des mots et des concepts.

Elle s'était posée dans une campagne retirée,

très à l'écart des agglomérations et des grandes voies de circulation.

Les premiers contacts furent avec des familles de rongeurs, des chats, des oiseaux, quelques reptiles. Ce fut comme un immense chœur de bienvenue réciproque, l'amitié joyeuse et active de la visiteuse des étoiles était ressentie par chacun au plus intime de sa nature. Elle apaisait et ravissait les habitants des champs, des forêts, des rivières. Les papillons et les abeilles dansaient d'allégresse. Les mammifères s'immergeaient dans cette onde bienveillante. Les oiseaux composaient des mélodies nouvelles, et planaient, enivrés, portés par ce courant de tendresse infinie. Même les serpents pointaient leur froid museau vers cette délicieuse et chaude source de bonheur.

Soudain la créature perçut une présence nouvelle, d'un caractère étrange et violemment dissonant dans cette suave symphonie d'échanges et de partages.

Les hommes, alertés par l'arrivée inopinée de cet objet volant non identifié, avaient envoyé sur place leurs services spéciaux, leurs techniciens, agents gouvernementaux et militaires, chargés d'isoler l'intrus et de le capturer en vue d'études ultérieures dans des laboratoires secrets. Ils avaient reçu la consigne, en cas d'une quelconque menace, de le neutraliser, voire de l'anéantir.

Par le réseau de ses capteurs ultra-sensibles, la créature entendit clairement les échos de la peur, de l'hostilité, de l'avidité, des pulsions d'agressivité meurtrières qui chagrinèrent et perturbèrent toute l'harmonie du site et de ses autres occupants.

Les hommes étaient à la fois terrifiés, cupides et violents.

La créature se replia sur elle-même et s'abîma dans une méditation profonde et sereine. Il n'était pas question pour elle de se frotter au flux amer de cette intelligence difforme et ténébreuse.

Enfermée dans un caisson étanche, elle fut conduite sous bonne escorte et avec mille précautions dans un endroit souterrain et ultra-secret afin d'y être livrée aux expériences d'une équipe de chercheurs considérés comme les plus performants dans chaque discipline concernée.

En dépit de bien de handicaps émotionnels et de nombreuses carences affectives, la plupart de ces gens n'étaient pas complètement insensibles. Malgré les moyens presque illimités qu'on avait mis à leur disposition, leurs travaux n'avançaient guère. Ils se heurtaient à des données incompréhensibles, à des mystères insolubles, car la nature même de l'extra-terrestre dépassait complètement leur entendement, débordait leurs repères, pulvérisait leurs références et leurs critères.

Les autorités commençaient à s'impatienter.

Au bout d'un certain temps, la créature sortit de son état contemplatif, les savants qui l'observaient sans relâche reçurent comme une décharge ardente et fraternelle, une sorte d'accolade extatique. Dans leur existence austère et studieuse, rien ne les avait préparés à un tel ravissement. Rires et torrents de larmes se succédèrent, proférant toutes sortes d'onomatopées bruyantes, s'enlaçant mutuellement, s'étreignant, s'embrassant avec force démonstrations euphoriques et gestes désordonnés qui provoquèrent une pagaille inouïe dans ces locaux peu propices à la fête.

Les agents de sécurité redoutant quelque attentat subversif ou soupçonnant les effets d'une contamination d'origine sidérale intervinrent sur-le-champ. Les fauteurs de trouble furent immobilisés, endormis, puis internés dans des unités psychiatriques ne figurant sur aucun annuaire.

Lasse du comportement chaotique de ces énergumènes butés, la créature s'esquiva discrètement et sans la moindre difficulté.

Elle était déjà loin quand ses geôliers constatèrent sa disparition.

L'espèce humaine l'intriguait par ses complexités, ses défaillances et ses contradictions. Elle l'attirait aussi, même si elle était gouvernée le plus souvent par l'ineptie, la rage prédatrice et l'illusion.

Après bien des tâtonnements infructueux, la créature d'outre-ciel finit par se fixer dans une petite salle d'école primaire.

Avec les enfants, le langage du cœur était tout naturel et spontané, la communion totale, l'osmose magique.

C'est ainsi que ce modeste établissement d'une banlieue sans attrait devint l'école du bonheur.

« Ma chère, j'ai un aveu à vous faire. J'aurais bien aimé vous rencontrer quand vous étiez petite. Vous deviez être une petite fille modèle, très mignonne, très sage, avec des moments imprévisibles de malice et de caprice. Nous serions certainement devenus amis, complices, confidents. J'aurais veillé sur vous et sur vos songes. Je vous aurais initiée à nos mystères et à nos subterfuges…

– Que signifient ces brusques accès de paternalisme ?

– Me croyez-vous incapable d'élans, sans équivoque et sans arrière-pensée ? C'est pourtant simple : nous autres chats aimons bien les enfants parce qu'ils nous ressemblent : curieux, magiques, insaisissables… »

Le Vieillard qui marchait sur l'eau

Bouddha Çakya Muni, l'Éveillé parfait, le Bienheureux, le très Compatissant, longeait les berges d'un fleuve avec un groupe de disciples, à la recherche d'un passeur, car il avait à faire sur l'autre rive.

Ses fidèles compagnons buvaient des yeux ses moindres gestes, et recueillaient avec dévotion chacune de ses paroles.

Soudain, ils aperçurent au beau milieu du fleuve, un vénérable vieillard, qui, sans support, demeurait assis sur la surface de l'eau, dans une impeccable posture de lotus et une totale immobilité. Son corps décharné portait les marques de la plus rigoureuse ascèse.

Le Bouddha le salua respectueusement et le questionna sur un ton déférent.

« Noble yogi, peux-tu nous dire le sens de ta quête ?

– Depuis des décennies, j'inflige à cette carcasse périssable d'innombrables austérités afin de rendre ce mental dérisoire et cette chair impure esclaves de ma seule volonté. À présent, je peux traverser n'importe quelle étendue d'eau, comme on sillonne une route, sans même être mouillé. N'est-ce pas un résultat remarquable ? »

Çakya Muni sourit sans répondre.

Quelques disciples s'écrièrent : « Mais c'est tout simplement merveilleux ! Ô Maître sage et infaillible, toi qui détiens tous les pouvoirs miraculeux, ne serait-ce pas gagner du temps et de l'énergie que de franchir le fleuve de cette manière ?

– Pas du tout ! s'exclamèrent d'autres disciples. Tout ceci n'est qu'un vulgaire tour de passe-passe, un numéro de cirque indigne d'un authentique chercheur spirituel ! De tels prodiges ne valent strictement rien ! »

Le Bouddha souriait toujours. Il dit enfin : « Mes amis, un peu de patience. Bientôt vous saurez très exactement ce que vaut un tel talent… »

Peu après le groupe atteignit la cabane du passeur, et la traversée du fleuve s'opéra sans encombre.

Quand tous eurent accosté sur l'autre berge, le Bienheureux régla au passeur le prix de ses services – deux roupies.

« Voilà, conclut le Bouddha, deux roupies : c'est très précisément ce que vaut le pouvoir de ce yogi… »

« Ma chère, je crois que je progresse ! »

Le chat semblait surexcité.

« Oui, je progresse. Lentement, certes, mais sûrement. La nuit dernière, la Lune m'a clairement adressé un clin d'œil. Prometteur. Elle a même entrebâillé son corsage de nuages, histoire de m'aguicher. Ensuite, elle a effeuillé quelques bouquets d'étoiles pour saupoudrer ma fourrure. J'en avais plein les oreilles et plein les yeux. C'était comme une invitation. Je sens que notre union est proche… »

Le Pacte

Il était une fois un vieux savant qui s'acharnait depuis des décennies à percer les ultimes secrets de la nature. Son rêve était en fait de découvrir un moyen d'accéder à l'éternelle jeunesse, et de vaincre ainsi l'usure, la déchéance, la mort.

Ses recherches magistrales et ses travaux brillants lui valaient l'estime de ses pairs, l'admiration générale, ainsi que toutes les distinctions et tous les titres honorifiques imaginables.

Mais son véritable objectif se dérobait jour après jour et demeurait désespérément hors de portée.

Le vieillard était prêt à tout pour parvenir à ses fins et obtenir la formule tant convoitée.

Belzébuth, seigneur des turpitudes et Prince des mouches, qui était toujours à l'affût des occasions exceptionnelles et des affaires de choix, se présenta au savant, sans dissimuler son identité ni déguiser son apparence pour le moins répugnante et pestilentielle.

« Voilà, dit-il, dans un long chuintement de crocs

pourris et un écœurant frétillement de ses multiples queues visqueuses, moi, le grand Belzébuth, je suis le seul à pouvoir t'aider à résoudre ton problème et à te sortir de ton marasme ! »

Un tourbillon de mouches grasses et lourdes formait une auréole vénéneuse derrière son crâne et son mufle difformes. Le savant ravala sa répulsion, contenant la nausée qui lui tordait la panse, et demanda : « Admettons que j'aie recours à tes services : qu'exigeras-tu en échange ?

– Oh, rien de plus simple ! »

L'archange obscur faisait crisser les membranes desséchées de ses ailes et déroulait lubriquement ses innombrables langues reptiliennes, tout en claquant des mandibules avec des gargouillements spongieux. « Il suffira que tu signes ce pacte où tu t'engages à me livrer ton âme…

– Et en retour, je posséderai enfin le secret de l'éternelle jeunesse ?

– Parfaitement ! Tu en seras bien sûr l'unique bénéficiaire. Pas question de le partager avec d'autres mortels.

– Un détail me chiffonne dans cet arrangement. Si j'acquiers de la sorte une promesse de vie illimitée, à quoi te sert de t'approprier mon âme ? Je serai désormais à l'abri de la mort ! Où est ton intérêt ? Ce n'est guère logique…

– Ne t'inquiète pas. La fin des temps sera bien

programmée un jour ou l'autre. Et l'Enfer est d'une patience infinie. »

Le vieillard accepta et signa. Il se disait au fond qu'il avait réussi à flouer son ténébreux partenaire, puisque jouissant d'une immunité charnelle et terrestre absolue, rien ne pouvait plus l'atteindre désormais dans son intégrité physique restaurée, doublée d'une énergie vitale inépuisable.

Le changement fut d'ailleurs immédiat et radical. Son image dans le miroir était bien celle d'un jeune homme vif, robuste, séduisant, dans la force bondissante et l'éclat pétillant du bel âge.

S'ouvrit alors pour lui une période euphorique où il collectionna les succès à la fois professionnels, amoureux et financiers. Rien ne semblait lui résister. Il triomphait facilement de tous les obstacles, de tous les défis.

On avait oublié l'illustre vieux savant mystérieusement disparu sans laisser la moindre trace, et découvert ce jeune scientifique dont le brio, le prestige et la fortune faisaient le bonheur des chroniqueurs des gazettes branchées. Les médias revendiquaient sa présence. Il fut invité sur les quatre continents. Les puissants de la terre recherchèrent son amitié. Les gouvernements et les multinationales lui proposèrent des fortunes pour s'offrir ses conseils. Son nom était régulièrement cité pour le Nobel.

Les années passèrent.

Bien sûr son visage ne prenait pas une ride. Sa vigueur, son entrain, sa pugnacité restaient inaltérables. Il possédait tout ce dont il avait pu rêver. Sa curiosité intellectuelle pourtant considérable, était de plus en plus repue, gavée.

Il avait lu tous les livres, visionné tous les films, écouté toutes les musiques, visité tous les musées, exploré tous les grands sites naturels archéologiques et historiques, rencontré les grandes figures charismatiques issues des horizons culturels et idéologiques les plus divers.

Il devenait progressivement une légende vivante, le temps n'ayant sur lui aucune prise apparente. Ceux qu'il avait fait sauter sur ses genoux étaient déjà sur le déclin. Ses femmes et ses maîtresses rejoignaient l'une après l'autre leur dernière demeure. Pour lui, rien ne changeait.

Belzébuth, le roi des mouches, le très fétide, avait scrupuleusement tenu parole et respecté les termes du contrat. L'homme était une curiosité mondiale, une sorte de miracle génétique officiel.

Quant à lui, son enthousiasme s'était lentement émoussé. Il avait peu à peu épuisé tous les artifices du plaisir, tous les sujets d'étonnement et d'excitation.

Il ne pouvait mourir.

Et maintenant de décennie en décennie, de siècle en siècle, il se retrouvait à court de ressource et d'invention pour épicer un peu l'existence, renouveler le champ des sensations, des expériences et des idées. Les jours se succédaient dans une monotonie affreuse, une étouffante répétition, un lancinant cauchemar où la réalité ne savait plus que bégayer. Et tout espoir d'y mettre fin était rigoureusement exclu. Il n'avait même plus cet ultime échappatoire – le suicide.

Alors il comprit le véritable sens du pacte et sa monstrueuse perversité.

Il était bien damné, de toute façon, damné de son vivant, son âme appartenait d'ores et déjà au roi des mouches. Il lui suffisait de continuer à vivre, et il ne pouvait que continuer à vivre, encore et encore.

« Cette fois-ci, ma pauvre amie humaine, vous qu'un sort funeste a privée de fourrure et de griffes rétractiles, je sens que je touche au but. La princesse Lune est de plus en plus proche, disponible, ouverte. Je vais bientôt me fondre dans ses longs falbalas, ses soieries et dentelles tamisées, ses lumières molles et lascives. Alors, je compte sur vous pour transcrire bien scrupuleusement le récit de mes nuits… »

Penche un peu la tête

Dans l'ancienne Chine, à l'époque reculée où l'Empire du Milieu était livré aux grandes manœuvres belliqueuses, aux expéditions sanguinaires et aux multiples exactions des satrapes et soldats de fortune dont les entreprises conquérantes ravageaient métropoles et campagnes, deux seigneurs de la guerre s'affrontaient depuis des années, avec une alternance de succès et de revers où nul ne réussissait à l'emporter durablement.

Les deux rivaux étaient habiles combattants, initiés à l'art subtil des plus savantes combinaisons stratégiques, aux subterfuges tactiques les plus complexes, les plus sophistiqués.

C'était aussi des chefs intrépides, audacieux, n'hésitant jamais à donner l'exemple et à payer de leur personne, des esprits inventifs et intuitifs, presque des artistes, sachant improviser, sortir des sentiers battus et transgresser les règles établies pour créer un effet de surprise et susciter l'effroi.

Tout a une fin, due à l'intervention du hasard, du karma, ou des dieux.

Un jour, l'un des deux généraux captura son ennemi de toujours. Il le fit comparaître chargé de chaînes, mais encore intact, inaffecté dans sa fierté, au milieu du désastre et de l'adversité.

« Pendant des années, dit le vainqueur, tu m'as posé bien des problèmes et valu bien des nuits blanches en déjouant mes plans les mieux conçus et mes plus astucieux calculs. Tu mérites donc largement la mort, et d'ailleurs c'est la règle. Nul ne peut s'y soustraire. Le commandant vaincu doit nécessairement périr. Mais tu as été le seul adversaire vraiment digne de moi. Et à ce titre, je te regretterai sûrement. Aussi pour te prouver toute mon estime, je vais te faire exécuter par mon premier bourreau, un homme très remarquable, et même exceptionnel, un visionnaire, un poète lyrique et hypersensible, qui pratique sa charge comme un art authentique, avec un raffinement sans borne et une exquise délicatesse. Cette attention particulière est une haute marque de considération, un hommage éclatant… »

Le bourreau, convoqué sur l'heure, s'inclina cérémonieusement devant l'illustre captif.

C'était un homme fluet, sautillant, minuscule, avec des gestes aériens, et des petits yeux noirs, luisants, très rapprochés.

Il brandit une lame courbe et mince, dont le fil acéré étincelait au soleil.

Avec un grand sourire, le petit homme se lança dans une prestation chorégraphique, exhibition impressionnante où étaient exposées les innombrables facettes et ressources de son art. C'était un véritable ballet, d'une exquise légèreté, avec une grande variété de rythmes et de cadences.

Le bourreau se laissait visiblement submerger par l'euphorie du créateur en plein élan.

Pour sa part, le prisonnier commençait à s'impatienter.

« Sache, dit-il, que j'apprécie ton précieux talent à sa juste mesure, mais il se fait tard. Il est temps d'en finir. Abrège si tu veux bien cet exercice, et passe donc sans plus tarder à la conclusion.

– Penche un peu la tête, soupira le bourreau : c'est déjà fait… »

Le chat furetait dans tous les coins, cherchant fébrilement un mystérieux et invisible intrus. Il m'avait certes habituée à des comportements inexplicables, mais il y avait cette fois dans sa démarche, une espèce de rigueur et de logique systématique assez troublante.

Il repérait un point, humait le voisinage, se postait, immobile, comme à l'affût d'une proie longuement convoitée, puis changeait brusquement de place, pour reproduire un peu plus loin le même cérémonial.

Ce petit jeu dura une bonne partie de la journée.

« Inutile d'essayer de comprendre, dit-il charitablement. Vous ne disposez pas des bons paramètres…

– Ah bon… Et vous êtes sûr que j'ai les bons paramètres pour m'occuper de vous ?

– Ces mesquineries ne sont pas dignes de vous ! Vaquez donc à vos petites affaires et laissez-moi m'occuper des miennes… »

Le Sphinx

Depuis toujours, le Sphinx régnait en maître absolu sur le désert, terrorisant les voyageurs et visiteurs des sables.

Fils du mystère et de l'abîme, supérieur aux titans en puissance et en ruse, éclipsant les démons en rage carnassière, il chevauchait les ouragans et dansait avec les mirages.

Au cours de ses longues nuits solitaires, il s'amusait à gober les étoiles filantes, à souffler les constellations comme des chandelles et à canonner la Lune de psaumes tonitruants. À l'aube, il étirait ses pattes monstrueuses pour éventrer le ciel dont il léchait sur l'horizon les viscères sanglants.

Depuis des millénaires, il posait des énigmes aux pèlerins et randonneurs égarés. Incapables de répondre, la plupart finissaient entre ses crocs.

Seul Œdipe avait réussi à éventer ses pièges, mais il avait connu par la suite un destin pathétique.

De temps à autre le monstre déployait ses ailes gigantesques, prenait son essor, escaladait l'azur, défiait les altitudes puis fondait sur la terre pour dévaster une cité ou ravager une province. Cette fureur apaisée, il retournait au cœur de son désert, guettant de sa prunelle étincelante et fauve, le passage d'une proie ou la chute d'un ange.

Il aimait aussi à s'abîmer dans une rêverie béante et hybride ponctuée d'interminables bâillements.

Les plus farouches cohortes et les plus fiers guerriers changeaient d'itinéraire pour éviter un affrontement avec ce dragon des sables, ce démiurge impitoyable et invincible.

Un jour, un voyageur très sage ou très fou, traversant le désert, n'hésita guère à l'aborder.

« Peux-tu me dire, petit homme, l'interpella le Sphinx, savourant d'avance la vivante friandise offerte, peux-tu me dire, toi qui oses t'aventurer dans ces lieux inhospitaliers, ce qu'est la mort? J'attends la vraie réponse sans quoi je ne ferai de toi qu'une bouchée!

– La mort? C'est ce qui arrive aux autres!

– J'ai coutume de soumettre quatre énigmes à la sagacité de mes interlocuteurs. Voici la deuxième: combien font un et un?

– Un et un font toujours un. Parce que dans l'univers il n'y a qu'Un.

– Voyons la troisième: qu'est-ce que la conscience?

– Dis-moi qui pose la question et tu auras toi-même la réponse…

– Enfin celle-ci : il suffit qu'on m'invoque pour m'abolir, qui suis-je ?

– Le silence ! À présent, puis-je à mon tour te poser une question ?

– J'y consens.

– Alors dis-moi : qu'est-ce que le temps ? »

Le Sphinx se mit à réfléchir. Le passé n'existait plus. Le futur n'existait pas encore. Le présent était insaisissable. Quelque chose en lui s'arrêta, se pétrifia. Son être se tétanisait.

Le Sphinx était à tout jamais devenu un monstre de pierre, balayé par les vents du désert, et mitraillé par les flashes des touristes.

Il ronronnait les yeux mi-clos, les pattes repliées sur les coussins du canapé.

« D'où vous vient ce bien-être inopiné ?

– La prière, une prière de louanges, un psaume, un cantique ! Je sais, les hommes n'en chantent plus, sauf des préfabriqués, lyophilisés, pasteurisés. Moi je prie pour remercier le jour et la nuit, le soleil et la pluie, les vastes horizons et les petits sentiers, les senteurs fraîches du petit matin, les odeurs épicées des sous-bois en été, les arômes lourds et faisandés des caves et des poubelles, le cri flûté des nouveau-nés, le souffle friable des moribonds, l'endroit et l'envers des choses. Vous voyez, je remercie. Je suis écarquillé, dilaté, exsangue de gratitude et de remerciements… »

La Nuit est en colère

Les Grands Anciens étaient excédés. Princes de l'abîme, souverains des ténèbres, seigneurs de l'invisible, puissances de la face obscure et cachée de l'univers, gouvernant les tribus de la Lune et commandant les escadrons de l'indicible, chevaliers de la brume avec leurs cohortes de spectres, sombres milices de l'incongru et du difforme, tous les vieux démiurges sillonnant les espaces noirs et peuplant les cavernes du rêve étaient exaspérés par les hommes et leur outrecuidance.

L'espèce humaine avait infesté la terre de ses machines polluantes, de sa rage prédatrice, multipliant les expériences les plus perverses, imposant son arbitraire et sa domination à la nature tout entière, réduisant faune et flore en esclavage, verrouillant l'univers dans un carcan de rationalité, l'étouffant dans une camisole de principes et de préceptes, balayant peu à peu toute liberté, toute spontanéité.

À force de se prendre pour une créature privilégiée, unique, supérieure à toutes les autres, au point de nier tout ce qui échappait aux limites étroites de son entendement et au champ exigu de sa petite logique, l'homme en était venu à saccager son propre domaine, à déprécier la vie, à vider la réalité de toute poésie. Son avidité insatiable, sa cupidité inouïe, avaient produit un océan de souffrances – misères, exploitations, persécutions, et génocides.

Du fond de leurs vertigineuses tanières, les Grands Anciens avaient décidé que cette nuisance avait trop duré et devait être éradiquée. Ils allaient déchaîner sur l'humanité un raz de marée de fantasmes, un ouragan de cauchemars, qui sèmeraient partout le chaos, le désastre et la mort. L'ange exterminateur aurait à brandir son glaive monstrueux.

Mais pour intervenir, les dieux avaient besoin des chats, mandataires de la Nuit, syndics de l'ombre, gardiens du mystère, portiers de l'invisible.

Or pour les chats, l'homme était à la fois un passionnant sujet d'observation, un objet d'étonnement et surtout d'hilarité sans cesse renouvelé. Le spectacle de la folie et de l'ineptie humaine provoquait chez les félins des fous rires qui pouvaient se prolonger indéfiniment. Et c'était pour eux une source de jouissance intense et raffinée.

Voilà pourquoi les chats s'opposèrent au projet des Grands Anciens.

Grâce à eux, l'humanité bénéficia d'un sursis.

« Vous qui êtes si songeur, si pensif, j'aimerais tellement savoir ce qui vous passe par la tête…

– J'explore mes existences précédentes.

– C'est passionnant ! J'aimerais pouvoir en faire autant…

– Qu'est-ce qui vous en empêche ? Vous pouvez oublier qui vous êtes. Vous faites l'impasse. Si votre petite vie actuelle occupe vos pensées, vous vous dérobez, vous vous absentez. Ensuite, pratiquez la rêverie oblique, l'image perpendiculaire, vous verrez défiler tous vos prédécesseurs. Masculins, animaux, angéliques, démoniaques, d'autres encore qui échappent à toutes catégories. Vous verrez, c'est très drôle, très savoureux, et très revigorant. Même les épisodes les plus scabreux et les plus consternants… »

Les Blancs doivent gagner

Il était une fois une très sage et très puissante magicienne qui vivait depuis des siècles au sommet d'une montagne inaccessible. Elle avait eu bien des maris successifs et donné le jour à d'innombrables rejetons qui, bien sûr, la quittaient à l'âge requis pour suivre leur destin.

Elle élevait, à l'époque, un joli marmot à l'âme pure et au cœur généreux.

Dans la vallée et dans la plaine, au pied de la montagne, s'étendaient deux royaumes qui se livraient depuis toujours une guerre sans merci.

Le premier vénérait les principes de justice, de bonheur, de liberté. Il incarnait les vertus d'ouverture et de tolérance. Son prince était le gardien de la lumière, le protecteur des arts, de l'équité, de la beauté, le bienfaiteur des faibles et des malheureux. Il commandait une armée de vaillants et loyaux chevaliers, vêtus de blanc, armés de glaives rutilants et d'écussons immaculés.

Le royaume adverse était celui de l'obscurité, de la tyrannie, de l'esclavage. On y pratiquait couramment le meurtre, le viol et la torture. Les geôles regorgeaient de captifs promis aux pires supplices. La population vivait sous la pression d'une terreur omniprésente. Tout n'était que chaos, ténèbres, hurlements d'agonie.

Dans le premier royaume régnait en permanence la clarté d'un azur sans tache, d'un éternel printemps.

L'autre était le domaine d'une nuit sépulcrale et glacée, d'un hiver sans fin et sans espoir, jalousement défendu par une milice de guerriers noirs, fourbes et sanguinaires qui brandissaient des squelettes en guise de bannière.

Depuis des temps immémoriaux, les chevaliers blancs et guerriers noirs étaient aux prises dans des combats titanesques dont l'enjeu était le triomphe définitif de la lumière ou des ténèbres.

La magicienne observait les deux camps, les alternances de succès et de revers, sans jamais prendre parti. Son jeune fils avait un caractère intransigeant et le sang chaud. Devenant adolescent, il s'émut de cette étrange neutralité, à ses yeux incongrue, car sa mère était compatissante, miséricordieuse et ne dissimulait en elle aucune zone d'ombre.

« Je dois m'engager, lui annonça-t-il, au service de la bonne cause. Je vais de ce pas offrir mon bras et mon talent au prince du royaume lumineux et à ses chevaliers blancs ! Il faut anéantir la menace des ténèbres. Les Blancs doivent gagner !

– Suis donc ta voie mon fils, si c'est là ce que te dicte ton cœur. Et agis pour le mieux sans jamais redouter l'échec, et sans attendre ni profit, ni récompense. »

Le garçon avait reçu une parfaite éducation, et c'était déjà un chevalier accompli, champion en arts martiaux, et initié aux plus savantes combinaisons stratégiques. Il fut reçu à bras ouverts par le prince du royaume lumineux qui ne tarda pas à lui confier le commandement de ses cohortes.

Une grande bataille était imminente. Mais avec leur nouveau général, les Blancs avaient cette fois un avantage majeur.

Les Noirs furent taillés en pièces, leur royaume, occupé, libéré. La nuit fut dissipée. L'azur égaya la campagne. L'harmonie et l'équité s'établirent partout.

Or peu à peu, bizarrement, le royaume vainqueur s'abîma dans l'ennui, l'oisiveté, la routine. Une espèce de grisaille mélancolique, de brume lancinante s'infiltrait dans les bourgs, polluait les chemins, brouillait le ciel jadis étincelant. Une insidieuse léthargie s'emparait des plus intrépides.

Le jeune homme désemparé alla consulter sa mère. « Les Blancs et les Noirs, lui dit-elle, sont tous deux indispensables au juste équilibre des choses et au mouvement du monde, comme le creux est nécessaire au plein, l'extérieur à l'intérieur, et le fini à l'infini. Abolir l'un revient à supprimer l'autre. Mesure bien cette vérité et agis en conséquence… »

Le fils de la magicienne redescendit pensivement vers le royaume obscur. Il y regroupa quelques rescapés clandestins de la vieille milice noire, et restaura l'empire des ténèbres.

En face, le royaume du jour retrouva aussitôt toute sa clarté.

La guerre allait pouvoir reprendre son cours.

« Ah ! les défunts sont ponctuels au rendez-vous…

– Vous voulez dire qu'il y aurait des fantômes circulant ici même en ce moment ?

– Vous avancez en permanence au milieu d'un tourbillon de trépassés dont vous ne pouvez détecter la présence, mais que nous autres chats voyons depuis toujours distinctement.

– Et une telle promiscuité ne vous gêne guère ?

– Oh, les morts ne sont pas bien encombrants. De toute façon, ils n'existent plus, ils n'ont plus rien à faire ni à dire. Ils sont gentils, polis, absents. Ils ont tout oublié, leur situation passée, leurs amours, leur état civil.

– Je ne vois pas tellement l'intérêt…
– Il n'y en a aucun. Pourquoi voulez-vous que les choses aient de l'intérêt ?
– Décidément, vous êtes un anarchiste, un nihiliste…
– Je suis tout simplement un chat… »

Le Rire

Depuis des lunes, la guerre faisait rage.

Les deux nations acharnées à s'entre-détruire ne savaient même plus pourquoi elles se battaient. Mais chaque année, des milliers de familles payaient un tribut sanglant à cette folie dévastatrice qui se propageait avec son noir cortège de fléaux – famines, épidémies et ruines.

Toutes les tentatives de tractations et pourparlers avaient échoué. De part et d'autre, les assauts étaient de plus en plus sauvages et massifs. Mais nul ne semblait en mesure de s'assurer un avantage décisif, de remporter une victoire définitive.

Le matin d'une grande bataille, un étranger d'allure très ordinaire, petit bonhomme plutôt malingre, un peu timide, balbutiant et distrait, mais avec une bizarre étincelle dans le regard, se présenta successivement aux deux monarques ennemis commandant les phalanges sur le point de s'entre-tuer.

« J'ai l'arme absolue qui arrêtera cette guerre, annonça-t-il.

– Mais est-ce que ce sera à mon avantage ?

– Tu auras tout à y gagner ! »

Il se plaça entre les deux armées et se mit à raconter une histoire tellement comique, d'une drôlerie si fracassante, que le champ de bataille se transforma bientôt en un immense fou rire.

Même les officiers, les généraux et les souverains, d'abord décontenancés, furent rapidement gagnés par cette hilarité générale.

C'était un rire convulsif, cataclysmique, un rire qui nouait les boyaux, déchirait les poumons, arrachait les yeux de leurs orbites, un rire qui lessivait les cœurs, calcinait les vanités, pulvérisait les vieilles rancunes.

La guerre était finie. À la satisfaction de tous, sans vainqueur, ni vaincu.

Le voyageur n'avait floué aucune des deux parties.

Avant de prendre congé des monarques réconciliés, il prospecta les villes et les campagnes des deux royaumes, et choisit une paire d'énergumènes à l'apparence la plus grotesque, à la voix la plus nasillarde, aux propos les plus insolemment incohérents. Il les conduisit auprès des souverains.

« Voici, dit-il, mon cadeau d'adieu. Ces hurluberlus seront vos bouffons. Chaque fois que l'un de vous sera tenté de trop se prendre au sérieux, ces paltoquets sauront utilement intervenir et vous remettre les idées en place. Ainsi la paix pourra se maintenir, bien mieux que par le truchement des négociateurs officiels qui ont vite fait d'envenimer les conflits potentiels. »

Ce matin-là, le matou se mit à miauler avec une insistance appuyée, croissante, presque angoissante. Je le pressais de questions, m'efforçant de comprendre ce qui le préoccupait et provoquait une telle effervescence. Mais lui, habituellement si disert, si prodigue de confidences et de révélations, restait obstinément muré dans son refus de dialogue.

Frottant son nez contre ma joue, esquissant sa pelote sur mes bras ou mon ventre, s'égosillant sans retenue ni raison apparente.

À la fin, après plusieurs heures de ce manège, je déclarai forfait.

Bien sûr, les miaulements s'interrompirent comme ils avaient commencé, sans le moindre motif plausible.

Les Dieux

Dame la Lune m'avait fixé rendez-vous au Port des Songes, sur le grand quai d'embarquement où stationnaient les navires en partance pour les archipels enchanteurs du mystère, les rivages de l'étrange et le détroit crépusculaire de la quête poétique. Cette invitation avait été pour moi aussi impromptue qu'inespérée.

Elle m'attendait, au bord de la jetée, dans sa robe de vapeurs chatoyantes, avec son voluptueux pelage de soieries liquides et mordorées. À petits coups rapides et sûrs de sa patte magique, dame la Lune s'amusait à dévider le fil des constellations et envoyait rouler les nébuleuses d'un bord à l'autre de l'horizon. Les courbes de sa silhouette si parfaitement lascive me plongeaient dans un trouble, un émoi indicibles. Mon échine frissonnait, mon panache avait doublé de volume, mes griffes s'étiraient et se rétractaient mécaniquement, tous mes muscles étaient parcourus d'insolites vibrations. J'avais l'âme quadrillée de prodiges.

« Viens avec moi, petit frère, susurra dame la Lune. Nous allons visiter le domaine des dieux, ceux qui gouvernent les sphères planétaires. »

Dans un long miaulement amoureux, je suivis la souveraine des nuits.

Elle m'entraîna dans une immense et vieille demeure, un château baroque et biscornu, un édifice tarabiscoté qui paraissait peuplé d'entités glauques et de chimères mélancoliques. C'était une enfilade de bâtiments, de tours, un dédale de toitures, façades et péristyles aux géométries absconses, aux espaces divergents et aux décors hybrides. Arches, ponts, belvédères, galeries et portiques se déployaient en symphonies d'ardoises, de tuiles, de briques, de marbres. Un opéra de verreries et de ferrures, un dévergondage de formes fantasmagoriques.

Notre première étape fut une rutilante féerie de tourelles cristallines, exquises constructions lumineuses et diaphanes, espaces nacrés aux contours délicats, aux torsades moirées baignant dans une triomphale canicule.

« Voici le fief du seigneur Apollon », me confia la Lune.

Dans un vaste théâtre en plein air, des ballets de clartés scintillantes improvisaient une chorégraphie de feu et d'or sur des rythmes d'extase. C'était un tourbillon jubilatoire et un brasier d'ivresse. Le dieu parut sur son char étincelant, jeune, vigoureux, superbe, éclatant d'une mâle et pure allégresse.

« Voici celui qui distribue à tout instant la semence torride fécondant le flanc béant de la terre, suscitant le mouvement, l'amour, la vie. Apollon, mon premier, mon très glorieux et impérial époux. »

Chaque hiver, sur son farouche destrier caparaçonné d'incandescence et brandissant bien haut son étendard de flammes échevelées, le dieu devait repousser les sombres puissances de la glace éternelle tendue aux commissures du néant par les archanges de la désolation et soufflée sur l'univers par l'esprit de négation.

La Lune me guida ensuite vers un petit palais, une délicieuse bonbonnière rococo où le moindre détail était d'un raffinement et d'une sophistication extrêmes. La douce lueur tamisée d'une tiède journée finissante donnait aux angles une langueur soyeuse. Des jets d'eau sveltes gazouillaient au milieu de bassins en forme de coquillages.

Une très jeune femme d'une beauté ineffable, aux traits d'une pureté inoubliable et à la grâce ensorcelante, rêvassait indolemment au bord de l'eau, étalant sa divine nudité en toute innocence. Un très léger sourire flottait sur ses lèvres pulpeuses. Sous ses paupières à demi closes infusaient mollement quelques songes d'amour.

« Regarde bien cette petite peste, cette allumeuse, grommela ma compagne, c'est Vénus. Toujours à mijoter un coup en douce. Les mâles sont tous à ses pieds. Elle est incurable. Combien de fléaux n'a-t-elle pas déchaînés ! Combien de tortures, de meurtres, de suicides ! La guerre de Troie et celle de Cent Ans. Jamais satisfaite, jamais repue ! Toujours plus de désirs fous, de passions fatales ! »

Dans ces propos sévères, je crus bien discerner quelques rivalités, peut-être une secrète jalousie. Car après tout Vénus inspirait également les grands élans du cœur et les plus chaudes visions artistiques.

Nous arrivions maintenant dans un bizarre dédale aux structures aériennes, presque translucides, où on devinait un réseau compliqué de corridors interminables, de vestibules et d'escaliers qui s'enroulaient dans toutes les directions ; caressées de senteurs matinales, de petites brises crépues et acidulées, des créatures affublées de déguisements hétéroclites sautillaient, virevoltaient, s'égosillaient, gesticulaient dans une fête pétillante et farfelue. Le maître de cérémonie était une sorte d'arlequin, agile, véloce, joueur, bavard, escamoteur, une espèce de farfadet espiègle et persifleur qui se livrait à mille galipettes, cabrioles, simagrées et grimaces, expert en faux-semblants, trompe-l'œil et facéties de toute nature.

« Voici mon petit frère Mercure, me précisa la Lune, le messager des dieux, grand communicateur, bonimenteur et farceur. Mais c'est aussi le plus intelligent, le plus subtil, le plus fin de nous tous. »

Nous pénétrâmes dans une orgueilleuse bâtisse fièrement dressée comme un défi de pierres. De longues salles voûtées servaient à l'entraînement des chevaliers qui s'y livraient des joutes sans répit ni merci. Les cloisons et les dalles résonnaient bruyamment des coups d'estoc et de taille au milieu de vociférations menaçantes, de halètements rauques.

L'arbitre et le seigneur des lieux était un rude géant aux traits barbares, à la face hirsute, labourée de cicatrices et de balafres.

« Voici le grand rapace, le carnassier indomptable, le guerrier téméraire, le prince des puissances agressives et viriles, le dieu Mars. Celui dont l'âme est synonyme de dangers, de conflits, de violences. Personne, pas même Apollon, ne saurait l'arrêter dans ses expéditions sauvages et ses féroces chevauchées. Ses désirs sont autant d'ordres de bataille. Mais il est également chargé d'une mission capitale. Empêcher les démons du chaos, de l'inertie, de l'entropie universelle d'investir le réel et de paralyser les mouvements de l'espace-temps. Si Mars ne veillait pas sur nous, une léthargie incoercible tétaniserait peu à peu les formes, et le monde sombrerait dans un coma profond irréversible… »

La Lune m'introduisit dans un palais grandiose où retentissait la joyeuse cacophonie d'un festin pléthorique.

Les agapes généreuses étaient présidées par un personnage rubicond, jovial, boursouflé, haut en couleur, qui vidait gaillardement des plats richement garnis, des coupes remplies à ras bord de vins capiteux et de liqueurs émoustillantes.

« Contemple, dit respectueusement la Lune, contemple notre père à tous, le grand Jupiter, géniteur, magistrat, prélat suprême. Certes, il est corpulent, volumineux, expansif, autoritaire, colérique, voire un peu paillard. Mais c'est le patriarche, le juge, le maître de la loi et des institutions. Le protocole lui accorde une préséance absolue. Il a le pas sur tous ses pairs, et ses verdicts sont sans appel. Souviens-toi, il peut infliger des châtiments exemplaires, exercer une coercition sans limite. Ne t'avise jamais d'attirer son courroux. »

Nous traversâmes une aire silencieuse et déserte, et je suivis la Lune dans un vieux donjon d'aspect rigide et maussade. Tout y respirait l'austérité, le dépouillement, une radicale sévérité.

Dans une cellule monacale, sans mobilier ni accessoire, se tenait un vieillard maigre, émacié, taciturne, avare de ses gestes, et le regard opaque entièrement tourné vers l'intérieur. C'était à l'évidence un solitaire, un misanthrope, méprisant tout échange frivole, tout propos inutile, voire un simple sourire. Tout paraissait chez lui strictement contrôlé, minutieusement élaboré, sans imprévu ni fantaisie d'aucune sorte.

Entre ses doigts noueux et crochus, le vieillard agrippait un énorme sablier, dont le contenu s'égrenait lentement, inexorablement.

« Voici l'aïeul, murmura ma compagne, le père monstrueux qui dévore ses enfants, le mal-aimé, l'indestructible, Saturne, maître du temps et des métamorphoses, sombre seigneur de la longue patience, usurier du silence et fossoyeur des mondes. Jamais son acharnement ne fléchit et rien n'entame son opiniâtreté. Tu crois sans doute qu'il ne nous prête guère attention, mais rien n'échappe à sa lucidité pénétrante. Sans lui, le réel se volatiliserait aussitôt, car il maintient imperturbablement le fil d'une implacable continuité. »

Plus loin, la Lune me fit escalader les murs d'enceinte d'une citadelle vertigineuse, une tour de verre et d'acier dont le sommet culminait au milieu des tonnerres, dans un jardin semé d'ouragans et de foudres.

« Nous sommes dans le domaine des crises, des paroxysmes et des révolutions. »

Un chercheur à crâne chauve et démesuré avait l'œil collé à des lunettes géantes braquées sur l'infini.

« Uranus, dit la Lune, prince des utopies, des subversions et des bouleversements majeurs. Mieux vaut se tenir à distance. »

Nous explorâmes encore tout un espace de greniers et de combles où s'entassaient vieilleries, souvenirs et chimères. Au milieu de ce bric-à-brac somnolait un énergumène entièrement vêtu d'algues et de coquillages. Sa tête baignait dans un nimbe de rêves évasifs, informes, qui se mélangeaient à la poussière des lieux.

« Chaperon des fantômes égarés dans la brume, seigneur du vague, de l'imprécis, du flou, de l'allusif, expert en confusion et affabulation, dieu des dissolutions ultimes dans les contours indiscernables du petit matin, je te présente Neptune, dont les mélanges hasardeux et les délires narcotiques ont initié le grand bouillon vital des origines… Avec celui-là, la méfiance est de rigueur… Mais il nous reste encore un domaine à prospecter. »

Cette fois il s'agissait de souterrains, de caves et d'égouts méphitiques où pullulaient toutes sortes de créatures innommables, qui grouillaient, rampaient, fuyaient furtivement à notre approche. Une entêtante puanteur imprégnait ces galeries comme un souffle de peste s'insinuant dans notre être. C'était un labyrinthe de perdition et de désespérance. « Tu ne verras pas le propriétaire de ces lieux, et c'est tant mieux pour toi. Sache seulement qu'il gouverne toute la population misérable des désirs interdits, des pulsions clandestines, des souvenirs censurés, toutes les sulfureuses puissances qui ne peuvent s'exprimer au grand jour et qui parfois explosent en démences terroristes, tous les déviances, les fanatismes et les dérèglements divers. Ce dieu invisible, c'est Pluton. »

Notre incursion tirait à sa fin. Nous avions fait le tour, ou presque, du domaine des dieux. Un seul restait à visiter, c'était celui de dame la Lune, ma compagne.

Nous étions près d'un lac aux eaux calmes et profondes, au cœur d'une nuit veloutée, embaumée d'essences rares et volatiles.

Dans le palais de la Lune, des formes évasives aux courbes alanguies déambulaient lentement avec le regard fixe des somnambules et des voyants. Des tourbillons de rêves et de souvenirs d'enfance composaient d'imprévisibles et changeantes féeries.

Les salles du palais étaient tapissées de sortilèges et d'énigmes. La déesse Lune, ma compagne, s'étirait langoureusement sur des coussins dont le moelleux invitait à l'enfouissement, à l'engloutissement.

Dans la salle du trône s'ouvraient les portes de l'imaginaire. Épouvantes et merveilles s'y donnaient libre cours. Il y avait toutes les tribus hallucinées, le bestiaire chiffonné du demi-sommeil, démiurges poreux, titans grumeleux, villes truquées, paysages illicites, anges du paradoxe et de l'inachevé. C'était les royaumes enchantés où les soldats de plomb livraient d'exquises batailles, où les ours en peluche faisaient la loi et où d'adorables poupées capricieuses annonçaient la météo. Gulliver y courtisait Cendrillon, et les trois petits cochons dansaient la farandole avec le grand méchant loup. Alice partait en voyage de noce avec le chapelier fou. Les objets inanimés parlaient couramment latin et grec. Le Père Fouettard, le Bonhomme de sable, Riquet à la houppe arpentaient le sentier de l'école buissonnière et pique-niquaient avec la princesse au petit pois. Les messagers de l'éternel jouaient à la belote avec les chevaliers des glaces. Sinbad cherchait l'île au trésor entre les récifs des constellations. Merlin et Viviane fêtaient leurs retrouvailles et leurs fiançailles. Les Schtroumpfs organisaient des parties de saute-mouton avec Dumbo, l'éléphant volant. E.T. initiait les Shadoks aux joies du V.T.T., Barbe Bleue auditionnait les Gremlins en vue d'une superproduction sur le mystère des armoires interdites. Les Pieds Nickelés se déguisaient en

Superman, Barbarella filait le parfait amour avec Polichinelle, Ali Baba louait ses tapis volants pour explorer le Livre de la Jungle.

J'allais pouvoir enfin bâiller et somnoler aux côtés de ma princesse Lune, en mélangeant nos pattes, nos fourrures, nos moustaches.

Je n'ai plus jamais revu le gros chat noir. J'ai vainement guetté son retour chaque matin pendant des semaines.

Je savais que sa disparition n'était imputable ni à un accident, ni à l'un de ces caprices dont les chats sont coutumiers. Mon ami était tout simplement ailleurs. Son étrange passion pour la Lune l'avait sans doute conduit derrière la face visible, de l'autre côté du décor, sur la rive incertaine et le versant crépusculaire de l'être.

Alors j'ai pris peu à peu l'habitude, surtout les soirs de pleine Lune, de me pencher à mon balcon pour contempler l'astre des nuits. Et il me semble bien parfois deviner une silhouette féline qui se moule et se love amoureusement au creux des voluptueuses rondeurs de sa gracieuse déesse mollement engourdie.

Table des matièes

éditions
CORPS 16

littera

Diabolus in musica Yann Apperry
Le Voyage d'Anna Blume Paul Auster
Tombouctou Paul Auster
Soie Alessandro Baricco
Accessible à certaine mélancolie Patrick Besson
Les Frères de la Consolation Patrick Besson
Cette aveuglante absence de lumière T. B. Jelloun
Labyrinthe des sentiments Tahar Ben Jelloun
L'Auberge des pauvres Tahar Ben Jelloun
Le Premier Amour est toujours le dernier Tahar Ben Jelloun
Le Mai, le joli mai Roger Bichelberger
Le Manuscrit de Port-Ébène Dominique Bona
Le Ciel de Bargetal Daniel Boulanger
Clémence et Auguste Daniel Boulanger
Les Mouches et l'âne Daniel Boulanger
Week-end de chasse à la mère Geneviève Brisac
Le Soir et le matin suivant Ève de Castro
Le Message Andrée Chedid
La Belle Écriture Rafael Chirbes
La Cinquième Montagne Paulo Coelho
Le Démon et mademoiselle Prym Paulo Coelho
Veronika décide de mourir Paulo Coelho
L'Île Madame Jean François Deniau

Sisters Stéphane Denis
Les Bonnes Intentions Agnès Desarthe
Cinq photos de ma femme Agnès Desarthe
Un secret sans importance Agnès Desarthe
Anchise Maryline Desbiolles
Le Petit Col des loups Maryline Desbiolles
Fleur de péché Geneviève Dormann
Mickey l'ange Geneviève Dormann
La Folie du roi Marc Clara Dupont-Monod
Je m'en vais Jean Echenoz
La Question humaine François Emmanuel
Des gens qui s'aiment Michèle Fitoussi
Gai-l'Amour Maurice Genevoix
Le Rire de l'ange Henri Gougaud
Les Sept plumes de l'aigle Henri Gougaud
Le Secret de l'Aigle Henri Gougaud/Luis Ansa
La Perle rouge Jean Grangeot
"Dentelles" Roger Hanin
Orlanda Jacqueline Harpman
La Correspondante Eric Holder
La Fille indigne Catherine Hervé-Bazin
Prodige Nancy Huston
Froides fleurs d'avril Ismail Kadaré
La Pourpre et le Jasmin Michèle Kahn
Allah n'est pas obligé Ahmadou Kourouma
Himmelfarb Michael Krüger
La Poussière du monde Jacques Lacarrière
Céleste Martine Le Coz
Dans ces bras-là Camille Laurens

L'Homme qui ne voulait plus se lever D. Lodge
Les Quatre Vérités David Lodge
Tu, Mio Erri de Luca
Les Échelles du Levant Amin Maalouf
La Musique d'une vie Andreï Makine
D'amour et d'exil Eduardo Manet
Rhapsodie cubaine Eduardo Manet
La Sagesse du singe Eduardo Manet
Les Filles prodigues Dominique Muller
La Petite Française Eric Neuhoff
Mercure Amélie Nothomb
Le Fantôme d'Anil Michael Ondaatje
Mon grand appartement Christian Oster
Un enfant Patrick Poivre d'Arvor
L'Irrésolu Patrick Poivre d'Arvor
Petit homme Patrick Poivre d'Arvor
Le Roi au-delà de la mer Jean Raspail
Arthur Michel Rio
Qu'a-t-on fait du Petit Paul ? Marie Rouanet
Le Chasseur Zéro Pascale Roze
Le Roman de la Belle et la Bête Bernard Simonay
Les Belles Âmes Lydie Salvayre
Le Sourire aux lèvres Robert Sabatier
Mazag Robert Solé
Ouvert au public Muriel Spark
Lambert Pacha François Sureau
Anielka François Taillandier
La Belle Endormie Elizabeth Taylor
Le Papier tue-mouches Elizabeth Taylor

Vue sur le port Elizabeth Taylor
Une expérience enrichissante Mary Wesley
Pays, villes, paysages Stefan Zweig

terroirs

La Maison Madeleine Chapsal
Les Loups du paradis Sophie Chérer
À travers champs Georges Clemenceau
L'Apollon de Marsac Louis-Michel Cluzeau
Les Voisins de l'horizon Didier Cornaille
Vigneron du Médoc P. Courrian et M. Creignou
Le Miroir de ma mère Marthe et Philippe Delerm
Bestiaire enchanté Maurice Genevoix
La Loire, Agnès et les garçons Maurice Genevoix
Tendre bestiaire Maurice Genevoix
Au bonheur du pain Robert Griffon
Mireille et Vincent Marcel Jullian
Patron pêcheur Michel Josié et Geneviève Ladouès
Une fille perdue Marcel Lachiver
L'Épée de Rocamadour Colette Laussac
Le Raconteur de monde Patrice Lepage
Le Matelot des fleuves R. Maillet et C. Piat
L'Enfance buissonnière Noëlle Marchand
La Dernière Neige Hubert Mingarelli
Une rivière verte et silencieuse Hubert Mingarelli
Les Amants Liam O'Flaherty
Paludier de Guérande Joseph Péréon
La Cabane aux fées Michel Peyramaure
Soupes d'orties Michel Peyramaure

La Braconne Jean-Claude Ponçon
Ulysse, le chat qui traversa la France
Philippe Ragueneau
Le Signe de la Pierre Évelyse Robin
Balades des jours ordinaires Marie Rouanet
Dans la douce chair des villes Marie Rouanet
Quatre temps du silence Marie Rouanet
Le Petit de l'ogre Lucette-Marie Sagnières
Le Chaudron de la sorcière Jean-Marc Soyez
Ma ferme andalouse Chris Stewart
Le Bougnat Marc Tardieu
L'Étranger alsacien Gisèle Tuaillon-Nass
À rebrousse-poil Henri Vincenot
Du côté des Bordes Henri Vincenot
Nouvelles ironiques Henri Vincenot
Récits des friches et des bois Henri Vincenot
Rempart de la Miséricorde Henri Vincenot
Toute la Terre est au Seigneur Henri Vincenot
Les Yeux en face des trous Henri Vincenot
Confidences des deux rivages Claudine Vincenot
Fossoyeurs d'étoiles Claude Vincent

police

La Comtesse de la nuit Béatrice de Boisanger
Dossiers très privés Roger Borniche
Le Bon, la brute et le notaire Luc Calvez
Le Frelon Maurice Chavardès
À propos de Max Amanda Cross
Le Complexe d'Antigone Amanda Cross

Les Amours auvergnates Charles Exbrayat
Au « Trois Cassoulets » Charles Exbrayat
La Belle Véronaise Charles Exbrayat
Ces sacrées Florentines Charles Exbrayat
Chewing-gum et spaghetti Charles Exbrayat
Des Amours compliquées Charles Exbrayat
Le Clan Morembert Charles Exbrayat
Les Douceurs provinciales Charles Exbrayat
Les Dames du Creusot Charles Exbrayat
Félicité de la Croix-Rousse Charles Exbrayat
Mets tes pantoufles, Roméo Charles Exbrayat
La Petite fille à la fenêtre Charles Exbrayat
Le plus beau des Bersagliers Charles Exbrayat
Le Quintette de Bergame Charles Exbrayat
L'Heure d'hiver Michel Grisolia
La Petite Amie du crime Michel Grisolia
Rendez-vous allée des brouillards Christine Haydar
La Piste Manson William Harrington
Qui a tué Régina ? William Harrington
Qui a peur d'Ed Garpo ? Fred Kassak
La Belle Inconnue Jean-Claude Lamy
La double mort de Thomas Stuart Mary London
Le Crime du corbeau Mary London
Un crime exemplaire Mary London
Le Mort de la Tamise Mary London
Le Parfum d'un crime Mary London
Meurtre par superstition Mary London
Sept ladies pour un meurtre Mary London
La Photo du bourreau Peter Lovesey

Le Baron les croque Anthony Morton
Le Baron et le receleur Anthony Morton
Le Baron est bon prince Anthony Morton
Noces pour le Baron Anthony Morton
Le Baron se dévoue Anthony Morton
Le Baron et le poignard Anthony Morton
Le Baron et le clochard Anthony Morton
Les Belles Infidèles Hubert Nyssen
Au bout des rues obscures Dorothy Salisbury-Davis
Sans espoir de retour Louis C. Thomas

HISTOIRE

Louis XIV artiste Philippe Beaussant
Le Siècle des Héros Général Bigeard
Lévénez Jeanne Bluteau
Marie et Julie Jeanne Bluteau
Le galant exil du marquis de Boufflers M.Brantôme
La Marion du Faouët Yvonne Chauffin
Cœur de Roc Olivier Chauvin
Douce et incomparable Joséphine B. Chevallier
Mémoires de Napoléon Robert Colonna d'Istria
Les Jeunes Amours de Louis XV Michel de Decker
Madame de Montespan Michel de Decker
L'Empire des illusions Régis Descott
La Bouche Yves Delaborde
Alexandra, la dernière tsarine C. Durand-Cheynet
Les Tsarines Vladimir Fedorovski
La Comtesse du Barry Christiane Gil
La Reine Christine Ivan Gobry

La Duchesse de Berry Monique de Huertas
Louis et Maximilien Marcel Jullian
Les Princesses vagabondes Frédéric Lenormand
Bel Ange Mireille Lesage
Sissi, une vie retrouvée Agnès Michaux
Portrait d'un homme heureux, Le Nôtre Érik Orsenna
Les Filles du Roi Colette Piat
L'Impératrice Eugénie Christophe Pincemaille
Elisabeth de Belgique Patrick Weber

latitudes

L'Accompagnatrice Nina Berberova
Le Livre du bonheur Nina Berberova
L'Enfant pied-noir Élie-Georges Berreby
Jonas Élie-Georges Berreby
Les Chiffons du rêve Madeleine Chapsal
Histoire du Mont-de-Piété Éric Deschodt
Le Chat qui désirait la lune Julia Deuley
Au bonheur des grand-mères Geneviève Doucet
Cézanne et Zola se rencontrent Raymond Jean
Du bon usage de la lenteur Pierre Sansot

DOCUMENTS

Mémoire d'un croyant Abbé Pierre
Mon royaume à Moi Stéphane Bern
La Véritable Joséphine Baker Emmanuel Bonini
La Véritable Romy Schneider Emmanuel Bonini
La Chartreuse de Valldemosa – George Sand et Chopin à Majorques B. Chovelon/C. Abbadie

« Dans Venise la rouge » - Les Amours de George Sand et Musset Bernadette Chovelon
Un certain jeune homme Bruno Crémer
Saint-Exupéry Eric Deschodt
Elizabeth reine de cœur Françoise Ducout
Coco Chanel Isabelle Fiemeyer
Pinay l'Indépendant Jean-Antoine Giansily
Renaître à la vie Joseph Gourand
Lettres à sa fille Calamity Jane
Sarah Bernhardt Claudette Joannis
Evita David Lelait
Maria Callas David Lelait
Sœur Emmanuelle Pierre Lunel
La Véritable Farah Vincent Meylan
La Véritable Audrey Hepburn B. Meyer-Stabley
La Véritable Jackie Bertrand Meyer-Stabley
La Véritable Grace de Monaco B. Meyer-Stabley
La Véritable Margaret d'Angleterre B. Meyer-Stabley
La Déclaration d'amour Madeleine Renaud
Les ténébreuses affaires du comte de Paris Prince Jacques d'Orléans
Conduite à gauche Pierre Tourlier
Mondes effacés Jusuf Vrioni avec Éric Faye

romance

Un caractère de femme Emmanuel Bove
La Fille d'Emma Claude-Henri Buffard
Amours d'automne Henriette Bernier
La Faute de Claire Henriette Bernier

Le Crime de Gardefort Nathalie Costes
Les Ombres du passé Nathalie Costes
Hauteloup Suzanne De Arriba
Le Pays bleu Suzanne De Arriba
Passent les nuages - Emma Suzanne De Arriba
Passent les nuages - Cécilia Suzanne De Arriba
Passent les nuages - Antonina Suzanne De Arriba
Ceux de la montagne Suzanne De Arriba
Campagne anglaise Marc Dugain
Silence coupable Claude Durussel
L'Importune François d'Epenoux
Amer Elisabeth Hennebert
Soledad Stéphanie Janicot
Une Traviata Stéphanie Janicot
Les Amants du Lac K.C. Mc Kinnon
Et monter lentement dans un immense amour... Katherine Pancol
Le Deuil de printemps Marie-France Pisier
Une femme de ménage Christian Oster
Le Mari dangereux Jane Shapiro
Jardin de nuit E.L. Swann
Le Jardin d'argile Jean-Max Tixier

Achevé d'imprimer en janvier 2002

JEDBURGH JUSTICE AND KENTISH FIRE

JEDBURGH JUSTICE AND KENTISH FIRE

Paul Anthony Jones

Constable • London

CONSTABLE

First published in Great Britain in 2014 by Constable

A CIP catalogue record for this book
is available from the British Library.

ISBN 978-1-47211-389-4 (B-format paperback)
ISBN 978-1-47211-622-2 (ebook)

Typeset in New Baskerville by Photoprint, Torquay
Printed and bound in Great Britain by Clays Ltd, St Ives plc

Constable
is an imprint of
Constable & Robinson Ltd
100 Victoria Embankment
London EC4Y 0DY

An Hachette UK Company
www.hachette.co.uk

www.constablerobinson.com

For Adam, *potiusque sero quam nunquam*

ACKNOWLEDGEMENTS

The material in this book has been compiled from a variety of different sources, but I am especially indebted to the writers and editors responsible for the *Oxford English Dictionary*; Chambers' monumental *Slang Dictionary*; Brewer's *Dictionary of Phrase & Fable*; Wilkinson's *Thesaurus of Traditional English Metaphors*; Grose's *Dictionary of the Vulgar Tongue*; and the many wonderful works of the late Eric Partridge. I encourage anyone with an interest in what this book has to offer to seek out any of these exceptional titles for themselves to unearth greater historical and etymological discussion than can be accommodated here.

Personal thanks to my agent, Andrew Lownie; to Hugh Barker, and all at Constable; to Nick Hopper for his countless content suggestions (some of which even made it into the final draft); and, as always, to my parents Leon and Maureen for their continued advice, support and encouragement.

CONTENTS

INTRODUCTION

Exploring the origin of a word is (on paper at least) a relatively straightforward process. All of the available written evidence is pieced together chronologically, often covering several centuries, and then any changes in spelling, meaning and context are used to formulate a conclusive explanation of its origin – or, at the very least, a best guess. Admittedly, a lack of textual evidence sometimes means that words remain complete mysteries, and frustrating dead ends and etymological question marks are by no means uncommon, but by and large the majority of English words can be confidently explained.

While word origins formed the basis of the first book in this series, *Haggard Hawks and Paltry Poltroons,* it is phrases and expressions that are our focus in *Jedburgh Justice and Kentish Fire,* and these prove much trickier subjects. There is frequently less written evidence, as idiomatic sayings and slang turns of phrase are typically the concern of spoken English, and their informality and 'clichédness' often precludes them from being widely used in print. They are often short-lived and faddish, and remarkably localized, with no comparable equivalents in foreign languages or even outside of a specific region or group. And while words might materialise and develop organically and predictably, phrases and sayings are often random and unpredictable, and etymologists must allow for their inventors and instigators to be witty, irrational, and just as unpredictable themselves. A reasonable explanation of *it ain't over till the fat lady sings*, for example, might try and connect it to Wagnerian opera, but as we shall see the evidence seemingly points in an entirely different direction.

For all of these reasons the origins of the 500 phrases collected here, in fifty allied groups of ten, are often speculative, inconclusive, and anecdotal – but that is not to say that they are any less worthwhile. Here are the remarkable tales of an itinerant Shakespearean morris dancer, a money-grubbing archbishop, a Glaswegian practical joker, an infectious cook, a fatally unlucky abstainer, a suicidal seafood chef, an Ancient Greek treasure hunt, and one of Thomas Jefferson's most memorable horse rides. Here you will discover how to host a Dutch feast, how a cat can predict a thunderstorm, where Gotham City really is, and what a fourth-century saint has to do with a promiscuous Victorian woman.

But, as always, let's start at home . . .

I

TEN PHRASES DERIVED FROM PLACES IN BRITAIN

All the expressions listed here mention somewhere in the British Isles, from JEDBURGH JUSTICE in the north to KENTISH FIRE in the south. Phrases like these are certainly not rare in English, and often simply make reference to some famous local industry (as in *coals to Newcastle* or *shipshape and Bristol fashion*) or else some peculiar tale from local lore (like the fishy story of the GLASGOW MAGISTRATE), but the ten examples here are among the more unusual that the language has to offer.

1. *To be* BORN AT HOGS NORTON

Accusing someone of having been *born at Hogs Norton* – or in full *born at Hogs Norton, where the pigs play the organs* – is an obscure sixteenth-century means of pointing out their ill manners or criticizing their bad language. How the people of Hogs Norton came to be associated with bad behaviour is unknown, but even greater mystery surrounds the whereabouts of the town itself. Some accounts claim it is actually Hook Norton in Oxfordshire, while others maintain that it is Norton-juxta-Twycross in Leicestershire, where it is even said (although sadly unproven) that the local organist was once a 'Mr Piggs'. Either way, since the expression has long since dropped out of common use, accusing someone of having been born in a perfectly pleasant rural English village today might not seem like such a bad thing.

2. CURSE OF SCOTLAND

To gamblers and card-players, *the curse of Scotland* has been a nickname for the nine of diamonds since the early 1700s. The name apparently refers to the nine diamonds depicted on the coat of arms of John Dalrymple, the Earl of Stair, who was not only embroiled in the Glencoe Massacre of 1692 but played a major part in the Union of Scotland with England in 1707, clearly cementing his reputation as the *curse of Scotland.* Other less likely theories claim that the Duke of Cumberland wrote down his orders on the eve of Glencoe on the back of a nine of diamonds during a card game, while popular history maintains that every ninth king of Scotland was a tyrant and a curse to his country.

3. GLASGOW MAGISTRATE

A *Glasgow magistrate* is a nineteenth-century nickname for a salted herring. The term apparently derives from a tale from local history in which, during a visit to the city by George IV in the 1820s, an anonymous practical joker placed a herring on a magistrate's carriage that was part of a delegation sent out to meet the king. Unnoticed, the herring was paraded through town atop the magistrate's coach as part of the king's procession and the *Glasgow magistrate* was born.

4. HERTFORDSHIRE KINDNESS

A *Hertfordshire kindness* is the return or exchange of an act of courtesy – 'the mutual return of favours received', as it was first described by the writer Thomas Fuller in 1661. Essentially it refers either to the repetition of a toast, in which a host twice drinks to the health of his guest, or to the reciprocation of a toast, in which a guest responds by toasting his host in return. Why this courtesy should be so specifically associated with Hertfordshire, however, remains a mystery.

5. JEDBURGH JUSTICE

Described by Sir Walter Scott in 1828 as 'hang in haste and try at leisure', the phrase *Jedburgh justice* has been used since the early eighteenth century to refer to a so-called summary execution, in which someone accused of a crime is executed before a fair trial can take place. This bloodthirsty brand of justice was presumably once customary in the Scottish border town of Jedburgh, although its residents will doubtless be relieved to know that it is by no means alone – *Halifax law, Abingdon law, Cupar justice* and *Lydford law* are all of identical meaning.

6. KENTISH FIRE

Although initially applied to any cheering or applause – an article in *New Sporting Magazine* in 1831 even used it as another name for 'three-by-three cheers' or 'hip, hip, hooray!' – more often than not *Kentish fire* describes derisive or disruptive handclapping, intended to drown out a public speaker or to show an audience's disagreement or impatience. It is said to derive from the jeering of local audiences who attended meetings debating the Catholic Relief Bill in 1829, which proposed allowing Catholics to sit in Parliament for the first time. The bill met with considerable opposition in the traditionally Anglican county of

Kent, with press reports of the audiences' disapproving *Kentish fire* popularising the phrase nationwide.

7. NORTHUMBERLAND ARMS

Northumberland arms – or the *Lord Northumberland's arms* – was an eighteenth–nineteenth-century northern slang name for a black eye. Local folklore claims it derives from a battle between Robert de Mowbray, an eleventh-century Earl of Northumbria, and the invading Scottish king Malcolm III, who was supposedly killed by having a spear (with the keys to Alnwick Castle hanging from it) thrust into his eye. The same tale also allegedly accounts for Northumberland's famous Percy dynasty who were said to take their name from the king's 'pierced eye', but sadly the entire story seems nothing more than legend. Instead, the Percys take their name from the town of Percy-en-Auge in Normandy, while *Northumberland arms* refers to a red-and-black spectacle-shaped design that once featured on the badge of the House of Percy and apparently resembled a bruised eye.

8. SCARBOROUGH WARNING

A *Scarborough warning* is really no warning at all – just another name for anything that takes place by surprise or at short notice. Dating from the mid-sixteenth century, the phrase was long supposed to have originated in a short-lived rebellion against Mary I by Thomas Stafford, a distant member of the Plantagenet dynasty, in 1557. Sailing from France, Stafford landed at Scarborough and quickly took control of the town's largely unprotected castle before many of the locals had even noticed his arrival. As plausible as this explanation is, however, the earliest mention of a *Scarborough warning* has since been traced back to 1546, predating Stafford's invasion by more than a decade and leaving the phrase's actual origin a complete mystery.

9. *To* SET UP SHOP ON THE GOODWIN SANDS

The Goodwin Sands is a large and notoriously treacherous sandbank off the Kent coast that stretches for around 16 km (10 miles) between Dover and Ramsgate. The Sands apparently once comprised a low-lying island owned by an ancient Earl Godwin that was protected from high tides by a great sea wall. After the Norman Conquest it was surrendered to a group of French clerics who failed to maintain the wall and the island was finally inundated during a storm in 1100. The entire area, which covers 4,000 acres 10–15 m (33–49 ft) below the waves, has been submerged ever since and has long been known as a danger to shipping; *to have set up shop on the Goodwin Sands* has meant 'shipwrecked' since the sixteenth century.

10. WHO HAS ANY LAND IN APPLEBY?

A 1785 *Dictionary of the Vulgar Tongue* defined *Who has any land in Appleby?* as 'a question asked [of] the man at whose door the glass stands long'. That is to say, along with similar expressions like *How lies the land?* and *How stands the reckoning?*, it is a request for another drink, with the Cumbrian town of Appleby presumably used as a pun for apple cider. The phrase seems to have all but disappeared by the mid-1800s.

II

TEN PHRASES DERIVED FROM PLACES IN LONDON

Arguably London's most celebrated contribution to the English language is Cockney rhyming slang, which first began to appear among Victorian street vendors and stall-holders in the mid-1800s. The earliest known 'Glossary of the Rhyming Slang' was an appendix to *A Dictionary of Modern Slang, Cant and Vulgar Words* published in 1859, which included the earliest written record of *apples and pears* ('stairs'), *mince pies* ('eyes') and *Cain and Abel* ('table'). Also included were a host of much less familiar expressions that have long since disappeared, like *flag unfurled* ('man of the world'), *top of Rome* ('home'), *throw me in the dirt* ('shirt') and *Battle of the Nile* ('roof tile', a slang name for a hat).

1. ALL LOMBARD STREET TO A CHINA ORANGE

Lombard Street in the City of London takes its name from the Lombards, inhabitants of the Italian region of Lombardy who for centuries operated across Europe as bankers and pawnbrokers. The area around Lombard Street has been associated with banking since the twelfth century and today it still stands just a few blocks away from the Bank of England. The eighteenth-century expression *all Lombard Street* referred to any vast amount of money, while a bet wagered at *all Lombard Street to a China orange* (an old name for a Seville orange) would once have implied that something is absolutely certain to happen.

2. A DRAUGHT ON THE PUMP AT ALDGATE

Reports of a well at Aldgate in central London date back to the thirteenth century, and it is thought that a mechanical pump has stood on the site since the mid-1500s. Located at the junction of Fenchurch Street and Leadenhall Street today, the Aldgate pump soon became a familiar London landmark and meeting place, and was once popularly said to mark the official boundary of the East End. The expression *a draught on the pump at Aldgate* dates from the eighteenth century and means simply 'a bad cheque', a pun on *draught* as both a drink and a withdrawal of cash.

3. GRUB STREET NEWS

According to Samuel Johnson, London's Grub Street was once 'much inhabited by writers of small histories, dictionaries, and temporary poems'. Although Johnson was writing in 1755, references to Grub Street's connection to mediocre literature and journalism date back to the early 1600s and in the centuries since has spawned a number of peculiar expressions: a *Grub Street crew* is a collection of gossipers or blabbermouths, and *Grub Street news* or *murmurs* are lies and slanderous rumours. Grub Street was renamed Milton Street in 1830 in honour of a local landlord, but its notorious association with writing has continued to this day.

4. KENT STREET EJECTMENT

In the sixteenth and seventeenth centuries, the area around Kent Street in Southwark was one of the poorest in London. Described as 'a miserable, wretched, poor place' by Samuel Pepys, the street was frequented by beggars, plague victims and peddlers of cheap goods, while as recently as the 1890s one Victorian commentator, Henry B. Wheatley, explained that 'the poor lodging-houses in this street continued till quite recently to be the most awful receptacles of the houseless in the country'. Reinforcing the street's sorry reputation, a *Kent Street ejectment* was a local nineteenth-century name for the unsympathetic practice of landlords removing the front doors of houses whose tenants had fallen more than two weeks behind in their rent. It remained in use until Kent Street was renamed Tabard Street in 1877.

5. MOORGATE RATTLER

Dating from the late 1890s, a *Moorgate rattler* was another name for a foppish or smartly dressed young man, the kind of gentleman who apparently frequented Moorgate in central London at the turn of the century. The phrase is believed to be a play on the earlier expression *morgan rattler*, the name of a popular eighteenth-century fiddler's jig that somehow by the mid-1800s came to refer to anything particularly striking or a fine example of its type.

6. NEWGATE FASHION

To walk *Newgate fashion* means to walk hand-in-hand, as inmates shackled together at London's Newgate prison would once have done. The earliest record of the phrase comes from Shakespeare's *Henry IV: Part 1* (III. iii), making this one of the oldest of an array of expressions referring to arguably London's most famous jail: a *Newgate collar* was a Victorian beard so-called as it encircled the neck like a noose; the *Newgate hornpipe* was the 'dance' of a man hanging from a gallows in the nineteenth century; a *Newgate nightingale* was a seventeenth-century 'jail-bird'; and a *Newgate saint* was a condemned man, proverbially said *to be canonised at the Old Bailey*.

7. ON CAREY STREET

In the 1840s the bankruptcy department of London's Supreme Court moved from Westminster to new premises on Carey Street, a narrow thoroughfare that ironically runs behind the London School of Economics today. *On Carey Street* soon became synonymous with financial woes or insolvency in London slang, although the phrase did not appear in print until the 1920s. Likewise *on Queer Street* means 'to be in financial trouble' and, although often presumed to be a variation of *Carey Street*, dates back to long before the Bankruptcy Courts opened and instead implies a crooked or peculiar state of affairs.

8. *To* RIDE THE MARYLEBONE STAGE

The nineteenth-century expression *Marylebone stage* actually has nothing to do with Marylebone in London, but is instead a pun on 'marrowbone'. *To ride the marrowbone stage* was an earlier slang phrase meaning simply 'to walk', in the sense of someone relying on their own strength or 'marrow' in order to travel from place to place.

9. WHITECHAPEL PLAY

Once one of London's poorest districts, Whitechapel is the subject of a number of old slang phrases and expressions referring to its poverty, its crime, and even its supposedly ill-educated inhabitants. *Whitechapel play* was an old name for a poor standard of play in card games or billiards, and even came to refer to a player accidentally potting his opponent's ball. Victorian men who could not afford a barber would have a *Whitechapel shave* instead, by disguising their stubble with whitening powder. And Whitechapel's notorious association with prostitution (it was the location of the Jack the Ripper murders in 1888) even led one eighteenth-century slang dictionary to define a *Whitechapel beau* as 'one who dresses with a needle and thread, and undresses with a knife'.

10. WESTMINSTER WEDDING

Like Whitechapel, Westminster was once notorious across London for its crime and poverty. It may be home to one of the most famous churches in the world, but as one seventeenth-century dictionary of London slang defined it, a *Westminster wedding* was one that witnessed 'a whore and a rogue married together'. A popular Elizabethan proverb meanwhile noted that *he who goes to Westminster for a wife and St Paul's for a man will meet with a whore and a knave.*

III

TEN PHRASES DERIVED FROM PLACES IN AMERICA

Some places in America have become so closely associated with a particular field or industry that their names are now entirely synonymous with it. *Hollywood,* most notably of all, has been used as a byword for the film industry since the 1920s. New York's *Madison Avenue* (1940s), *Broadway* (1880s) and *Wall Street* (1800s) have each given their names to America's advertising industry, theatre business and financial market respectively. And *Foggy Bottom,* a district of Washington DC, is both home to and a nickname for America's Department of State.

1. BRONX CHEER

Giving a *Bronx cheer* is a 1920s American equivalent of 'blowing a raspberry'. Taking its name from the northernmost of New York's five boroughs (itself named after a seventeenth-century Swedish landowner named Jonas Bronck), the *Bronx cheer* apparently derives from its use among disgruntled baseball fans at New York's Yankee Stadium. *Blowing a raspberry* dates from the late nineteenth century, and is derived from the London rhyming slang *raspberry tart* meaning (for obvious reasons) 'fart'. It was first recorded in an 1890 *Dictionary of Slang, Jargon & Cant,* which explained that 'the tongue is inserted in the left cheek and forced through the lips, producing a peculiarly squashy noise that is extremely irritating'.

2. CHICAGO OVERCOAT

Overcoat as a slang name for a coffin dates from the late nineteenth century, although even earlier euphemisms like *wooden doublet* and *wooden surtout* (a type of long hooded coat) date back as far as the 1700s. *Chicago overcoat* is just one of a number of variations on this theme and dates from the 1920s and 30s, when Chicago was infamous across Prohibition-era America as a hotbed of organized crime; in fact the phrase is often specifically used to refer to the clandestine disposal of a body encased in a concrete block, a practice allegedly once employed by the city's gangsters. Similarly, *Chicago typewriter, Chicago piano, Chicago mowing-machine* and *Chicago atomizer* are all 1930s nicknames for machine guns referring to their rattling sprays of bullets, while *Chicago lightning* was once another name for gunfire.

3. *To go* DOWN THE SWANEE

America's Suwannee or 'Swanee' river flows for 400 km (250 miles) from Georgia into northern Florida before emptying into the Gulf of Mexico. As well as giving its name to the *Swanee whistle*, the river is also the origin of *down the Swanee*, meaning 'ruined', 'bankrupted', or 'gone to waste'. The phrase is a relatively recent coinage, dating from the mid-1900s, which likely began as a variation of earlier expressions like *down the drain, sent upriver* (referring to convicts being shipped up the Hudson to New York's Sing Sing prison) and *sold downriver* (referring to rebellious slaves being transported down the Mississippi to plantations further south as punishment for their insubordination). So why the Suwannee river and not any other? A likely explanation is that the Suwannee was already well known thanks to the old American folk-song 'Old Folks At Home', which famously begins 'Way down upon the Swanee river, / Far, far away'.

4. HOLLYWOOD NO

Hollywood's long-standing association with cinema is the origin of a number of English expressions including *Hollywood ending*, another name for a film's happy conclusion (and in particular one that is schmaltzy or contrived), and *Hollywood science*, the artistic licence taken by film-makers who bend the rules of science in order to better serve a plot. Actors attempting to attract the attention of producers and directors might also receive a *Hollywood no* – namely an implied 'no', such as one inferred by an unreturned telephone call or an unanswered message.

5. I'M FROM MISSOURI

Little used outside America, *I'm from Missouri* is a late-nineteenth-century expression used to show scepticism; the full phrase is usually said to be *I'm from Missouri, you'll have to show me.* It is associated with an American Congressman named Willard D. Vandiver, who represented Missouri from 1897 to 1903. While attending a naval banquet in Philadelphia in 1899, Vandiver famously delivered a speech in which he queried an earlier speaker's comments, declaring, 'I come from a country that raises corn and cotton ... and frothy eloquence neither convinces or satisfies me. I'm from Missouri, and you've got to show me.' His words stuck and quickly became a popular American catchphrase that has remained in use ever since.

6. KENTUCKY BREAKFAST

Like the colloquial *liquid lunch*, a *Kentucky breakfast* is one comprised only of drink – or, as one popular nineteenth-century definition explained, 'three cocktails and a chew of terbacker'. The phrase is said to have been inspired by the (apparently true) story of a noted Kentucky colonel who took a breakfast of 'six brandy cocktails, tea and toast' at a lavish Cincinnati hotel in the late 1800s. Perhaps the best definition, however, comes from a 1913 article in the *Pittsburgh Press*, which explained that a *Kentucky breakfast* should consist of 'a three-pound sirloin steak, a bottle of whisky, and a good-sized dog' – with the dog there to eat the steak.

7. MICHIGAN BANKROLL

A *Michigan bankroll* is a roll of low-denomination or even fake banknotes wrapped inside a single large-denomination bill, giving the false impression of a vast amount of cash. The term probably originated among American criminals in the nineteenth century, when just such a bankroll was proverbially said to contain *more dollar bills than there're rabbits in Michigan*, before it was picked up by petty gamblers and hustlers who would carry a *Michigan bankroll* or 'mish' in order to cheat their opponents. The phrase has since been extended to *California, Chicago, Minnesota, Missouri* and *Philadelphia*, each of which has its own equally fraudulent *bankroll*.

8. NEW YORK MINUTE

Meaning 'an instant', the phrase *New York minute* dates from the early 1900s and simply refers to the city's famously bustling pace. That being said, some New Yorkers claim *a New York minute* is actually the length of time between a traffic light turning green and the waiting driver blaring his horn, while in Texas it is said that New Yorkers do in an instant what it would take a Texan a minute to do.

9. PHILADELPHIA LAWYER

The expression *Philadelphia lawyer* has been used since the late eighteenth century to refer to any very skilful, persuasive or ruthlessly successful lawyer; anything particularly confusing would likewise be said *to puzzle a Philadelphia lawyer.* It is believed to refer to Andrew Hamilton, a Scottish-born lawyer working in Colonial America in the early 1700s who came to national renown when he defended the New York publisher John Peter Zenger against charges of libel in 1735. Zenger had earlier printed several articles in his *New York Weekly Journal* criticizing the city's oppressive and avaricious governor, but Hamilton managed to have him acquitted of all charges and to this day the case is regarded as a landmark in the freedom of the press in America.

10. *To make a* VIRGINIA FENCE

In America, a *Virginia fence* is another name for what is otherwise known as a 'split-rail' or 'snake' fence, a barrier comprising a chain of logs or timbers laid flat, one on top of the other, in a long zigzag so that the ends of each set of posts are interlocked with those that follow. This zigzag layout is the inspiration for the phrase *to make a Virginia fence*: an eighteenth-century term listed in Benjamin Franklin's *Drinker's Dictionary* in 1737 describing the meandering walk of a drunk.

IV

TEN LATIN PHRASES USED IN ENGLISH

From stock phrases like *et cetera* ('and the rest'), *ad hoc* ('for this') and CARPE DIEM to more obscure examples like some of those listed here, hundreds of Latin expressions have made their way into the English language. A great many are found in the language of law, with Latin legal terms like *ipso facto* ('by the fact itself') and *modus operandi* (a 'method of operation') even having slipped into more general use. Among the many less familiar legal terms are *scandalum magnatum* (the 'scandal of the magnates'), an ancient law preventing defamation of peers of the realm; *id quod plerumque accidit* ('that which generally happens'), a term for the most obvious outcome of an action; and *cuius est solum, eius est usque ad coelum et ad inferos,* a Latin maxim of property ownership, literally meaning 'whoever owns the soil, it is theirs up to Heaven and down to Hell'.

1. AB OVO

Meaning 'from the egg', the Latin *ab ovo* has been used in English texts since the late sixteenth century to mean 'from the very beginning'. Its full version, *ab ovo usque ad mala,* is a quote from the Roman poet Horace that literally means 'from the egg to the apples', a reference to a custom in Ancient Rome of beginning a meal with eggs and ending with a dessert of apples. Although much rarer than its shorter counterpart, Horace's *ab ovo usque ad mala* is nevertheless sometimes used in English to mean 'from the start to the very end'.

2. CARPE DIEM

Carpe diem, meaning 'seize the day', is another quotation from the Roman poet Horace taken from the first of his four books of *Odes* written in the first century BC. It appears in a poem addressed to Leuconoë, a young woman worrying about her future: 'Do not ask what end the Gods have granted to me or you,' Horace advises, but instead, 'seize the day, trusting as little as possible to the next.' The phrase is one of a number of Latin expressions of similar sentiment used in English, including *dum vivimus, vivamus* ('while we live, let us live'), *nunc est bibendum* ('now is the time to drink'), *memento vivere* ('remember to live', the opposite of a *memento mori*), and *collige, virgo, rosas* ('pick, girl, the roses'), from which the familiar expression 'gather ye rosebuds while ye may' is derived.

3. CONNUBIALIS AMOR DE MULCIBRE FECIT APELLEM

The Latin epithet *connubialis amor de mulcibre fecit apellem* is attributed to a sixteenth-century Flemish painter named Quentin Matsys, best known for his portrait of *A Grotesque Old Woman,* or *The Ugly Duchess,* housed in London's National Gallery. Matsys was originally a blacksmith who according to tradition fell for the beautiful daughter of a local artist. When her father forbade him from marrying her because of his lowly profession, Matsys set about proving his devotion by painting the girl's portrait. Despite being untrained, he produced such an incredible work that her father gave the couple his blessing and they were married, and Matsys went on to become one of the most celebrated artists of his time. Loosely meaning 'love turned the blacksmith into an artist', this Latin line appears on a memorial dedicated to Matsys outside Antwerp Cathedral, and has been used in English ever since to refer to any fine work of art unexpectedly produced by someone apparently unskilled or inexperienced.

4. CROCUM IN CILICIAM FERRE

Crocum in Ciliciam ferre is essentially a Latin equivalent of *to carry coals to Newcastle.* It means 'to carry saffron to Cilicia' and (as with coal and Newcastle) refers to the fact that saffron and the crocus flowers from which it is obtained were once so abundant in Cilicia, an ancient region of Turkey, that taking any more there would be foolishly unnecessary. Similarly *noctuas Athenas ferre,* 'to carry owls to Athens', and *Alcinoo poma dare,* 'to give apples to Alcinous' (a king of Corfu renowned for his orchards), were both popular Roman expressions.

5. DAVUS SUM, NON OEDIPUS

A Latin line from an obscure Ancient Roman play might not seem the most obvious phrase to drop into everyday conversation, but *Davus sum, non Oedipus* was once a popular proverbial expression across Europe. It is taken from the opening act of *Andria,* or *The Girl from Andros,* a comedy by the Roman playwright Terence written in the second century BC. In the play Davus is a slave who, when quizzed by his master about his son's complicated love life, replies *Davus sum, non Oedipus* ('I am Davus, not Oedipus'), implying that he is an unworldly man rather than a great intellectual like the Greek hero Oedipus, who famously solved the riddle of the Sphinx. The phrase soon caught on as a proverbial response used by anyone presented with a particularly complicated problem that is beyond their comprehension.

6. ODERINT DUM METUANT

Popular history claims that *oderint dum metuant* – 'let them hate me, so long as they fear me' – was a favourite maxim of the Roman emperor Caligula. The line sums up Caligula's apparently fearsome and notorious reputation, but given that so little is actually known of his life – and that much of his legacy was tarnished after his assassination in AD 41 – whether these words were ever actually his is doubtful. In more general use, they have since become associated with many other tyrannical leaders and their regimes.

7. PERSONA NON GRATA

Meaning literally 'person not acceptable', the Latin *persona non grata* has been used in English since the mid-nineteenth century. It derives from the same Latin root, *gratus* (meaning 'welcome'), as words like *gratitude* and *congratulations*, and first appeared in diplomatic contexts to refer to a foreign representative no longer accepted by their host nation's government. In this context, it was coined as an opposite to the earlier expression *persona grata*, describing diplomats who *are* accepted by a foreign government, but it has since become a much more generalized term used for anything that is unwanted or unwelcome.

8. POST HOC, ERGO PROPTER HOC

First appearing in English in the seventeenth century, *post hoc, ergo propter hoc* – usually cut just to *post hoc* – is an example of a logical fallacy, an argument based on poor reasoning from which inadequate or misleading conclusions are drawn. It literally means 'after this, therefore because of this', and is intended to warn against presuming that just because one event happened after another then the previous event must have caused it. Although this can sometimes appear true (like a flood following a rainstorm) in other cases this kind of reasoning is clearly misinformed – thinking of someone before they telephone you, for example, does not mean that you actually caused it to happen.

9. QUIS CUSTODIET IPSOS CUSTODES?

Meaning 'who will guard the guards themselves?' – or more loosely 'who guards the guards?' or 'who will watch the watchmen?' – *quis custodiet ipsos custodes?* is a famous quote from the Roman poet Juvenal taken from the sixth and longest of his sixteen poems known as the *Satires*, written in the late-first–early-second centuries AD. In its original context, the quote was part of a deep discussion of fidelity and promiscuity, but in English is generally used to imply a doubt or distrust of those in charge.

10. SIC TRANSIT GLORIA MUNDI

Meaning 'thus passes the glory of the world', the familiar saying *sic transit gloria mundi* is often used in English as an acknowledgement of the passing of time or as a tribute when something remarkable draws to a close. It is believed to derive from a similar line in *The Imitation of Christ*, a famous work by a fifteenth-century German cleric named Thomas à Kempis, but likely gained greater recognition when it began to be used at the coronation ceremonies of newly elected Popes in the Vatican several centuries later.

V

TEN FRENCH PHRASES USED IN ENGLISH

Some French phrases used in English might not appear to be French at all: *a-go-go,* for instance, derives from the French colloquialism *à go-go,* meaning 'galore' or 'aplenty'. Others are used in entirely different contexts in English than in their native French, like *cinq à sept*: an extramarital affair in English, but an after-work meeting with friends in Canadian French. Perhaps strangest of all are those used in English that are not found in their native French at all – *double entendre,* for instance, is considered ungrammatical and meaningless in French where the correct form *à double entente* or *double sens,* 'with double meaning', is used instead.

1. C'EST LA VIE

C'est la vie ('that's life') has been used in English since the mid-nineteenth century to express a laid-back resignation or acceptance of events or circumstances. Said to be more popular in English than in French, it is likely that *c'est la vie* actually originated in Britain as a flippant French translation of *such is life,* an older English expression dating from the early 1700s. Of similar meaning is *c'est la guerre* ('it's the war'), which became a popular catchphrase across wartime France as people became used to tolerating a poor quality of life under German occupation. It soon slipped into use in English and remained popular even after the Second World War as a French equivalent to acceptant English sayings like *what can you do?* and *that's the way it is.*

2. CHERCHEZ LA FEMME

Meaning literally 'look for the woman', *cherchez la femme* implies that if a man is seen to be acting out of character, then a woman is usually the cause of it; find the woman, and the issue will be solved. Its origin is disputed, with conflicting accounts and anecdotes variously crediting it to the Napoleonic diplomat Charles Maurice de Talleyrand, the eighteenth-century French writer Jean-Baptiste Dupaty, and Alexandre Dumas, whose crime drama *Les Mohicans de Paris* contains its first written record: 'There is a woman in all cases; as soon as a report is brought to me I say, "*Cherchez la femme!*"' Whatever its origin, the phrase had slipped into popular usage in English by the late 1800s and soon became synonymous with uncovering the root cause of any problem.

3. ÇA NE FAIT RIEN

Ça ne fait rien, roughly meaning 'it doesn't matter', is thought to have been borrowed into English during the First World War via British troops serving on the continent. It soon became distorted in military slang and even today is more familiar to English speakers as *san fairy Ann*, a popular expression of indifference or lack of concern often mistakenly said to be a corruption of *sans faire rien*, meaning 'without doing anything'.

4. COUP DE FOUDRE

Borrowed into English in the late eighteenth century, *coup de foudre* is the French phrase for a thunderbolt or fork of lightning but is used in both French and English as an equivalent to 'love at first sight', or A BOLT FROM THE BLUE. *Coup* literally means 'strike' or 'blow' and is the origin of dozens of other phrases used in English, of which arguably the most familiar, *coup d'état*, is also the oldest, dating back to the early 1600s. Elsewhere, a *coup de maître* (mid-1600s) is literally a 'masterstroke'; *coup d'essai* (late 1600s) is another term for a first attempt or test; a *coup de grâce* (late 1600s) is a mercy blow that finishes off a dying man; a *coup d'œil* (mid-1700s) is a swift glance; and a *coup de vent* (early 1800s) is a violent gale or whirlwind. Regrettably English has yet to adopt the French *coup en vache* ('a hit from a cow'), used of a dirty or unsportsmanlike trick, *coup de pied de l'âne* ('a kick from a donkey'), describing an attack on an already defeated or defenceless opponent.

5. NOM DE GUERRE

Both *nom de guerre* and *nom de plume* are used in English to describe a pseudonym, but *nom de guerre* predates its much more familiar cousin by more than 200 years and was originally borrowed into the language in the mid-1600s. It literally describes a 'name of war', and initially referred to a pseudonym adopted by someone involved in some clandestine scheme or wartime plot, allowing them to remain anonymous. As its meaning suggests, such names were originally military and by the early 1700s, long before the introduction of service numbers and dog-tags, had become mandatory for every new recruit, allowing individuals to be identified without confusion. Other aliases and pseudonyms borrowed from French include a *nom de théâtre* (mid-1800s), another name for an actor's stage name, and *nom de vente* (literally 'name of sale', mid-1900s), a fake name used by a buyer who wishes to remain anonymous at an auction.

6. PLUS ÇA CHANGE

The expression *plus ça change* – or in full *plus ça change, plus c'est la même chose* ('the more it changes, the more it is the same thing') – was coined by a French journalist named Alphonse Karr in an 1849 edition of his satirical pamphlet *Les Guêpes* ('The Wasps'). Karr was widely celebrated in nineteenth-century France as a social commentator and wit, and this saying – usually given as 'the more things change, the more they stay the same' in English – originally appeared in an article decrying France's current political situation. It has since been adopted into English to imply a pessimistic, world-weary acceptance of the current state of events, suggesting that although things may appear to change or improve, beneath it all they remain much the same.

7. POUR ENCOURAGER LES AUTRES

Meaning 'in order to encourage the others', the French expression *pour encourager les autres* is used ironically in English to refer to any action (and in particular a punishment) carried out as an example to others to *discourage* any future discord or rebellion. It was first used in this context by eighteenth-century French writers commenting on the execution of John Byng, an otherwise well-regarded English admiral who was deemed not to have done his utmost in preventing French forces from invading Minorca in 1757, and was quickly court-martialled and executed. Byng's death sentence proved hugely controversial at the time and Prime Minister Pitt the Elder even petitioned the king to have it overturned, but it went ahead nonetheless and at the height of Britain's Seven Years War against France proved a major news story across Europe.

8. RECULER POUR MIEUX SAUTER

Derived from an old French proverb dating back to the thirteenth century, *reculer pour mieux sauter* means 'to draw back in order to leap better'. It is used figuratively in both French and English to refer to a temporary withdrawal or pause in activity that allows time to regroup or reassess a situation, and so make a better attempt at it in the future. The phrase first appeared in English in the early seventeenth century when it tended only to be used in reference to military manoeuvres to describe a retreat that gives time to prepare for a later and better-organised attack.

9. REVENONS À NOS MOUTONS

Modern speakers might be confused by someone stating 'let us return to our sheep', but *revenons à nos moutons* has been used figuratively in English since the early 1600s (and in French since the mid-1400s) to mean 'let us return to the matter at hand'. It comes from an anonymous fifteenth-century French stage comedy, *La Farce de Maître Pierre Pathelin,* which proved massively popular across Europe in its day, no doubt helping this line – lifted from a central courtroom scene in which a character accused of stealing sheep is advised by his lawyer to answer all of the prosecutor's questions by baaing – to catch on in both French and English.

10. LA VIE EN ROSE

The expression *la vie en rose* was popularized in the mid-1900s by the song of the same name written and recorded by Édith Piaf in 1947 (although it is unlikely that she coined the phrase herself). It literally translates as 'life in pink' but its closest English equivalent is probably *life through rose-coloured glasses,* describing an idealistic or overly optimistic worldview. The colour pink, as well as adjectives like *rosy* and *rose-coloured,* have long been associated with sentimentalism, with references to 'the rosy time of the year' and 'rose-coloured thoughts' recorded in literature as far back as the seventeenth century. No one is quite sure where this association comes from, although various explanations point to everything from the blooming of pink roses at the best time of the year to the pink protective lenses apparently once worn by mapmakers, who would literally 'see the world' through them.

VI

TEN SHAKESPEAREAN EXPRESSIONS

A full list of the expressions Shakespeare's works have given the language would include such familiar sayings as *a sorry sight* (*Macbeth,* II. ii), *a foregone conclusion* (*Othello,* III. iii), *forever and a day* (*The Taming of the Shrew,* IV. iv), *thereby hangs a tale* (*As You Like It,* II. vii), and even *in stitches* (*Twelfth Night,* III. ii). In fact Shakespeare's contribution to English is so great than he is often wrongly credited with inventing some phrases that were already present in the language long before he used them. In *King Lear* (III. iv) for instance, Edgar cries out, 'Fie, foh and fum / I smell the blood of a British man' – but the story of *Jack the Giant-Killer* was already well known by Elizabethan times. The warning that *all that glitters is not gold* might appear in *The Merchant of Venice* (II. vii), but derives from a much earlier medieval saying – Chaucer warned that '[it] is not al golde that glareth' as early as 1379. And even *all's well that ends well* was an English proverb long before Shakespeare used it as the title of one of his plays.

1. ALL GREEK TO ME

Describing anything unintelligible as 'Greek' originated in the early Middle Ages, when knowledge of Ancient Greek among ecclesiastical scholars and translators was a dying art. Faced with an obscure and utterly indecipherable Greek word, scholars translating ancient manuscripts would often write *Graecum est, non legitur* – literally 'it is Greek, it is not read' – in the margin. This idea was picked up by Shakespeare in *Julius Caesar* (I. ii), in which Cassius and Casca, both among Caesar's eventual assassins, discuss a speech given in Greek by the Roman statesman Cicero: 'Those that understood him,' Casca explains, 'smiled at one another and shook their heads. But, for mine own part, it was Greek to me.' Referring to anything beyond comprehension as *all Greek to me* soon became idiomatic in English, although other languages have different ideas: in French, unfathomable language is described as *du chinois* (Chinese) or *l'hébreu* (Hebrew); in Italian it is *arabo* (Arabic); in Czech and Slovak the equivalent is *it's all a Spanish village*; and in Bulgarian *to speak Patagonian* means 'to talk indecipherably'.

2. BE-ALL AND END-ALL

In the opening act of Shakespeare's *Macbeth* (I. vii), the title character delivers a lengthy soliloquy in which he contemplates his plan to murder King Duncan and assume the throne himself: 'If it were done when 'tis done, then 'twere well / It were done quickly [. . .] that but this blow / Might be the be-all and the end-all here'. Shakespeare's *be-all* essentially means 'the entirety of something', while *end-all* refers to anything capable of bringing about a conclusion. These two are rarely encountered separately, but together comprise a popular expression in use in English since the early nineteenth century.

3. *To* DIE LAUGHING

Expressions that imagine exaggerated injuries being caused by fits of laughter, like *splitting your sides* or *laughing your head off*, first began to emerge in English in the eighteenth century. *To die laughing*, however, was a Shakespearean coinage first used in *The Taming of the Shrew* (III. ii): as the eponymous Kate and her ludicrous new husband Petruchio leave the stage, one of their wedding guests comments, 'Went they not quickly, I should die with laughing.' Tales of famous historical figures *literally* dying laughing date back into antiquity, and it is likely that at least one of these stories inspired Shakespeare's words; perhaps strangest of all, the Greek philosopher Chrysippus is said to have died of laughter after suggesting giving wine to a donkey that had just eaten all of his figs.

4. *To* EAT OUT OF HOUSE AND HOME

The phrase *house and home* dates back to the Old English period, but the idea of *eating someone out of house and home* – implying that someone has more than consumed their fill and left little for their host – is a quote from Shakespeare's *Henry IV: Part 2* (II. i), in which the innkeeper Mistress Quickly complains that Falstaff 'hath eaten me out of house and home; he hath put all my substance into that fat belly of his'. The phrase soon became proverbial in English and is today the only context in which the earlier *house and home* still tends to be found.

5. *To* GILD THE LILY

Meaning 'to embellish unnecessarily', in the sense of adding improvements to something that is already perfectly adequate, *to gild the lily* is actually a misquotation as Shakespeare's original words were 'to paint the lily'. It first appeared in a famous speech from *King John* (IV. ii), in which the Earl of Salisbury scorns John's wasteful self-indulgence after he arranges an entirely unnecessary second coronation: 'To gild refined gold,' he explains, 'to paint the lily, / To throw a perfume on the violet, / To smooth the ice, or add another hue / Unto the rainbow . . . / Is wasteful and ridiculous excess.'

6. GREEN-EYED MONSTER

Green has long been considered the colour of enviousness and jealousy, which is personified as a *green-eyed monster* in Shakespeare's *Othello* (III. iii). This association apparently derives from the ancient belief that jealousy or anger is brought on by an excess of bile in the body, which would give the skin a sickly greenish-yellow colour. The same idea is the origin of the nineteenth-century expressions *green with envy* and *to have the green eye*, meaning 'to look at something jealously'.

7. *To* LAY IT ON WITH A TROWEL

As modern as *laying it on with a trowel* might seem – and despite the popular belief that it was coined by Benjamin Disraeli, who famously quipped, 'Everyone likes flattery; and when you come to royalty you should lay it on with a trowel' – it was actually invented by Shakespeare and first appeared in *As You Like It* (I. ii). Meaning 'to flatter excessively' or 'to labour a point', the phrase plays on the idea of applying a thick coat of plaster and covering something entirely, an image carried into more recent variations like *to lay it on thick* or *with a spade.*

8. ONCE MORE UNTO THE BREACH

Once more unto the breach, dear friends is a famous rallying cry from the 'Cry "God for Harry, England, and Saint George"' speech that opens the third act of Shakespeare's

Henry V, and accompanies Henry's assault on the French port of Harfleur ahead of his victory at the Battle of Agincourt. The *breach* in question is a hole in the town walls, which Henry encourages his troops to continue attacking or else 'close the wall up with our English dead'. The speech is one of the most memorable and rousing in all of Shakespeare's works which no doubt helped this, its opening line, to become a popular expression of encouragement in its own right. The same speech is also the origin of *to stiffen the sinews* and *like greyhounds in the slips*, both essentially meaning 'braced for action'.

9. SALAD DAYS

Describing any period of inexperience or youthful naivety, the expression *salad days* was coined by Shakespeare in *Antony and Cleopatra* (I. v), in which Cleopatra, now enamoured with Marc Antony, calls her earlier infatuation with Julius Caesar her 'salad days / When I was green in judgement, cold in blood'. The phrase is a play on the association between greenness and youthfulness or immaturity, which dates from the early 1500s. The same idea is the basis of words and phrases like *greenhead* (late 1500s), 'an inexperienced fool'; *greenhorn* (late 1600s), 'a newly enlisted soldier', 'a novice'; *green man* (mid-1600s) or *green hand* (mid-1700s), 'a new naval recruit'; and *greener* (1870s), an American slang name for a recently arrived immigrant.

10. *To* SHUFFLE OFF THIS MORTAL COIL

A familiar euphemism for death, *to shuffle off this mortal coil* comes from perhaps the most famous speech in all of English drama, namely Hamlet's 'To be, or not to be' soliloquy: 'For in that sleep of death what dreams may come / When we have shuffled off this mortal coil / Must give us pause' (III. i). In this context, *coil* is often wrongly presumed to be a reference to the passing of time and the spinning of the Earth, but in fact it is merely an old-fashioned word meaning 'commotion' or 'confusion'.

VII

TEN LITERARY EXPRESSIONS

From a paradoxical *Catch-22 situation* to the ever-watchful *Big Brother*, literature of all types is a particularly fruitful source of English expressions. The ten examples listed here take in novels, nursery stories, plays, fables and poetry, and range from an obscure character from the *Arabian Nights* to some of the most famous lines in English literature.

1. ABANDON HOPE ALL YE WHO ENTER HERE

The famous words *abandon hope all ye who enter here* are taken from *Inferno*, the first of the three sections or *canticas* of Dante's *Divine Comedy*. Written over the thirteen years leading up to Dante's death in 1321, *The Divine Comedy* recounts an imagined journey taken by the author through Hell, Purgatory and Heaven in 14,000 lines of verse, of which this – the last of nine inscribed above the entrance to Hell – is by far the most famous. Dante's work was not fully translated into English until the eighteenth century, when this line was originally rendered as 'Ye who here enter to return despair', and it was not until 1814 that a jumbled 'All hope abandon, ye who enter here' first appeared in a translation by the English author Henry Francis Cary.

2. ALNASCHAR DREAM

Alnaschar is a character from the *One Thousand And One Nights* whose tale, 'The Barber's Fifth Brother', is an example of the old warning not to count your chickens before they are hatched. Alnaschar is introduced as an idle dreamer who spends all of his father's inheritance on a basket of glassware that he intends to sell piece by piece until he has doubled his investment. As his tale unfolds, Alnaschar remains sat at his market stall and lets his mind wander, imagining how he will continue reinvesting his money in glassware, each time doubling his money, until he is rich enough to win the heart of a beautiful woman. He imagines a lavish wedding and his married life, until finally he envisages an angry confrontation with his wife and in his imagined rage kicks over the basket, smashing everything and leaving himself penniless. Alnaschar's name has since become synonymous with any unrealistic or timewasting idealist, while an *Alnaschar dream* has been used as another name for a daydream since the early 1800s.

3. BE STILL MY BEATING HEART

The famous line *be still my beating heart*, an expression of breathless excitement, is taken from a little-known play called *Zelmane, or the Corinthian Queen* written in the late seventeenth century by an actor named William Mountfort. Given that both Mountfort and his work are so unfamiliar today it is tempting to wonder how something so obscure could have become so well known – but while staying in London in 1692 Mountfort was murdered by two men, Charles Mohun and Captain Richard Hill, who stabbed him to death in the street. Hill was described at the time as 'an adventurer', who had long been jealous of the attention Mountfort had been receiving from one of London's most famous actresses, Anne Bracegirdle. Both Anne's involvement and the fact that Mohun was Fourth Baron Mohun and a member of the House of Lords made the crime a national scandal and ignited a posthumous interest in Mountfort's work, from where this memorable phrase is thought finally to have dropped into everyday use.

4. GOOD RIDDANCE TO BAD RUBBISH

Riddance is an obscure sixteenth-century word literally describing a 'ridding' or removal of something. The earliest reference to *a good riddance* comes from Shakespeare's *Troilus and Cressida,* while the saying *good riddance to bad rubbish* is a quote from Dickens' 1848 novel *Dombey and Son. Riddance* itself is rarely encountered anywhere else in English, making it – alongside the *pale* of *beyond the pale* (a fourteenth-century word for a fence-post), the *luke* of *lukewarm* (a Middle English word meaning 'not quite hot') and THE BE-ALL AND END-ALL – one of a handful of so-called 'fossil words', namely old-fashioned words found almost exclusively in just one context today.

5. GOODY TWO-SHOES

Describing an excessively virtuous or sycophantic person, *goody two-shoes* dates from the mid-eighteenth century and is derived from an old nursery story, *The History of Little Goody Two-Shoes,* published anonymously in 1765 but usually credited to the playwright Oliver Goldsmith. It tells the story of an impoverished young girl named Margery who is so poor that she can only afford one shoe, so when a brand new pair of shoes is given to her by a rich gentleman she runs through town showing them to everyone she meets, 'and by that means obtained the name Goody Two-Shoes'. Originally used as a nickname for any young or naïve girl in the late 1700s, by the mid-1800s *goody two-shoes* had come to imply a drearily or overly righteous person.

6. HELL HATH NO FURY LIKE A WOMAN SCORNED

The famous saying that *Hell hath no fury like a woman scorned* is based on lines taken from *The Mourning Bride*, a play by the English dramatist William Congreve first performed in 1697. Congreve's only tragedy, *The Mourning Bride* tells the story of a young Spanish princess named Almeria, whose father so disapproves of her marriage to her lover, Alphonso, that he has him imprisoned and sentenced to death, only for the king to be mistakenly executed in his place. The lines 'Heaven has no rage, like love to hatred turned, / Nor Hell a fury, like a woman scorned' close the play's third act.

7. I THINK YOU ARE A WITCH

In the early seventeenth century, *I think you are a witch* was a popular English catchphrase used in response to someone who had made an unexpectedly perceptive remark which, it implies, they could only have known through some supernatural means. The line is taken from *The Fair Maid of the West*, a 1631 play by the writer Thomas Heywood, and comes from a scene in which Clem, the play's clown, meets Tota, a Moroccan queen, who correctly supposes that he is English: 'I think you are a witch,' he replies, before going on to explain that the expression is 'a foolish proverb we use in our country;

which, to give you in other words, is as much as to say you have hit the nail on the head.'

8. IT WAS A DARK AND STORMY NIGHT

'It was a dark and stormy night; the rain fell in torrents – except at occasional intervals, when it was checked by a violent gust of wind which swept up the streets.' This is the opening line of *Paul Clifford*, an 1830 novel by Edward Bulwer-Lytton telling the story of an upper-class gentleman who leads a double life as a highwayman. The novel might not be particularly well known but its snappy opening seven words have gone on to become one of the most familiar phrases in all English literature, nowadays typically used as a clichéd beginning to any overly dramatic or sensational story.

9. NO MAN IS AN ISLAND

No man is an island is a quotation from *Meditation XVII*, a work by the renowned English poet John Donne. Published in 1624, Donne's *Meditations*, twenty-three in all, comprise what are collectively known as his *Devotions Upon Emergent Occasions*, a series of thought-provoking essays written in the months during and after which he had battled an unknown illness. Having come close to death, the *Meditations* explore themes of birth, death, immortality and sin, as Donne (like many devout Elizabethan Christians) saw illness of any kind as a punishment from God. In *Meditation XVII*, he remarks that the illness or death of any other person, signified by the tolling of a bell, should always be of concern to everyone as, 'No man is an island, entire of itself; every man is a piece of the continent, a part of the main.' He goes on to famously explain, 'therefore, never send to know for whom the bell tolls; it tolls for thee'.

10. A THING OF BEAUTY IS A JOY FOREVER

'A thing of beauty is a joy forever' is the opening line of *Endymion*, a vast 4,000-line poem written by John Keats in 1818. Based on Greek myth, the poem tells the story of a handsome young shepherd named Endymion who is visited in a dream by a goddess of the moon, Cynthia. Having fallen in love with her, Endymion embarks on an epic journey to track her down, journeying into the Underworld and to the bottom of the sea. Along the way, he falls in love with a mortal woman whom it is eventually revealed is his beloved Cynthia in disguise. Although slated by critics on its publication, today *Endymion* remains one of Keats' most popular works.

VIII

TEN PHRASES FROM COMICS AND CARTOONS

Comic books and cartoon strips might seem an unlikely source of English turns of phrase (and certainly some of those listed here will be far from familiar to modern speakers) but as expressions like CURATE'S EGG and KEEPING UP WITH THE JONESES prove, cartoons can be a surprisingly inventive and important resource.

1. BANG GOES SIXPENCE!

In late-nineteenth-century London, *bang goes sixpence!* was a popular catchphrase describing a sudden or unexpectedly costly expense. It was coined in a caption to a cartoon by the Victorian artist Charles Keene, first printed in *Punch* magazine in 1868, which lampooned two contemporary stereotypes: the increasingly extortionate cost of living in London and the clichéd miserliness of Scots. Depicting a meeting between two Scottish men, one of whom has apparently returned earlier than expected from a visit to the capital, the caption read, 'It's just a ruinous place, that! A had na' been there abune twa hours when – *bang* – went saxpence!' The expression soon caught on in Victorian London before dying out in the early 1900s.

2. BROWN, JONES AND ROBINSON

Created by the English artist and illustrator Richard Doyle, *Brown, Jones and Robinson* were three middle-class

Englishmen who featured in a long-running comic strip first printed in *Punch* in 1850. The cartoons, originally called *The Pleasure Trips of Brown, Jones and Robinson*, satirised the narrow-mindedness and awkwardness of social climbers and would-be gentlemen, and soon the trio's names became a popular nineteenth-century expression typifying the English middle classes.

3. CURATE'S EGG

Like the curate's egg – good in parts is a familiar expression used to refer to something that, although outwardly bad, has at least some redeeming features. It has been current for over a century, having first appeared in a cartoon by the artist George du Maurier (grandfather of the author Daphne du Maurier) in *Punch* in 1895. The image depicted a nervous-looking curate having breakfast with a bishop, who comments, 'I'm afraid you've got a bad egg, Mr Jones', to which the curate replies, 'Oh no, my Lord, I assure you! Parts of it are excellent!' Almost a century later, the same cartoon was reprinted in the final edition of *Punch* in 1992, but making light of changes in manners since the Victorian era was given the more modern caption: 'Curate: This fucking egg's off!'.

4. DRAGON LADY

Describing any domineering or strong-willed woman, the expression *dragon lady* was originally the name of a character in *Terry and the Pirates*, an action-adventure comic strip created by the American cartoonist Milton Caniff in 1934; the Dragon Lady character, a beautiful but treacherous East Asian piratess, was introduced the following year. Originally a villain, when Caniff cleverly began to work the real-life events of the Second World

War into the comic's storylines in the 1940s, the Dragon Lady allied herself to the main protagonists and was depicted fighting against invading Japanese forces in China. Her name soon entered into common use in American English as a byword for any aggressively powerful or commanding woman, and in more recent years has begun to be used with increasingly positive connotations to refer to any strong-willed or unflappable woman.

5. HORSE FEATHERS

Horse feathers, American slang for 'nonsense' or 'lies', is often wrongly credited to the Marx Brothers, who used it as the title of their fourth full-length feature film in 1932. In fact its earliest record comes from a 1927 cartoon by the American artist Tad Dorgan, which featured the caption 'The cashier's department – Bah! – horse feathers'. The following year, the same phrase was used as the title of a short animated film by the American cartoonist Billy DeBeck, who claimed it as his own. As both writers were well known for creating their own words and phrases in their work – Dorgan coined *drugstore cowboy* and *cat's pyjamas,* while DeBeck invented *the heebie-jeebies* – which of the two men is truly responsible remains a mystery.

6. *To* KEEP UP WITH THE JONESES

Expressing the natural competitiveness of neighbours, *keeping up with the Joneses* was originally the title of a comic strip created by the American cartoonist Arthur 'Pop' Momand in 1913. Based on Momand's own experience of growing up in one of the wealthiest parts of New York, the strip ran for almost thirty years and was adapted into books, films, and even a musical comedy. The eponymous *Joneses* – whom Momand originally wanted to call 'the

Smiths' before deciding that 'Joneses' sounded better – were the neighbours of the cartoon's principal characters and were never actually seen.

7. LEAD BALLOON

In British English, a complete failure is often said *to go down like a lead balloon*, while in America it is said *to go over like a lead balloon*, a change of words thought to have originated in the theatre where a poor joke was said to 'go over' the audience's heads. The original expression, however, was *to go up as fast as a lead balloon*, first used in an edition of the comic strip *Mom 'n' Pop* by the American cartoonist Loren Taylor in 1924. From there, it soon slipped into use in US slang before being adopted into British English during the Second World War.

8. MUTT AND JEFF

Before it became rhyming slang for 'deaf' in the 1960s, in the early 1900s the names *Mutt and Jeff* were used to refer either to any two visibly dissimilar people, or to a 'good-cop, bad-cop' means of interrogation. It derives from the name of a popular comic strip created by the American cartoonist Bud Fisher in 1907. Recounting the various misadventures and get-rich-quick schemes of its two mismatched leads – the tall, slim Augustus Mutt and his short, bald companion known only as Jeff – the series ran for almost eighty years, during which time it spawned several books, spin-off cartoons, songs and a musical stage show.

9. PIP, SQUEAK AND WILFRED

Pip, Squeak and Wilfred were the names of a dog, a penguin and a rabbit who featured in a children's comic strip in the *Daily Mirror* from 1919 to 1955. Created by the cartoonist Austin B. Payne, the series proved hugely popular in the 1920s, around the same time that a series of First World War medals were introduced by the British government: the 1914–15 Star became known as *Pip*; the British War Medal was *Squeak*; and the Allied Victory Medal became *Wilfred*. The nicknames were soon established in military slang, and by the 1960s *Pip, Squeak and Wilfred* had come to be used simply for any connected group of three people or things.

10. SADIE HAWKINS DAY

Created by the American cartoonist Al Capp in 1934, the *Li'l Abner* comic series ran for more than forty years, chronicling the lives of a group of hillbillies in the fictional Arkansas town of Dogpatch. Thirty-five-year-old spinster Sadie Hawkins was the town's 'homeliest gal', whose father, worried that she was never going to marry, decided to organize a *Sadie Hawkins Day* on which a footrace was held for all the town's unmarried men with Sadie in pursuit. The first man Sadie caught would ultimately become her husband. What began as a one-off joke soon became an annual occurrence in the comic strip and eventually inspired real-life *Sadie Hawkins Days*, on which women are encouraged to propose to their partners, and *Sadie Hawkins dances*, in which women are obliged to invite male guests, all across America.

IX

TEN PHRASES FROM SONGS

The popularity of old music hall numbers in Victorian and Edwardian Britain (DADDY WOULDN'T BUY ME A BOW-WOW) and the worldwide popularity of songwriters like Cole Porter (THE BIRDS AND THE BEES, MISS OTIS REGRETS) and George and Ira Gershwin (POTATO, POTAHTO) have led to a number of song titles and lyrics being adopted into the language. The ten listed here have their origins in genres as diverse as jazz, folk music and opera, and take in national anthems, musical theatre and even protest songs.

1. The BIRDS AND THE BEES

The reappearance of the birds and bees each spring has long been used as a metaphor for courtship in literature, with vague references to *the birds and the bees* dating back as far as the seventeenth century. More recently however *the birds and the bees* has become a familiar euphemism for sex, and in particular sex education, and in this context is usually said to have developed from the lyrics to Cole Porter's 1928 song 'Let's Do It (Let's Fall in Love)', which famously begins, 'Birds do it, bees do it'.

2. DADDY WOULDN'T BUY ME A BOW-WOW

The song 'Daddy Wouldn't Buy Me a Bow-Wow' was written in 1892 by an English songwriter named Joseph

Tabrar for Vesta Victoria, one of the most popular singers and entertainers of the time. Its lyrics tell of a young girl who takes her pet cat to school with her each day, and when her teacher asks her why, the girl huffily replies, 'Daddy wouldn't buy me a bow-wow!' The song proved hugely popular in late-nineteenth-century London and its title soon became an equally popular London catch-phrase, used as a jokingly sulky or petulant reply to someone who has turned down a request or suggestion.

3. GOODNIGHT VIENNA

Goodnight Vienna is a British expression dating from the 1930s that is usually taken to mean 'it's all over!' or 'that's that!', often with the implication that nothing can be done to change the outcome. Originally it was the title song of a 1931 operetta written for BBC radio by the English entertainer Eric Maschwitz (who went on to co-write 'A Nightingale Sang in Berkeley Square' in 1939), which told the story of two lovers trapped in Austria who become separated by the First World War. The production proved hugely successful and the following year became the first British musical ever adapted for cinema.

4. IT TAKES TWO TO TANGO

The first written reference to the *tango* comes from an 1896 travelogue that described it as a dance 'requiring unusual agility . . . [that is] popular in the lower class' of venues across Spain. The expression *it takes two to tango* dates from the 1950s, and was originally the title and refrain of a song written in 1952 by the American song-writing partnership Al Hoffman and Dick Manning: 'There are lots of things that you can do alone,' the song explains, 'but it takes two to tango.' The track soon became a popular standard while the idiomatic use of its title to refer to the need for cooperation between two opposing parties was popularized by Ronald Reagan in 1982, when he used it in reference to America's uneasy diplomatic negotiations with Russia.

5. MISS OTIS REGRETS

Miss Otis Regrets is the title of a 1934 song by Cole Porter that became a popular catchphrase in the mid-1900s as a means of politely turning down an invitation or proposal. Porter was supposedly inspired to write the song when he overheard a waiter in a restaurant tell a fellow diner that 'Miss Otis regrets she's unable to lunch today.' Based on this single line, he went on to write one of his most famous songs – all the more famous due to its notorious subject matter, with the eponymous Miss Otis portrayed as a high-society lady who shoots her cheating lover, is thrown in jail by an angry mob and hanged. Her last words, and those of the song, are 'Miss Otis regrets she's unable to lunch today.'

6. OPEN THE DOOR, RICHARD!

The catchphrase *open the door, Richard!* began life as a comedy routine performed by an African-American vaudeville entertainer named Dusty Fletcher in the early 1900s. In his act, Fletcher played a soliloquizing drunk dressed in oversized shoes and a top hat and tails who, having drunk more whisky than he can handle, attempts to wake up his housemate, Richard. Fletcher's routine proved hugely popular in the thirties and forties, and in 1946 the American bandleader Jack McVea reworked his monologue into a musical number, 'Open the Door, Richard!', which soon became one of the biggest hits of the decade. The track went on to be recorded by more than thirty different artists (including jazz pianist Count Basie, for whom it was his only US Number One) and Fletcher's catchphrase soon slipped into everyday language as a joking reply to someone who has knocked on an already open door. It took on an altogether more significant meaning amid the upheaval of America's Civil Rights Movement (no doubt due to its lengthy association with predominantly black artists and performers) and became a popular slogan rallying against outdated, discriminatory rules and conventions; anyone failing to recognize the social changes of the 1950s and 1960s would be told to *open the door, Richard!* and acknowledge them.

7. PIE IN THE SKY

The colloquialism *pie in the sky* has been used in English since the 1940s to refer to a pipe dream or fantasy, or else to some wonderful but unrealistic ambition unlikely ever to come true. It was coined by an American labour activist and songwriter named Joe Hill, who used it in the lyrics to his 1911 song 'The Preacher and the Slave' which mocked the Christian idea of heavenly rewards following a virtuous yet impoverished life on Earth. Hill's song was a parody of a popular nineteenth-century hymn 'In the Sweet By-and-By', which described Heaven as 'a land that is fairer than day', where 'we shall meet on that beautiful shore'. In 'The Preacher and the Slave', however, Hill speaks of 'long-haired preachers' who 'when asked about something to eat' by penniless workers will answer, 'You will eat, by and by, / In that glorious land above the sky. / Work and pray, live on hay, / You'll get pie in the sky when you die.'

8. POTATO, POTAHTO

Potato, potahto – or *tomayto, tomato* – is a familiar colloquialism used to indicate that there is no real difference between two possible alternatives. It comes from the George and Ira Gershwin number 'Let's Call the Whole Thing Off', which the Gershwins wrote for the 1937 musical comedy *Shall We Dance.* The song famously plays on the contrary pronunciations of a series of words to highlight the differences between an ill-matched couple, played on screen by Fred Astaire and Ginger Rogers – one says 'ee-ther', the other says 'eye-ther'; one says 'vanilla', the other says 'vanella'. Ira's lyrics were supposedly inspired by similar differences between him and his wife, although later accounts have suggested that the song was more likely inspired by a similar scene in the Marx Brothers' comedy *Duck Soup.* Whatever its origin, the song's clever lyrics, its memorable melody and the remarkable dance routine it accompanied on screen – a quickstep tap dance performed on roller skates – all ensured its adoption into everyday English.

9. *The* TUNE THE OLD COW DIED OF

Often used simply to refer to any cacophonous noise or a poor-quality musical performance, the nineteenth-century expression *the tune the old cow died of* originally referred to the doling out of pointless advice instead of actual assistance. In this context it derives from an old Irish folksong that tells of a farmer who was unable to feed his starving cow. Instead of doing anything proactive, he 'took up his fiddle and played her a tune', singing '"Consider, good cow, consider, / This isn't the time for the grass to grow."'

10. UNITED WE STAND, DIVIDED WE FALL

The rallying words *united we stand, divided we fall* have been used as a motto for various civil and political movements for almost 250 years. They are taken from 'The Liberty Song', a patriotic tune of the American Revolution written in 1768 by a former Governor of Delaware and Pennsylvania named John Dickinson. Remarkably, the words do not appear until the song's sixth verse – 'Then join hand in hand, Americans all, / By uniting we stand, by dividing we fall' – but despite their obscurity, they were quickly recognized as a rousing and effective slogan and have remained so ever since.

X

TEN WAYS OF SAYING 'WOW!'

As an exclamation of astonishment or surprise, *wow* dates back to the sixteenth century when it is thought to have first appeared as an alteration of *vow*, which was also once used to express emphasis or earnestness. The derivative *wowee* first appeared in the 1960s, while the use of *wow* as both another name for anything spectacular and as a verb meaning 'to impress' or 'to excite' dates from the 1920s.

1. BY JINGO!

Jingo first appeared in English in the late seventeenth century as a conjuror's exclamation, *hey jingo!*, used to accompany the sudden appearance of something on stage; *hey presto!*, oppositely, was used when something suddenly disappeared. This magical use of *jingo* died out in the early 1700s, but its use as a general exclamation of surprise or wonder in forms like *by jingo!* or even *by the living jingo!* remained long into the twentieth century. Appropriately enough, *jingo*'s sudden appearance in the language remains a mystery – if not simply invented by conjurors so as to sound exotic and enigmatic, it is perhaps an old naval term derived from the Basque word for 'God', *Jinko* or *Jainko.*

2. BY THE PIPER!

By the piper! is an Irish-English exclamation from the 1700s, although it became especially popular in the nineteenth century when it was often embellished into more exaggerated expressions like *by the piper that played before Moses!* and *by the piper that shook the Giant's Causeway!*. Quite why a piper should be the subject of such an expression is debatable, but it is likely that phrases like these are all related to the old slang use of *piper* to refer to a wheezing, out-of-condition horse, or to someone who is out of breath, thereby implying that any sudden shock or surprise would make a person temporarily breathless.

3. GREAT SCOTT!

The mystery of who the *Scott* of *Great Scott!* is has remained unsolved for more than a century. Since it first appeared in the 1850s, various explanations have attributed it to everyone from Sir Walter Scott to Prince Albert (who supposedly popularized the similar-sounding German greeting *grüß Gott* in English), but the general understanding today is that the original *Great Scott!* was General Winfield Scott, an eighteenth-century commander-in-chief of the United States Army. A prominent and highly decorated figure of the American Civil War, Scott further assured his 'greatness' by running for president, serving as governor of Mexico City, becoming the longest actively serving general in American military history, and being the first man since George Washington to be promoted to the unique three-star rank of Lieutenant General. Scott also stood 6 foot 5 inches tall, and remains the tallest person ever to have run for the American presidency.

4. HOLY MACKEREL!

Most exclamations beginning *holy . . . !* first appeared in the language in the early nineteenth century. Among the earliest to emerge were religious exclamations like *holy*

Christ!, *holy Moses!* and *by the holy poker!* (a reference to one of the instruments of torture supposedly used in Purgatory) but towards the turn of the century many of these had been replaced by a peculiar array of euphemisms: *holy Christ!* became *holy Christmas!* (1900s) and *holy cow!* (1910s), and *holy Moses* became *holy moly!* (1920s). This trend continued long into the twentieth century, with ever more random words cropping up in ever more unusual exclamations like *holy Toledo!* (1950s), *holy monkey!* (1950s), *holy hailstones!* (1960s) and even *holy pretzel!* (1960s). *Holy mackerel!* dates from the 1890s making it one of the earliest of these variations, but its origin is not as random as it might appear – *mackerel* was a Victorian slang nickname for a Catholic, inspired by the Catholic tradition of eating fish on Fridays.

5. JUMPING JEHOSHAPHAT!

A great-great-grandson of King Solomon, Jehoshaphat was one of the earliest leaders of Judea who ruled Jerusalem in the ninth century BC. His reign is recounted in several books of the Old Testament, and is celebrated both for his quest for a peaceful alliance with the neighbouring Kingdom of Israel and for his nation's miraculous victory over the Kingdom of Moab: according to the Bible, on what should have been the day of a great battle Jehoshaphat's army discovered the Moabites had slain one another amid quarrels and infighting, leaving Judea untouched. Aside from his fairly eventful reign, quite why Jehoshaphat's name should have become such a familiar expression is unclear, although it is likely that it is simply intended to be a euphemistic replacement for 'Jesus'. Originally an American expression, the earliest record of *Jumping Jehoshaphat!* dates from 1857.

6. MAMMA MIA!

Mamma mia! literally means 'mother of mine', and in its native Italian first appeared as an exclamation of amazement in the mid-sixteenth century before working its way into English in the 1800s. Among many other foreign exclamations to have been borrowed into English over the years are the French *mon Dieu!* ('my God!'), which dates back to the 1600s, and its German equivalent *mein Gott!*, which first appeared in the late 1700s. The French *sacré bleu!* ('holy blue', with *bleu* acting as a euphemistic replacement for *Dieu*) dates from the mid-1800s.

7. MY STARS AND GARTERS!

In reference to their supposed effect on our fate and fortune, stars have been a popular subject of English exclamations and expressions since the sixteenth century. The first recorded example of such – *O, my starres!* – comes from Christopher Marlowe's 1593 play *Edward II*, and since then phrases like *bless my stars!*, *curse my stars!* and *thank your lucky stars* have all become common additions to the language. *My stars and garters!*, however, does not refer to astronomical stars, but rather to the trappings and showy symbolism of knighthoods and similar decorations; Jonathan Swift originally coined *stars and garters* in reference to these elaborate ornaments as far back as 1739.

8. SNAKES ALIVE!

Other than that it is almost certainly American – its earliest written use comes from an 1853 edition of New York's *Yankee Notions* magazine – very little is known of the origin of *snakes alive!*. Among an array of potential explanations is the idea that it was originally rhyming slang for 'fifty-five', as it is in bingo, with the two S-shaped fives said to resemble a pair of snakes. As an American invention, alternatively, it might have first referred to the snakes that hikers and explorers would have stumbled across in the American wilderness. Or maybe it was originally an Irish-American expression, somehow intended to refer to the fable of St Patrick ridding Ireland of its snakes. Perhaps the most likely idea, however, is that *snakes alive!* – along with *saints alive!* – is simply a variant of *sakes alive!*, an earlier Americanism descended from older English expressions like *for God's sake!* which date back to the 1400s.

9. STONE THE CROWS!

Used as an exclamation of annoyance as much as it is of surprise, *stone the crows!* first appeared in the language in the early 1900s and is thought to be of Australian origin, coined around the turn of the century alongside an array of similar Australianisms like *stiffen the lizards!*, *starve the wombats!* and *starve the bardies!*. It is probable that it originally referred to farmers literally shooing birds off their land with a shower of stones, but alternative explanations have since claimed that *crows* might be a corruption of *cross*, making this some kind of vague reference to the crucifixion of Jesus, or else a misspelling of *croze*, an old name for the groove around the lid of a barrel. If this latter suggestion is true, then *stone the crows!* might originally have been a fairly unsubtle demand for a drink.

10. THIS BEATS MY GRANDMOTHER!

Family members are common subjects of phrases and sayings, and grandmothers prove no exception. *To see your grandmother* once meant 'to have a nightmare' (1850s); *to shoot your grandmother* means 'to be mistaken' or 'dis-appointed' (1860s); and in the early 1900s *do I know my grandmother?* emerged as an alternative form of 'IS THE POPE CATHOLIC?'. *This beats my grandmother!* meanwhile has been used as an expression of astonishment since the 1830s. It originated in America where it first appeared in an anonymous poem, 'Logic', in an 1833 collection of elocutionary texts called *The United States Speaker*. In the poem, a student of logic cleverly outlines a logical argument to his uncle who responds, 'Bravo! Bravo! . . . Logic forever! / This beats my grandmother – and she was clever.'

XI

TEN WAYS OF SAYING 'NONSENSE!'

The English language is home to a whole host of words and phrases meaning 'nonsense', many of which are appropriately nonsensical inventions like *flim-flam, slip-slop, flummadiddle, fible-fable, skimble-skamble, fiddle-faddle* and *diddle-daddle.* Unfortunately, the origins of many of these somewhat ridiculous words and dozens more like them are either unknown, or else defy explanation; in fact, despite all being less than a century old, *codswallop, malarkey, baloney, hokum, hooey* and *phooey* are complete mysteries.

1. ALL MY EYE AND BETTY MARTIN!

Londoners have been using *all my eye!* to mean 'absolute nonsense' since the early 1700s, and since then a seemingly random array of suffixes have been added to it to create ever more elaborate expressions like *all my eye and my grandmother!* (1860s), *all my eye and my elbow!* (1780s) and *all my eye and Betty Martin!* (1780s). Precisely who (or what) *Betty Martin* was remains a mystery. As the earliest record of *all my eye and Betty Martin* describes it as 'a sea phrase', perhaps it was originally a nickname for some obscure piece of naval equipment. Alternatively it might be a corruption of an old Latin prayer, *Ora pro mihi, beate Martine* ('pray for me, blessed St Martin') or *O mihi Britomartis* ('help me, Britomartis', an obscure Greek goddess of fishing and sailing). Even more tenuously, it might once have been *Betty and Martin*, the names of two love-struck servants in a popular eighteenth-century French stage romance, *The Whimsical Lovers*, adapted into English in 1762. The most likely explanation, however, is that Betty was a real person, in which case she can probably be identified with an eighteenth-century eccentric Irish actress and travelling-theatre manager named Elizabeth Grace. According to the memoirs of her fellow actor Charles Lee Lewes, Elizabeth met and married 'a young gentleman of the name of Martin' in Ireland in 1741, thereby becoming the original *Betty Martin*.

2. ALL ROUND MY HAT!

In Victorian London the exclamation *all round my hat!* was used as a derisive reply to anyone apparently talking nonsense or telling lies. Although its exact origin is debatable, the phrase was probably lifted from the lyrics to an old London folksong 'All Around My Hat', described by Charles Dickens as 'a plaintive air' that was 'just beginning to form a recognized portion of our national music' in 1835, around the same time that *all round my hat!* first began to emerge. The song itself dates back to 1830 when, appropriately enough, it appeared in a fascinating nineteenth-century guidebook entitled *An Illustrated History of the Hat*.

3. BOIL YOUR HEAD!

A clutch of expressions like *fry your feet!*, *fry your face!* and *bag your head!* began to appear in the late 1800s as exclamations of exasperation, essentially meaning 'rubbish!', 'nonsense!' or 'don't be stupid!'. The earliest of all of these – and from which all the others are likely derived – was *boil your head!*, which is usually said to have originated as a fiery euphemism for 'go to Hell!'.

4. FLEMINGTON CONFETTI!

Flemington is a suburb of the Australian city of Melbourne, and since 1840 has been home to one of the country's oldest and most famous racecourses. The expression *Flemington confetti!* dates from almost a century later and first appeared in Australian English in the 1920s as a slang term for 'nonsense'. It apparently alludes to the litter-strewn state of the racecourse after it has hosted a major meeting, covered with utterly useless torn-up betting slips and other debris. A similar phrase, *farmyard confetti!*, dates from the 1960s.

5. GAMMON AND SPINACH!

Meaning 'nonsense!' or 'humbug!', *gammon and spinach!* dates from the early 1800s. It derives from the old use of *gammon* in London criminal slang as a verb meaning 'to swindle' or 'to cheat', which dates from almost a century earlier. In this context, *gammon* probably began as a pun on 'game' or 'backgammon', or else figuratively referred to 'tying someone up' by deceiving them, in the same way that a joint of ham or gammon would be tied with string before being cooked. Similar expressions include *to stand gammon*, meaning 'to distract someone while they are robbed by an accomplice' (early 1700s); TO GAMMON THE TWELVE, meaning 'to cheat a jury' (late 1700s); *to pitch gammon*, meaning 'to invent a story' (mid-1800s); and *to gammon the draper*, an early nineteenth-century term referring to an impoverished man tucking a handkerchief into the collar of his jacket to give the impression that he is wearing a shirt underneath.

6. MOONSHINE ON THE WATER!

Moonshine has been used to mean 'nonsense' since the fifteenth century, when it was often found in the old phrase *moonshine on the water!*; later variations included *a bag of moonshine!* and even *moonshine in a mustard pot!*. In all of these, *moonshine* alludes to the fact that the moon itself does not produce light but only appears to shine because it reflects the light of the sun. Ultimately *moonshine* became associated with anything fake or lacking any real substance in English, and hence 'nonsense!' or 'rubbish!'. The later use of *moonshine* to refer to illicit or smuggled alcohol dates from the late 1700s.

7. PULL THE OTHER ONE!

Pull the other one! is a familiar British expression used to indicate scepticism or a suspicion that something that has been said might not actually be true. Its origin is unknown, although the fact that the full phrase was originally *pull the other one, it's got bells on!* is often said to prove that it alludes to the belled hats worn by court jesters. The phrase itself however dates from as recently as 1936 when it first appeared in a German dictionary of idiomatic English that neatly explained that *pull the other one!* means 'Are you teasing me? Only continue if it amuses you.' A more likely explanation is that it is somehow related to *pull your leg*, meaning 'to deceive' or 'tease', which is in turn said to derive either from criminals being tackled to the ground by grabbing their legs, or from the practice of hastening a hanging person's demise by pulling down on their legs, tightening the noose.

8. TELL THAT TO THE MARINES!

Tell that to the marines! is an old nineteenth-century phrase used, like PULL THE OTHER ONE!, to show doubt or disbelief. For many years it was widely claimed to have originated in a conversation between Charles II and Samuel Pepys in which the king told Pepys how a member of his Maritime Regiment (the precursor to the Royal Marines) had been able to confirm the existence of flying fish. In reality, this story was the invention of a Victorian writer named W. P. Drury who, as a former lieutenant colonel of the Royal Marines, was probably trying to conceal the fact that the phrase is actually based on a long-standing joke among civilian sailors that the Marines were once considered a particularly gullible and dim-witted bunch who would believe almost anything anyone said to them; indeed the full phrase, dating from the early 1800s, was *tell that to the marines, because the sailors won't believe it.*

9. TIE THAT BULL OUTSIDE!

Tie that bull outside! is a 1920s American expression meaning 'nonsense!' or 'tell me another one!'. In this context, *bull* is unsurprisingly short for 'bullshit', which has been used to mean 'rubbish!', in the sense of something utterly worthless, since the early 1900s. Of similar origin are the Americanisms *to peddle* or *spin the bull,* meaning 'to deceive with words'; *to toss* or *shoot the bull,* meaning 'to gossip' or 'talk nonsense'; and *to spread the bull,* meaning 'to boast', all of which likewise date from the early twentieth century.

10. VERY LIKE A WHALE!

Used as a derisive or sceptical reply to being told something utterly unbelievable, *very like a whale!* is another of Shakespeare's contributions to the language. It is taken from the third act of *Hamlet* (III. ii), and comes from a discussion between the eponymous prince and the king's counsellor, Polonius, as they mull over the appearance of a passing cloud. Hamlet first decides that it looks 'almost in [the] shape of a camel', before changing his mind to 'a weasel', and finally 'a whale', to which Polonius wearily replies, 'Very like a whale.'

XII

TEN WAYS OF SAYING 'SHUT UP!'

As a means of telling someone (in no uncertain terms) to stop talking, *shut up!* first appeared in the mid-1800s, with one of its earliest recorded uses coming from the otherwise well-mannered world of Jane Austen's *Mansfield Park.* Before then a host of unusual alternatives were used in its place, some of which are listed here.

1. CUT THE CACKLE AND COME TO THE HORSES!

Cut the cackle and come to the horses! essentially means 'stop talking and come to the point!', or else 'get to the action!'. It is attributed to a nineteenth-century circus showman named Andrew Ducrow, whose elaborate displays of horsemanship at Astley's Amphitheatre in London are considered the origin of all modern circus horse acts and made him one of the most famous entertainers of his day. Ducrow's love of horses and extravagant entertainment was so great that while once watching a rehearsal of *Hamlet* at the theatre in the early 1800s he reportedly shouted up from the auditorium, 'Cut the dialect and come to the horses!' His heckle soon became a catchphrase among Astley's many actors and performers, and eventually slipped into common use in nineteenth-century London.

2. GIVE YOUR EARS A CHANCE!

Give your ears a chance! is one of a number of variations

of 'shut up!' (or in this case 'stop talking, and listen!') that appeared in Armed Forces slang during the First World War. It is also one of the most polite – an Australian alternative dating from the same period was *give your arse a chance!*, while a popular version from the Second World War was *shut your arse and give your mouth a chance!*, or in other words, 'stop talking rubbish!'.

3. HOLD YOUR WHISHT!

Alongside *sh!*, *hush!* and *st!*, *whisht!* is one of a number of sounds and exclamations listed in the dictionary as meaning 'silence!'; its earliest written use oddly comes from John Wycliffe's Bible in the late fourteenth century. Thought to be either Irish or Scots in origin, *whisht!* has been used in a variety of different expressions over the years, of which the sixteenth-century *hold your whisht!* or *haud yer wheesht!* is just one.

4. KNOCK IT ON THE HEAD!

To knock something on the head is a familiar English idiom often used to mean simply 'to stop' or 'to prevent something from happening', as well as 'quiet!' or 'shut up!'. It is often wrongly said to be an Australian invention, supposedly referring to killing a snake or a fish with a swift blow to the head, but in fact it dates back to the sixteenth century in British English when it was originally a euphemism for execution or, equally grimly, for beating someone to death.

5. MUM YOUR DUBBER!

More than two centuries before it became another word for 'mother', *mum* first appeared in English in the fourteenth century to describe someone's utter inability or refusal to speak; it was originally onomatopoeic, intended to imitate a sound made through tightly closed lips. Since then it has appeared in a number of English expressions all bearing some sense of keeping quiet or silent, including *mum is counsel*, a sixteenth-century version of *mum's the word*; *to keep mum* (or originally *to play* or *stand mum*), meaning 'to be silent'; *mum for that!*, a seventeenth-century exclamation meaning 'silence!'; and *mum your dubber!*, a nineteenth-century slang expression literally meaning 'shut your mouth!'. Similarly, *mum-tip* was a slang name among Victorian criminals for 'hush-money', a payment made to ensure someone's silence.

6. PIPE DOWN!

Pipe down! has been used as a request for silence or calm since the nineteenth century, although the phrase itself – often in the old expression *pipe down the hammocks* – dates from more than a century earlier. Originally, *pipe down* was a naval expression used on board ships as a signal that the crew were dismissed for the day and could retire to bed; the actual *pipe* would ultimately have been a boatswain's whistle or bugle. In the mid-1800s this old nautical phrase slipped into general use in Victorian English and has remained a familiar expression ever since.

7. SAVE YOUR BREATH!

The idea of *saving* or *keeping your breath*, thereby avoiding wasting time or effort on some pointless concern, dates from the late sixteenth century, and *save your breath!* (or, in the nineteenth century especially, *save your wind!*) appeared soon after. Of similar age is the old Scottish saying *to save your breath to cool your porridge*, a proverbial warning to keep your opinions to yourself.

8. SOFT AND FAIR!

Soft! was once a familiar English expression meaning 'silence!' or 'quiet!', used in much the same way as *hush!* or *sh!* would be today. It frequently appears in this sense in Shakespeare (most notably in Romeo's famous line 'But soft! What light through yonder window breaks?') and in the sixteenth and seventeenth centuries would often be used in phrases like *soft and fair!* or *soft and peace!* as a request for calm or silence.

9. SLACKEN YOUR GLIB!

When it first appeared in English in the late 1500s, the adjective *glib* originally meant 'smooth', 'slippery' or 'constantly moving'. Although this sense of the word has long since disappeared, in the mid-nineteenth century it nevertheless inspired the use of *glib* in Victorian slang to refer to the tongue, and in particular the constantly moving tongue of a chatterer or gossip. *Slacken your glib!* ultimately meant 'be quiet!', or literally 'give your tongue a rest!'.

10. STUBBLE YOUR WHIDS!

Dating from the early 1500s, *whid* is an old slang name for a word or a lie. It has appeared in a number of different expressions over the years, most of which dropped out of use long before the twentieth century, including *to crack a whid*, meaning 'to speak' or 'tell a story'; *to hold your whid*, meaning 'to stop talking'; a *whidding cheat*, a slang name for a liar's tongue; and *whiddler*, Victorian thieves' slang for a police informant. *Stubble it!* or *stubble your whids!* was a seventeenth-century expression meaning 'shut up!' or 'be quiet!', playing on an earlier use of *stubble* as a verb meaning 'to cut short' or 'crop'.

XIII

TEN WAYS OF SAYING 'CHEERS!'

Different cultures and languages around the world each have their own way of making a toast, a handful of which – like the Irish *sláinte* and French *santé*, both meaning 'health' – have slipped into occasional use in English. The Spanish *salud*, Italian *salute* and Portuguese *saúde* also mean 'health', while other equivalents around the world include the German *prosit* and Dutch *proost*, both taken from the Latin *prosit*, meaning 'may it be good for you'; the Japanese *kanpai* and Chinese *ganbei*, both meaning 'empty (the) cup'; and *skål*, the name of an old Nordic drinking bowl now used as a toast in Norway, Sweden and Denmark.

1. BOTTOMS UP!

Bottoms up! has been a popular English toast since the nineteenth century and probably began as a nautical expression among sailors referring to the undersides of drinkers' glasses, which are naturally turned upwards when a drink is taken. Alternatively, as the earliest written record of *bottoms up!* in an 1875 American magazine article explains, after a shout of *bottoms up!*, 'the glasses were emptied in silence, and turned bottoms uppermost on the bar'. Ultimately it might originally have been a command to drain a glass completely, with the glass then upturned to prove that it is empty.

2. BUNG HO, TROOPS!

Bung ho! has been used as a toast in English since the 1920s, often with the addition of *troops!* as a humorous reference to the other drinkers involved. Although its origin remains a mystery, various explanations suggest that it refers to the cork stopper or 'bung' of a barrel or wine bottle, or else derives from the earlier nineteenth-century use of *bung* to mean 'to throw' or 'to move quickly', like someone throwing back a drink. It is more likely, however, that *bung ho!* was originally a goodbye, probably based on earlier terms like *cheerio!* or *cheer-o!*, which later became associated with drinking from the tradition of toasting someone's departure.

3. CHIN CHIN!

As a toast *chin chin!* was first used in the late 1800s before becoming particularly popular among the upper classes after the turn of the century. It dates back to the late 1700s when it was originally used as a greeting, derived from the Chinese *t'sing-t'sing*, which was borrowed into the language via sailors and merchants travelling to the Far East in the eighteenth and early nineteenth centuries.

4. DOWN THE HATCH!

In naval slang *hatch* has long been used as a humorous name for the mouth or throat, derived from the old nautical use of *hatch* to refer to a trapdoor or grated opening in the deck of a ship. As a toast or an order to finish a drink, *down the hatch!* is likewise presumed to have been a naval expression that probably originated in America in the 1920s and 1930s before slipping into common use elsewhere.

5. HANS IN KELDER!

Hans in Kelder! is an old toast adopted into English from a Dutch expression, *Hans-en-Kelder*, referring to an unborn child. The phrase literally means 'Hans in the cellar', with *Hans* used as a generic name for a young boy as 'Jack' or 'John' would be in English. Borrowed into the language in the mid-1600s, *Hans in Kelder* was originally used in English in much the same way as it would in the Netherlands, but by the eighteenth and nineteenth centuries it had become a popular toast used to offer best wishes to a pregnant woman and her child.

6. HERE'S LOOKING AT YOU!

Toasts beginning *here's to . . . !* (a shortened form of *here's a health to . . . !*) have been popular in English since the sixteenth century. All manner of different variations and endings have been recorded over the years, from straightforward examples like *here's luck!*, *here's hoping!* and *here's how!* to more outlandish lines like *here's to your face!*, *here's hair on your chest!*, HERE'S MUD IN YOUR EYE! and even *here's fluff in your latch-key!*, which comes from the Second World War. *Here's looking at you!* dates from the late nineteenth century but will forever be associated with the classic 1942 film *Casablanca*. Popular history claims Humphrey Bogart's famous line 'Here's looking at you, kid' was not in the original script, but came from conversations between him and his co-star, Ingrid Bergman, as they played poker on set between takes.

7. HOB AND NOB!

Hob and nob! dates from the early seventeenth century but is derived from the even earlier expression, *hab and nab*, which first appeared in the 1500s. Both forms have been used in a variety of different contexts over the years, but always tend to refer to some sense of 'this or that' or 'back and forth' – to do something *by hab or by nab* means 'in any way necessary'; to do something *by habs and nabs* means 'intermittently' or 'bit by bit'; and to carry out a *hob-nob* venture is to not care how it ends, 'win or lose'. Likewise in the eighteenth century *to drink hob and nob* came to mean 'to drink back and forth' or 'to drink to one another in turn', and eventually *hob and nob!* became a popular toast, implying that all those involved are mutually wishing each other well.

8. MAY ALL YOUR TROUBLES BE LITTLE ONES!

The expression of good wishes *may all your troubles be little ones!* – often followed by *and all your little ones be trouble free!* – dates from the late nineteenth century. Although all of its earliest records come from America the toast is believed to have originally been an old Irish saying, or even a line lifted from some long-lost Irish folksong. The phrase inspired a number of humorous and short-lived variants in the early twentieth century, including *may all your roosters lay eggs!*, *may all your ups and downs be between the sheets!* and *may all your days be circus days!*, originally used as an advertising slogan for an American circus in the 1960s.

9. MUD IN YOUR EYE!

The popular toast *here's mud in your eye!* is often said to have arisen among troops in the First World War. If this is the case then the mud in question is presumably that of trenches and battlefields, and it has even been suggested that the toast was intended to point out that having 'mud in your eye' was a relatively insignificant problem compared to what else could happen in the course of battle – better to merely have mud in your eye than anything else. The exact origin of the phrase is, however, unknown, and the alternative suggestion that it alludes to the winning horse in a race having kicked mud into the faces of its opponents could be just as likely.

10. SKIN OFF YOUR NOSE!

Here's to the skin off your nose! and its many variations date from the early 1900s. Its origin is unclear, and various suggestions claim that it refers to a glass touching the bridge of a person's nose as they drink, or else to the toasting of a victorious boxer despite his injuries. Perhaps the most likely explanation, however, is that it is somehow related to the expression *no skin off my nose*, meaning 'that's not my problem', which originated in America at the turn of the century. If so, the carefree toast *the skin off your nose!* might have originally implied a disregard of any problems or issues, and an intention to celebrate instead.

XIV

TEN WAYS OF SAYING 'DRUNK'

Drunkenness is often claimed to be one of the most variably described subjects in the entire English language, with more words and phrases used for being *tiddly, toppy, foggy, hazy, snuffy, swipey, rosy, boozy, stinking, well-oiled, well-cornered, half-shaved, half-channelled, half-cocked, pegged too low, pegged out, in the down-pins, in your altitudes, Mickey Finished, squizzled, plastered, befuddled, smashed, sloshed, soused, kaylied, lustick, groggified, tipsified, off the nail, stinko, pinko, how-come-ye-so, hiccius doccius, rouzy-bouzy, rumdum* and *thumped over the head with Sampson's jawbone* than almost anything else.

1. ALDERMAN LUSHINGTON IS CONCERNED

In the late eighteenth century a society of Covent Garden actors and writers called the City of Lushington would routinely meet to drink in a tavern on Russell Street near London's Royal Opera House. Inside, the drinkers would divide into four groups or 'wards', which would each elect its own leader or 'alderman', while the entire enterprise was presided over by a 'Lord Mayor'. The tradition of the society continued long into the nineteenth century, when *Alderman Lushington is concerned* – in the sense that a person is absolutely engrossed in or 'concerned' with their drink – became a popular expression in London slang.

2. ALL MOPS AND BROOMS

All mops and brooms has been English slang for 'drunk' since the early nineteenth century. It apparently refers to the so-called 'mop fairs' long held across England, where unemployed servants and domestic staff – alongside shepherds, dairymaids, farmhands and all manner of other workers – would set themselves up for hire. Each one would identify him or herself to prospective employers by holding some symbol of their work, and so while the shepherd would carry his crook and the cart-driver his whip, maids would usually carry mops and brooms. The fairs became increasingly disorderly over time and were evidently accompanied by a considerable amount of drink, and soon *all mops and brooms* was born.

3. CONTENDING WITH PHARAOH

Contending with Pharaoh is an old eighteenth-century phrase meaning 'drunk' that was first cited in the *Drinker's Dictionary*, a glossary of drunkenness compiled in 1737 by Benjamin Franklin. Some accounts suggest it might originally have come from some long-lost biblical textbook or pamphlet, perhaps one retelling the stories of Joseph or the Exodus from Egypt, but a more likely idea is that *pharaoh* is simply a misinterpretation of 'faro', the name of a type of Belgian wheat-beer flavoured with sugar or caramel that was popular across England in the 1600s and 1700s. Quite why a drunk should be said to be *contending* with their beer is debatable, although it could be a humorous reference to fighting (albeit unsuccessfully) to stay sober.

4. DOWN AMONG THE DEAD MEN

In the sense that they have lost their 'spirit', empty glasses and bottles have been known as *dead men*, *dead marines* or *dead soldiers* in military slang since the early 1600s. *To be down among the dead men,* conjuring up the image of a drunkard collapsed among empty bottles on the floor or table, is a later expression from the mid-1800s which probably came from a popular Victorian drinking song: 'Come let us drink it while we have breath, / For there's no drinking after death. / And he that will this health deny . . . / Down among the dead men let him lie.'

5. FIVE OR SEVEN

Throughout the nineteenth century, *five or seven* was a popular London slang name for a drunkard, while *to be (found) five or seven* meant simply 'to be drunk'. Although some explanations wrongly claim that it refers to the number of drinks a person might have consumed, it originated among London policemen in the early 1800s at a time when the standard penalty for public drunkenness was either a fine of five shillings or a sentence of seven days in prison. The phrase appears to have survived for a short time into the early 1900s, but has long since disappeared.

6. *To have* GONE TO BUNGAY FAIR (AND BROKEN BOTH LEGS)

A huge number of old expressions of drunkenness imply some sense of 'going' or having 'been' somewhere. *To have gone to Geneva* for instance was a seventeenth-century pun on 'Jenever', a type of Dutch gin; *to have gone to France* was an eighteenth-century way of saying 'drunk on wine'; and in the nineteenth century the characteristic untidiness of heavy drinkers inspired the phrase *to go to Jericho,* a reference to a biblical story in which King David told his servants not to leave the city until their beards had grown. *To have gone to Bungay Fair* was another

Victorian expression, referring to the small market town of Bungay on the Norfolk–Suffolk border. Although *Bungay* might simply be a pun on 'bung', the stopper in a barrel or cask, a more likely explanation is that the phrase derives from the earlier exclamation *go to Bungay!*, meaning 'go to Hell!' – although its origin in turn remains a mystery. The later addition of *and broken both legs* comes from the long-standing connection between intoxication and injury – in fact, in Victorian English a *breakyleg* was another name for a drunkard.

7. LOADED FOR BEAR

To be loaded for bear or *loaded for rhino* began as a gambler's term in late nineteenth-century America, when it originally meant 'to be holding a good hand of cards'. Alluding to the image of a big-game hunter fully armed and equipped, over time the expression came to mean simply 'well prepared' or 'ready for any eventuality' before finally coming to refer to drunkenness in the 1940s, in the sense of someone being 'fully loaded' with drink.

8. *To have* SEEN THE FRENCH KING

Seeing the French king is a peculiar expression of drunkenness dating back to the mid-1600s. Thought to have originally been a naval term, its precise origin and meaning is unclear, although different explanations suggest that it refers to someone having had so much to drink that they begin hallucinating fantastic images, or else is simply a reference to someone drunk on French brandy or wine.

9. THREE SHEETS TO THE WIND

Three sheets to the wind is almost certainly an old naval expression dating from the mid-nineteenth century (if not even earlier), although precisely what these *sheets* are is open to question. One possible explanation is that they are simply sails, as a ship with three sails fully open 'to the wind' would often prove top-heavy and unstable on the water, much like someone who has drunk more than they can handle. Alternatively these *sheets* might have originally been the ropes or chains used to secure the lower edge of a sail. If one of these ropes were to come undone, the sail (as well as the *sheet* itself) would become loose and be liable to flail dangerously across the deck; and the looser the sails, the larger and more erratic the ship's movements. Likewise, the drunker a person becomes, he can be said to have *four, five* or *six* or more *sheets to the wind.*

10. *To have drunk* WINE OF APE

The expression *wine of ape* is one of the oldest euphemisms for drunkenness in the entire English language, with its earliest record found in 'The Manciple's Tale', the penultimate story in Chaucer's *Canterbury Tales,* written in the late fourteenth century. The phrase was apparently borrowed into English from French but originally derives from an ancient Jewish fable in which Satan appeared before Noah while he was planting grapevines. According to the story, Satan sacrificed a lamb, a lion, an ape and a pig in front of Noah, with each creature said to represent the different stages of drunkenness – initially quiet and docile like the lamb, a person slowly becomes louder and braver like the lion, then foolish like the ape, and finally ends up in the dirt like the pig. Ultimately *wine of ape* (a literal translation of the French *vin de singe*) refers to a drunken person's foolish monkeying behaviour.

XV

TEN WAYS OF SAYING 'MAD'

Someone who is 'mad' (in the sense of insanity rather than anger) can be compared to any one of an array of random things in English, including *a hatter, a fish, a weaver, a hornet, a cut snake, a March hare, a brush* and even *brewer's hops.* Hatters became associated with madness in the nineteenth century, when the mercury once used in the manufacture of felt hats was found to be the cause of all kinds of neurological disorders that the hat-makers often suffered from. Hares become 'mad' in March and early spring in the run up to their mating season, during which time the males participate in extraordinary boxing matches in order to assert their dominance. Quite why anyone should be said to be *as mad as a brush,* however, is a mystery.

1. BARMY ON THE CRUMPET

On its first appearance in the language in the early 1500s, *barmy* literally meant 'resembling or covered in barm', namely the yeasty froth that forms on top of ale as it ferments. In the 1600s, this literal meaning gave way to a figurative sense of 'active' or 'turbulent', and then in the 1800s – probably with some influence of *balmy* (with an L) to mean 'soft' or 'weakened' – to the more familiar sense of 'excitable' or 'crazy'. It is this that is found in the Victorian English expression *barmy on the crumpet,* meaning 'mad' or 'deranged'; *crumpet* is an old British slang name for the head, presumably in reference to its round shape.

2. BEDLAM RIPE

Bedlam, describing a scene of absolute havoc, is a corruption of St Mary of Bethlehem, the name of an old mental hospital and asylum that opened in Bishopsgate in London in the mid-thirteenth century. The term is the origin of a number of English expressions, all of which carry some sense of madness or derangement: a *Tom* or *Jack o' Bedlam* is an old name for a madman; a *bedlam-house* is literally a madhouse; and a *Bedlam beggar*, as mentioned in Shakespeare's *King Lear* (II. iii), is a beggar who has escaped the asylum and returned to the streets. The adjective *bedlam ripe* dates from the early sixteenth century when it literally described someone ready or 'ripe' enough to be taken straight to Bedlam Hospital.

3. BESIDE YOUR GRAVITY

Dating from the eighteenth century, *beside your gravity* is one of a whole host of English expressions of madness that bear some sense of being in the wrong place or position, many of which date back hundreds of years. As well as being *beside your gravity*, you can also be *beside your wits*, *beside your patience*, and *beside yourself*, a familiar phrase that dates back as far as the 1400s. Likewise, you can be *out of your mind*, *out of your wits*, *out for lunch* and *out of the envelope*; *round the bend* and *round the twist*; *up the pole* and *up the creek*; *over the edge* and *away with the fairies*; *off your head*, *off your onion*, *off your rocker*, and *off your trolley*, the latter being an early twentieth-century Americanism originally referring to Manhattan's electric trolley cars.

4. DOOLALLY TAP

Doolally dates from the late nineteenth century in English, when it first began to appear in British soldiers' slang as another way of saying 'mad' or 'senseless'. It is a corruption of Deolali, the name of a small town and former British–Indian transit camp around 190 km (120 miles) east of Mumbai. How it came to refer to madness is debatable, with various explanations ranging from reports of a sanatorium for mentally unstable soldiers in the camp to the maddening boredom that would set in as troops waited out the weeks and months before transportation back to Britain. The full expression *doolally tap*, however, is thought to contain a corruption of the local Urdu word for malarial fever, *tab*, and so the phrase might actually refer to the delirium experienced by patients suffering from the disease.

5. EAST HAM

Perhaps one of the most tenuous synonyms for madness in the entire English language is *East Ham*, the name of a suburb of London in the East End borough of Newham; *Upton Park*, another Newham suburb one mile further west, is of similar meaning. To understand how both these London locations became associated with madness (and to fully appreciate their tenuousness) requires knowledge of the London Underground and in particular the District Line, one of the oldest on the entire system dating back to 1868. The District Line connects Ealing, Richmond and Wimbledon in the west and south of London to Upminster in the east, via Kensington, Westminster, Whitechapel, Upton Park, East Ham and, crucially, Barking. Presumably in reference to the wild behaviour of rabid dogs, *barking* has been a slang term for madness since the early 1900s, and hence describing someone as *East Ham* implies that they are literally 'one stop before barking', that is, 'almost entirely mad'; describing someone as *Upton Park* meanwhile means 'two stops before barking', and so not quite as mad as *East Ham*.

6. HALF A BUBBLE OFF PLUMB

Like BESIDE YOUR GRAVITY and a great many other expressions referring to some sense of being 'out of place', phrases like *half a bubble off plumb* or *one bubble left of level* allude to the bubble in a spirit level, indicating how straight (or crooked) something is – and so metaphorically, how mad or foolish a person is. A handful of phrases along these lines began to appear in the mid-nineteenth century, with *half a bubble off plumb* often said to have been coined by Mark Twain.

7. *To have* LOST YOUR MARBLES

In English slang *marbles* has at one time or another been used to refer to spots or blisters (late 1500s, probably from the French *morbilles*); items of furniture (mid-1800s, from the French *meubles*); gambling stakes or poker chips (US, late 1800s); money (1930s); and even testicles, derived (for obvious reasons) from the old London rhyming slang *marble halls. To have lost your marbles* is a much more straightforward expression originating in nineteenth-century America as simply a metaphor for losing your wits.

8. NON COMPOS MENTIS

Both *non compos mentis* and its less common opposite *compos mentis* date from the early seventeenth century in English, and were originally coined as legal terms referring to the relative soundness or unsoundness of a person's mind. The phrase literally means '(not) the master of one's mind' and derives from the same Latin root, *mentis* or *mens*, as words like *mental*, *demented* and *dementia*. *Non compos mentis* is also sometimes claimed to be the origin of the word *nincompoop*, but this theory remains uncertain.

9. A SHINGLE SHORT

A common trait among expressions of madness or foolishness is some sense of being deficient or short of something. Examples like these seem first to have arisen in Australian English in the nineteenth century, with the expression *a shingle short* – referring to a tiled roof, and probably based on the slightly earlier 1840s expression *to have a loose tile* – being among the first to appear. Since then, the familiar *x*-short-of-*y* formula has yielded an array of seemingly random expressions like *a sandwich short of a picnic, a card short of a full deck, a sixpence short of a shilling, a crayon short of a full box, an inch short of a foot* and even *a sultana short of a fruitcake*.

10. WIRED TO THE MOON

In English slang, the adjective *wired* has a lengthy history dating back to the late 1800s, when it initially meant simply 'irritated' or 'wound up'. Through the twentieth century this meaning developed to refer to the frenzied symptoms associated with drug use and addiction, and ultimately in the seventies and eighties to complete insanity or distress. *Wired to the moon*, meaning 'mad' or 'senseless', is an Irish slang expression first recorded as recently as the 1990s.

XVI

TEN WAYS OF SAYING 'DEAD'

Like drunkenness and madness, death is a particularly fruitful source of English expressions and euphemisms, with speakers often tactfully wanting to avoid broaching the subject too obviously. Listed here are ten examples of precisely that, lifted from as typically varied sources as Victorian London, the Navy, gamblers' slang, Ancient Greece and the American Air Force.

1. *To have gone to* ABNEY PARK

Abney Park is the name of a grand Victorian cemetery in north London which is one of the city's so-called 'Magnificent Seven' cemeteries built in the 1800s to accommodate the capital's rapidly expanding population; by the end of the twentieth century, these seven cemeteries alone had witnessed well over a million burials. Unsurprisingly the Victorian phrase *to go to Abney Park* meant simply 'to die' and appears to have remained in common use until the 1930s. As neither the largest nor the oldest of the 'Magnificent Seven', it is unclear why Abney should have warranted its own phrase, but perhaps it is somehow derived from the fact that it was London's principal non-denominational cemetery for 'non-conformists': William and Catherine Booth, the founders of the Salvation Army, are famously buried there alongside their son.

2. *To have* BOUGHT THE FARM

Buying the farm – or *the ranch, the plot* or even *the mall* – is an unusual euphemism for death originating in 1950s America. It is often mistakenly presumed that it refers to a person cashing in their life savings and retiring to a farm or rural estate, but as logical as this suggestion is *buying the farm* actually derives from American Air Force slang, where it began as a joke among jet-fighter pilots who would often train and test their jets in the skies above remote ranches and farms. If a jet crashed onto one of these the litigious farm-owner would routinely sue the US government for the damage to his property, and the resulting payment would often be more than enough to clear all his debts and buy the farm outright. As the crash would almost always be fatal to the pilot he would be said to have *bought the farm* with his life.

3. *To have gone to* PEG TRANTUM'S

Peg Trantum is an old seventeenth-century nickname for a boisterous or tomboyish girl. *Peg* is a diminutive of 'Margaret', while the invented surname *Trantum* is presumed to be a play on 'tantrum'. The expression *gone to Peg Trantum's* is almost as old as the name itself and means simply 'dead', but how these two entirely different meanings are connected remains a mystery. One possible (albeit fairly tenuous) explanation refers back to an old proverb of the early 1700s that warned *set a beggar on horseback and he'll ride to Peg Crancum's* – but why the change of name? As unpleasant as it might seem, *crancum* is a variant of *crinkums,* an old English name for venereal disease or pox; *crinkums* is in turn a corruption of *grincome,* a seventeenth-century name for syphilis; the similarity between *crancum* and *Trantum* presumably made them interchangeable; and ultimately it seems *having gone to Peg Trantum's* would have been enough to bring about a man's demise.

4. *To have* KICKED THE BUCKET

Dating from the eighteenth century at least, *kick the bucket* is such a well-known euphemism for dying that it might be surprising to find that there is no definitive explanation of its origin. The most commonly held theory is that it refers to an execution by hanging; a person sent to the gallows would be made to stand atop an upturned bucket with the noose around his neck, and as the bucket was kicked out from under him he would be killed. Another explanation alludes to an old Catholic custom in which a bucket of holy water would be placed at the foot of a recently deceased person as they lay in bed. Visitors would sprinkle the water over the body as they paid their last respects, but if the deceased was merely sick or dying rather than dead they might suddenly *kick the bucket*, spilling its contents. (As outlandish as this explanation might seem, in its defence the Spanish equivalent of *kick the bucket* is *estirar la pata*, literally meaning 'stretch the leg'.) Other alternatives claim that the *bucket* in question is not a pail but rather a wooden beam from which a slaughtered pig was suspended; it might instead be a reference to an old children's game called *kick the can*, similar to hide-and-seek; or else it might derive from an ancient Latin saying, *capra Scyria*, referring to the ill-tempered goats of the Greek island of Scyros – when the goats would be milked, they would often jump back and kick out violently, knocking over the bucket of fresh milk behind them.

5. *To be* LAID IN THE LOCKERS

Laid in the lockers is an old naval slang expression meaning 'to die' dating from the early nineteenth century and probably inspired by the much earlier eighteenth-century expression *Davy Jones's locker.* In naval parlance, a *locker* is a chest or container variously used to house a sailor's possessions, money or ammunition – *to still have shot in your locker* alternatively means 'to still be active' or 'still in with a chance'. The origin of Davy Jones himself, however, is more complicated and various different legends claim he was originally the ghost of some long-dead pirate or sailor; that he was the ghost of the prophet Jonah; or that he was a demon who presided over the spirits of the sea and whose appearance on board a ship supposedly foretold a disaster.

6. *To* NEED PARSLEY

As unfamiliar a phrase as *needing parsley* might seem to most people today, the connection between parsley and death is a particularly ancient one that originates in Ancient Greece. *He has need of nothing but parsley* was an old proverb recorded in the works of the Greek historian Plutarch as far back as the first century AD that referred to the practice of decorating graves and headstones with parsley as it retained its bright green colour much longer than other flowers and plants. In English, this proverb and a number of variations were commonly used up to the nineteenth century, since when they seem to have all but disappeared from the language.

7. *To have* PAID CHARON'S FARE

In Greek mythology, Charon was the ferryman who transported the souls of the departed across the River

Acheron, one of the five great rivers of the Underworld that separated the living from the dead. In Greek tradition an *obol*, a small coin worth one-sixth of a drachma, would be placed inside a dead person's mouth so that they had money to pay their way across the river; those unable to pay would be left to wander the shores for 100 years before being permitted to cross. Someone who has died was once proverbially said *to have paid Charon's fare*, a phrase dating from the eighteenth century in English, while later scholars who identified Charon's river as the Styx rather than the Acheron inspired the similar phrase *to have crossed the Styx.*

8. PUSHING UP THE DAISIES

Dating from the early 1900s, the familiar expression *pushing up the daisies* is descended from a long line of similar Victorian euphemisms for death like *under the daisies* and *to turn your toes up to the daisies,* some of which date back as far as the 1840s. The image is obviously that of a body buried beneath flower-covered ground and more recent variations have taken this a step further, including *kicking* or *shoving up the daisies, pushing up the weeds* or *the poppies* and even *grinning at the daisy roots.* A *daisy-pusher* meanwhile is a later twentieth-century slang term for a dead body, while saying that something will not happen until you are *looking up the daisy roots* implies 'not until I'm dead', or 'over my dead body'.

9. SIX FEET UNDER

A reference to the customary depth at which coffins are laid in the ground, the earliest written record of being *six feet under* dates from 1839 and a story published in *Bentley's Miscellany*, a renowned early-Victorian literary magazine once edited by Charles Dickens. As an expression in its own right however, *six feet under* seems not to have fully caught on until the 1930s.

10. *To have* THROWN A SEVEN

To throw or *chuck a seven*, or *to throw a seven-spot*, is an old Australian military slang expression meaning 'to die' which dates from the late nineteenth century. It alludes to gambling and dice-throwing games, and is presumed either to refer to the impossibility of *throwing a seven* with a six-sided die or else comes from the game of craps, in which any player who throws seven with a pair of dice – except on their first throw – loses. *To throw six-and-a-half* is a more recent Australian invention, predictably meaning 'to come close to death'.

XVII

TEN WAYS OF SAYING 'NEVER'

English contains a number of unusual and colourful ways of implying that something is unlikely ever to occur, many of which are the names of entirely fictitious events or feasts, like TIB'S EVE or ST GEOFFREY'S DAY, on which something implausible would proverbially be said to take place. Some of these 'dates' seem at least to have some historical reasoning behind them (IN THE REIGN OF QUEEN DICK), or else have been inspired by a genuine date from the calendar (LATTER LAMMAS), but more often than not are simply random examples of utterly implausible situations, like WHEN PIGS FLY. In these cases, phrases like this can be classed as an example of *adynaton*, an extreme form of hyperbole in which something is compared to an absolute impossibility – like *when Hell freezes over.*

1. GREEK KALENDS

In the Roman calendar, the *kalends* was one of three basic dates used to divide up the month. It referred to the first of the month, usually reckoned to correspond with the new moon, and was followed by the *nones*, falling roughly around the time of the half-moon, then the *ides*, on either the thirteenth or fifteenth day, which tended to match the full moon. The use of *kalends* to refer to the first day of the month was eventually adopted into English, and in the seventeenth century saying that something will occur *on the Greek kalends* came to mean that it will simply never occur – the Greek calendar, which predates that of Ancient Rome, did not use a *kalends* in its design.

2. LATTER LAMMAS

Lammas is an ancient Christian harvest festival celebrated on 1 August. Derived from *hlafmas*, an Old English word literally meaning 'loaf-mass', for centuries it was customary to take a loaf of bread made from the first harvest of the year to church on Lammas Day so that it could be blessed. As there is only one Lammas festival a year, *Latter Lammas* literally refers to a date sometime in the future that simply does not exist, and so saying that something will occur *at Latter Lammas* has been used since the sixteenth century to imply that it will never come to pass.

3. NARROWDALE NOON

To put something off until *Narrowdale noon* means to defer it indefinitely, or else implies that it will simply never take place. The phrase is a seventeenth-century expression from central England that is said to refer to an extremely deep and narrow valley on the River Dove in the Derbyshire Peak District that runs almost exactly north to south. Consequently the valley remains in darkness for most of the day even at the height of summer, and so a *Narrowdale noon* would seem much later than it would elsewhere.

4. REIGN OF QUEEN DICK

Anything that will occur *in the reign of Queen Dick* will proverbially never happen – not least because there will likely never be a queen of England who chooses to be called Richard. The *Queen Dick* in question however is

Richard Cromwell, the son of Oliver Cromwell who succeeded his father to the position of Lord Protector of the Commonwealth in September 1658. By this time the Commonwealth was already beginning to show signs of weakness – Parliament and the largely royalist Army had drifted apart and Richard, who had little military know-how, lacked the experience and charisma to resolve the situation. His rule ultimately lasted just nine months, and in May 1659 he was ousted from his position and the Commonwealth finally collapsed the following year. With Charles Stuart happily restored to the throne as King Charles II, in the years that followed Richard became known across England by a number of unflattering nicknames including 'Tumbledown Dick' and, as here, 'Queen Dick'.

5. ST GEOFFREY'S DAY

There is no 'St Geoffrey', and so since the seventeenth century something said to happen *on St Geoffrey's Day* will simply never occur. But why 'Geoffrey'? One suggestion is that it is a reference to Geoffrey of Monmouth, a twelfth-century English cleric and one of the first prominent figures to chronicle the history of Britain, but this question will likely never be conclusively answered.

6. TIB'S EVE

Thought to have originally been a pet form of Isabel, *Tib* or *Tibby* is a girl's name dating from the early 1500s. It soon came to be used as a general name for any young girl or sweetheart, but by Shakespeare's time almost exclusively referred to a mistress or a prostitute, or any similarly promiscuous woman. The phrase *on Tib's Eve* dates from the mid-1700s and refers to the day before the feast day of the fictitious 'St Tib' – who, given the name's negative connotations, is an ironically unlikely character.

7. WHEN DUDMAN AND RAMHEAD MEET

When Dudman and Ramhead meet is an old Cornish expression alluding to two headlands – Dodman Point near St Austell and Rame Head near Plymouth – that stand around 30 km (18 miles) apart on the south coast of Cornwall. As these two fixed points will never come together, this phrase has been used to mean 'never' since at least the eighteenth century, although it was likely in use locally much earlier than that. A more familiar equivalent is *when Dover and Calais meet*, referring to the English and French ports that stand around 50 km (30 miles) apart on opposite sides of the English Channel, which dates from the early 1700s.

8. WHEN PIGS FLY

Flying pigs are perhaps one of the most familiar examples of impossibility in the entire English language, having been referenced everywhere from *Alice's Adventures in Wonderland* to The Beatles' 'I Am the Walrus' and even a joke on *The Simpsons*. The earliest record of a phrase of this kind dates back to 1732, when the English writer Thomas Fuller included 'That is as likely as to see an Hog fly' in his *Gnomologia*, an eighteenth-century collection of *Adages and Proverbs, Wise Sentences and Witty Sayings*, although an even earlier saying, 'Pigs fly in the ayre with their tayles forward', appears in a *Dictionary for Young Beginners* dating from 1616. The phrase even has equivalents in a number of foreign languages: a German proverb, *Wenn Schweine Flügel hätten, wäre alles möglich*, literally means 'If pigs had wings, everything would be possible', whilst in Spanish anything improbable is said to occur *cuando las vacas vuelen*, or 'when cows fly'.

9. WHEN THE DEVIL IS BLIND

Like Shakespeare's *when the world's grown honest* (*Hamlet*, II. ii), saying that something will occur *when the Devil is blind* is a figurative reference to a time when there will be no evil in the world, implying that something will either never occur or only at some infinitely distant time in the future. The full phrase, which dates from the mid-seventeenth century, is *when the Devil is blind – and he has not got sore eyes yet*.

10. WHEN TWO SUNDAYS COME TOGETHER

As the holy day of the Christian church, Sunday is the subject of a number of old English sayings and expressions, many of which refer to an indefinite or impossible period of time. *When two Sundays come together* has been an expression of implausibility since the early 1600s, and similarly *a month* or *week of Sundays* has been a byword for a seemingly endless amount of time since the mid-eighteenth century; the earliest record of the saying *not in a month of Sundays* dates from 1852.

XVIII

TEN INITIAL PHRASES

As well as THE THREE RS, classical musicians have *the Three Bs*: Bach, Beethoven and Brahms. Sailors were once told to be aware of *the Three Ls*: 'lead, latitude and look-out'. *The Three Fs* were once 'fair rent, free sale and fixity of tenure', the basic tenets of a campaign for land reform in nineteenth-century Ireland. *The Four Cs* are 'carat, colour, clarity and cut', the four qualities dictating the value of a diamond. And *the Five Ws* are the five basic journalistic questions used to establish fact: 'who?, what?, where?, when? and why?' Similarly, all ten of the expressions listed here, from A LITTLE FROM COLUMN A to CATCHING SOME ZS, contain at least one individual letter of the alphabet.

1. *To* CATCH (SOME) Zs

The association between a droning *zzz* sound and the dull sound of sleeping or dozing dates from the early 1900s in English, with one of the earliest citations recorded in 1909 in *Tono-Bungay*, a semi-autobiographical story by H. G. Wells, which featured a character who 'had a way of drawing air at time through his teeth . . . a sound I can only represent as a soft Zzzz'. *To catch*, *bag* or *stack some Zs* or *zees*, meaning 'to snooze' or 'take a nap', is a more recent invention from 1960s America; similarly, *to be Z'd out* means 'to be completely tired' or 'unable to wake'.

2. *To* GO ON THE Q

To go on the Q is Victorian criminals' slang meaning 'to swindle' or 'to trick'. Unlike *on the QT* (a later nineteenth-century expression meaning 'on the quiet'), here *Q* is a pun on 'billiard cue', which is in turn a reference to an even earlier and equally obscure expression *on the billiard slum*, meaning 'to hoax' or 'defraud'. *Slum* has long been a slang name for deceptive chatter or blarney, but quite how billiards came to be associated with criminal activities is unclear – one suggestion is that a swindler might go from person to person in much the same way that billiard balls continuously knock together during a game.

3. *To not* KNOW B FROM A BATTLEDORE

In sixteenth-century England, saying that someone *doesn't know B from a battledore* implied that they were illiterate and had little or no knowledge of the alphabet. Later variations included *to not know B from a bull's foot, B from a broomstick* and even *B from A*, but *B from a battledore* – the name of a large wooden bat or mallet-like implement used in washing or 'beetling' clothes – appears to be the earliest of all.

4. A LITTLE FROM COLUMN A, A LITTLE FROM COLUMN B

A relatively recent American expression, probably dating from no earlier than the 1980s, *a little from column A and a little from column B* implies that when presented with or asked to choose between two alternatives, both are equally applicable or accurate: 'Did it rain yesterday or was it sunny? / Well, *a little from column A, a little from column B.*' The phrase is popularly said to derive from the set menus of Chinese restaurants which sprang up across the United States in the 1960s and 70s, which were typically divided into two columns, A and B, from each of which customers would be asked to select one dish.

5. *To be* MARKED WITH A T

If someone were widely known to be a thief or felon in nineteenth-century England, they would be said *to be marked with a T*. The phrase alludes to an old and once common practice of branding a letter T onto the hands of criminals who had been convicted but had escaped a more severe punishment through so-called 'benefit of the clergy', an obscure loophole in English law originally established to ensure that members of the clergy were only ever tried in ecclesiastical courts. Eventually, however, this loophole allowed almost anyone to escape a harsher sentence by reciting a Latin biblical verse, thereby demonstrating their schooling, their intelligence or their faith. The playwright Ben Jonson was famously branded on his left thumb with the so-called *Tyburn T*, a reference to London's Tyburn gallows, despite being found guilty of the manslaughter of Gabriel Spenser in a duel in 1598.

6. *To* MIND YOUR Ps AND Qs

Essentially meaning 'to mind your manners', *to mind* or *watch your Ps and Qs* dates from the eighteenth century in English although an alternative form, *to be on* or *in your Ps and Qs*, meaning 'to be alert' or 'to be at your best', dates back as far as the early 1600s. In either case, the exact meaning of *Ps and Qs* is a complete mystery. Even on its earliest appearance in the language both the spelling and context of *Ps and Qs* were ambiguous, with 'Now thou art in thy Pee and Kue' used in a play of 1602, and the completely different 'at her p. and q.' used in another play written just five years later and by the same dramatist, Thomas Dekker. Unsurprisingly – given such inconsistency – a number of rival theories as to what *Ps and Qs* means have been suggested over the years, among them the suggestion that it stands for 'pints and quarts', a reference to publicans keeping an eye on the rowdy behaviour of their customers; *ps and qs*, individual letters of printers' type that could easily be confused; 'peas and queues', old naval names for a sailor's overcoat and ponytail; *pieds et queues*, old French military terms for feet and wigs; and even 'please and thank yous', the cornerstones of good manners. There is however no solid proof to support any of these ideas.

7. SMALL-L LIBERAL

Particularly used in reference to a person's politics or beliefs, phrases like *small-l liberal, small-d democrat* and *small-c conservative* began to appear in the language in the late nineteenth century to indicate a person's general rather than specific views, highlighting that 'liberal' ideas are different to 'Liberal' ones. Oppositely, expressions like *busy with a capital B* or *mad with a capital M* are used to emphasize a point, with the earliest example – 'Society with a capital S' – recorded in an edition of *Punch* magazine in 1859.

8. THE THREE Rs

The notion of *the Three Rs* – reading, (w)riting and (a)rithmetic – was invented by the eighteenth–nineteenth-century politician Sir William Curtis in a speech made to the House of Commons in 1807, in which he stated that 'The House is aware that no payment is made except on the "three Rs".' Curtis's neat expression of the three basic principles of education (complete with its ironic misspellings) soon caught on and has remained in use ever since, even inspiring several alternative definitions: Franklin D. Roosevelt's New Deal policy to escape the Great Depression was based on *the Three Rs* of 'relief, recovery and reform', while computer technicians often employ their own *Three Rs*, namely 'reboot, reformat, reinstall'.

9. *The* V SIGN

The history of *the V sign* – and its two very different meanings depending on which way round the hand is held – is on the one hand (no pun intended) very well documented, but on the other is open to considerable debate. As a sign of peace, the V dates from 1941 and was the brainchild of a former Belgian politician named Victor de Laveleye. At the time, de Laveleye was working for the BBC on their French-language broadcasts when he shrewdly suggested that the letter V, the initial letter of the word for 'victory' in all the languages of the European Allies, could be used as a means of rallying the nations together. The 'V for Victory' campaign quickly took off and a Morse-code V (· · · –) was added to all the BBC's wartime radio broadcasts; it was eventually replaced by the opening bars of Beethoven's Fifth Symphony, which famously shares the same rhythm.

The opposite *V sign*, with the palm facing inwards, is often said to have originated at the height of the Hundred Years War in the fourteenth and fifteenth centuries. According to legend, English archers who were captured by French forces would have their middle finger and forefinger cut off, making it impossible for them to use their bows again, and so gesturing to the French with the same two fingers became an obvious symbol of defiance. Sadly this ingenious tale seems to have been concocted as recently as the 1980s, and in truth the insulting *V sign* cannot be dated any further back than the late 1800s, when it is thought to have originated among criminal gangs in Victorian England. What its original use or meaning was, however, will likely never be known.

10. X MARKS THE SPOT

Although vague references to crosses or Xs marking locations on maps and charts date back to the early 1800s, popular history credits the clichéd phrase *X marks the spot* to Robert Louis Stevenson and his 1883 novel *Treasure Island*. The problem with this explanation, however, is that it is completely untrue. Stevenson's novel undoubtedly popularized the image of Xs drawn on treasure maps, but he never used the phrase *X marks the spot* himself, and instead simply describes 'three crosses of red ink', beside one of which is written 'Bulk of treasure here'. The first independent use of the phrase *X marks the spot* dates from the early 1910s.

XIX

TEN NUMERICAL PHRASES

Numbers are a common point of reference in English phrases and expressions, but often trying to explain what the number (or numbers) in question actually relate to can prove tricky, if not impossible. No one is quite sure for instance why *cloud nine* should be so heavenly, or why your *twopenneth* or *two cents' worth* of advice should be so valuable, and even of those listed here, being DRESSED TO THE NINES and at SIXES AND SEVENS are both mysteries.

1. *To* BEAR SIX AND SIX

An obscure Jacobean comedy called *The Spanish Curate*, co-written in the early 1620s by John Fletcher (one of Shakespeare's frequent collaborators), makes reference to an unusual expression that has puzzled writers, editors and actors for years: 'He's the most arrant beast,' one character comments of another, to which a companion replies, 'Let him bear six and six, that all may blaze him.' The context suggests that *bearing six and six* is some kind of humiliating punishment (here 'blaze' is used in an old-fashioned sense to mean 'ridicule'), but what it actually alludes to is unclear. One suggestion is that the *six and six* are perhaps meant to resemble the curled horns of a goat or ram (*66*), but what Fletcher truly intended this phrase to mean will probably never be known for sure.

2. *To be* DRESSED TO THE NINES

One popular explanation of how being *dressed to the nines* came to mean 'smartly' or 'elaborately attired' is that it refers to a nineteenth-century infantry of the British Army, the 99th Wiltshire, who were supposedly known for their immaculate appearance. As neat an explanation as this is, however, the earliest written record of *dressed to the nines* dates from the 1830s, long before the 99th Wiltshires were established in the 1880s. Instead, the phrase is apparently a development of the earlier eighteenth-century expression *up to the nines*, meaning simply 'to the highest degree' or 'quality', in which case *nines* is perhaps a corruption of *eyen*, an old form of 'eyes'.

3. FIFTEEN PUZZLE

Invented by a New York postmaster named Noyes Palmer Chapman in 1874, the *fifteen puzzle* was the Rubik's cube of its day. The puzzle comprised a wooden four-by-four frame containing fifteen identical numbered blocks and one empty space. The aim was simple: tip out the blocks, place them back in the box in a random order, and then slide them one at a time into the single vacant space to reassemble the numerical sequence. A straightforward yet surprisingly challenging puzzle, Chapman's invention proved to be the biggest craze of its day, and his *fifteen puzzles* sold in their millions across America and Europe in the late 1800s. Further interest was fuelled in the 1890s when an American mathematician and chess master named Sam Loyd offered $1,000 (equivalent to more than $25,000 today) to anyone who could solve a fifteen puzzle that began with all the blocks in numerical order except for the 14 and 15, which would be reversed; as tantalizing as Loyd's challenge was, he knew all too well that such a combination is impossible to solve. Eventually the *fifteen puzzle* fad died out, but its name was retained in the language long into the 1920s and 1930s as a popular metaphor for any intricate device or complicated situation, or anything impenetrably difficult to comprehend.

4. FORTY WINKS

Meaning 'a nap' or 'short sleep', especially one taken during the day, the familiar expression *forty winks* raises two simple questions: why *winks*, and why *forty*? The modern use of *wink* to mean 'a quick closing of one eye' is a fairly recent invention dating from the early 1800s. Before then, a *wink* was simply 'a short amount of time' (the same sense as in *to not sleep a wink*), while the verb *to wink* meant the same as 'blink' or, on its earliest appearance in the language more than 1,000 years ago, 'to close your eyes to sleep'. So why forty of them? One popular explanation is that this is some kind of ironic reference to the dreariness of the Thirty-Nine Articles, the basic doctrines of the Anglican Church first outlined in the sixteenth century. However, this theory seems only to be based on a quote from an 1872 edition of *Punch* magazine – describing 'a conscientious, right-minded man [who] after reading steadily through the Thirty-Nine Articles, [was] to take Forty Winks' – which was long considered the phrase's earliest use. In fact, 'a 40 winks nap in a horizontal posture' was described as 'the most reviving preparative for any extraordinary exertion of either the mind or the body' in an 1821 fitness manual called *The Art of Invigorating and Prolonging Life* written by William Kitchiner, one of the foremost lifestyle writers of the time. But the question still remains – why forty? Well, in the sixteenth and seventeenth centuries *forty* was colloquially used to mean 'any large amount' (perhaps inspired by the 'forty days and forty nights' of the Bible), and it seems this relatively more straightforward explanation is the most likely.

5. *To* GAMMON THE TWELVE

Like GAMMON AND SPINACH!, *to gammon the twelve* is another early nineteenth-century expression that derives from the even earlier use of *gammon* to mean 'to swindle' or 'to deceive'. The *twelve* here are the twelve members of a jury, and so a criminal who has been tried in court but acquitted and escaped prosecution – or who has been found guilty but has dodged a death sentence or transportation in favour of a relatively less severe punishment – would once have been said *to have gammoned the twelve.*

6. NINE DAYS' WONDER

In 1600, an English comic performer named William Kempe, one of Shakespeare's fellow actors and collaborators, abruptly left his theatrical company, The Lord Chamberlain's Men, and took it upon himself to morris dance from London to Norwich (a distance of 177 km/110 miles). His extraordinary undertaking, carried out on nine separate days over the course of several weeks in February and March, soon became national news and Kempe was met by cheering crowds in almost every town he came to on what eventually became known as his 'Nine Days' Wonder'. As brilliant as this (entirely true) story is, regrettably Kempe's was not the original *nine days' wonder*, nor does the phrase refer to some great achievement or triumph. Instead, a *nine days' wonder* was originally a passing craze or novelty, which attracts attention only for a brief time before vanishing. In this context, the first *nine days' wonder* comes from the fifteenth century, although the idea that such crazes are only of interest for *nine days* (or *nine nights*) dates back to the early 1300s.

7. NINE TAILORS MAKE A MAN

A popular eighteenth-century fable told the story of a young orphaned boy who was taken in by a company of nine London tailors who raised him and eventually helped him open a market stall, from which he became considerably wealthy. When questioned about his success, the stallholder would always answer that 'it takes nine tailors to make a man'. Unfortunately this pretty sentimental story has nothing at all to do with the nineteenth-century expression *nine tailors make a man*, which was instead a snide reference to the difference between the physiques of soldiers and labourers compared with tailors and other men whose jobs did not demand as much physical effort, the implication being that it would take *nine tailors* to do the work of a single man. Although the fable of the orphan who became a gentleman dates from more than a century earlier, the addition of the nine benevolent tailors appears to be a later invention – perhaps added by tailors trying to improve their feeble reputation.

8. THE PROBLEM IS 30

The problem is 30 is a modern American slang expression originating among office employees and computer technicians in the early 2000s. The *30* in question is thirty centimetres, a reference to the typical distance between a computer monitor and its user. So if *the problem is 30*, then an apparent technical fault is not the fault of the computer, but rather the inexperienced person using it.

9. SEVEN-SIDED ANIMAL

In the late eighteenth and nineteenth centuries, a *seven-sided animal* was an unusual and fairly derogatory nickname for someone with only one eye, an apparently common injury among soldiers and sailors who had served in any one of the numerous wars of the time. According to a contemporary *Dictionary of the Vulgar Tongue* of 1795, a *seven-sided animal* was someone left with 'a right side and a left side, a fore side and a back side, an outside, an inside, and a blind side'.

10. SIXES AND SEVENS

In 1516, London's forty-eight existing livery companies – tradesmen's and merchants' corporations, each established by its own royal charter – were ranked by the Lord Mayor in order of precedence, with the most important comprising what became known as 'The Great Twelve'. Among them, ranked in sixth and seventh place, were The Guild of Merchant Taylors (that is, tailors and 'linen armourers', who made the fabric linings for suits of armour) and The Worshipful Company of Skinners (traders of fur and skins). These two companies were apparently dissatisfied with the mayor's ordering, and so decided among themselves to alternate sixth and seventh place annually. This curious tale is often claimed to be the origin of *at sixes and sevens*, meaning 'disordered' or 'in disagreement', but the phrase in fact dates back almost another two centuries to the late 1300s. In its earliest form, the phrase was *to set on six and seven*, meaning 'to risk everything', and while its precise origin remains unclear it seems likely that it derives from some long-forgotten dice game in which a score of six or seven was either particularly risky or particularly profitable.

XX

TEN NATIONAL PHRASES

National stereotypes – sometimes positive, but more often than not negative – are frequently encountered in slang and idiomatic language not just in English but all around the world. Ten different nationalities mentioned in English phrases and expressions are listed here, many of which derive from some notorious historical event or scandal, or else first appeared in the language when Britain was at war. The trend often works both ways, however, as the French equivalent of TAKING FRENCH LEAVE is *filer à l'anglaise*, 'to take an English'.

1. *To* CATCH A TARTAR

Nowadays the Tatars are the natives of Tatarstan, a small landlocked Russian republic around 950 km (600 miles) north of the Caspian Sea. Historically however the term *Tartar* was used to refer to any of the various peoples of Tartary, a vast generic region extending across much of Asia from the Ural Mountains to the Pacific coast and which included the Turks, Kazakhs, Cossacks and Mongols among its many inhabitants. To English minds, the Tartars were known as exceptional warriors and unassailable opponents, and so the seventeenth-century phrase *to catch a Tartar* was variously used to mean 'to (attempt to) catch something uncatchable', 'to catch something that proves too hard to handle', or essentially 'to punch above your weight'. A popular nineteenth-century anecdote purporting to be the origin of the phrase (but more likely inspired by it) told of a soldier who, while fighting a battle against the Turks, shouted back to his companions that he had 'caught a Tartar'. 'Bring him along!' his commanding officer answered. 'I would,' the soldier replied, 'but he won't let me!'

2. CHINESE WHISPERS

The children's game *Chinese whispers* – in which a short whispered message is passed from player to player, often becoming distorted along the way – goes by a number of different names around the world, including 'grapevine', 'operator', 'whisper-down-the-lane' and 'telephone' or 'the phone game', by which it is usually known in America. The name *Chinese whispers,* presumed to be a reference to the indecipherability of Chinese languages to English speakers, is all but confined to British English and apparently dates from as recently as the 1950s and 1960s. The game itself is considerably older and dates from the mid-nineteenth century, when it was originally known as 'Russian scandal' to British speakers.

3. DUTCH FEAST

The hostility between Britain and the Netherlands during what became known as the Anglo-Dutch Wars of the 1600s and 1700s led to a whole host of *Dutch* expressions entering the language throughout the eighteenth century. Unsurprisingly, many of these were either uncomplimentary or at the very least carried some sense of an absurd reversal or overturning of the norm; a *Dutch auction,* for instance, is one in which the asking price is deliberately set high and then lowered until a single winning bid is made. Likewise, *Dutch consolation* or *comfort* is merely being thankful that things are not worse than they already are (late 1700s); a *Dutch bargain* only benefits the one side (mid-1600s); a *Dutch concert* is a cacophony (early 1800s); *Dutch courage* is courageousness induced by an alcoholic drink (mid-1800s); and a *Dutch feast* is one at which the host becomes drunk before his guests (late 1700s).

4. *To take* FRENCH LEAVE

To take French leave generally means 'to act without permission', but it is often used more specifically to refer to someone shirking their work or responsibilities. It dates from the eighteenth century and although it is easy to presume that it might have its roots in the good-humoured rivalry that has long existed between Britain and France, early descriptions of *taking French leave* explain that it derives from an old custom in France of leaving a party without saying goodbye to the host. This would have appeared the height of discourtesy to English guests, but to the French it was considered an act of considerable politeness as it meant not disturbing your obviously very busy host.

5. INDIAN SUMMER

Describing a period of unseasonably warm weather towards the end of autumn, the phrase *Indian summer* is often mistakenly associated with the hot, dry weather of the Indian subcontinent and so is wrongly assumed to be a colonial expression dating from the era of British rule in India. In fact, it is of North American origin and dates from the late 1700s, predating the British Raj by several decades. Although its precise meaning is unclear, *Indian summer* is thought to refer to a period of unusually hot and calm weather often observed in late October or early November in what are today the westernmost states of America and Canada, but at the time would have largely comprised land still occupied by Native Americans. The phrase did not catch on in British English until the mid-nineteenth century, before which any period of warm weather towards the end of the year was typically known as either *St Luke's summer*, referring to St Luke's Day on 18 October, or *St Martin's summer*, referring to St Martin's Day on 11 November.

6. ITALIAN QUARREL

Italy's notorious Borgia dynasty grasped and connived their way into becoming one of the most famous and most powerful families in Renaissance Europe in the fifteenth century. Even after their downfall in the early 1500s tales of their treachery, their murderous plotting and their unrelenting quest for power at any cost continued to spread, and they became popular subjects of drama and debate. Interest in the Borgias peaked in the early nineteenth century, likely spurred on by a clutch of contemporary literary and musical works including a play by Victor Hugo, a novel by Alexandre Dumas and an opera by Gaetano Donizetti, all based on the Borgias' story. Among Victorian criminals, the slang phrase *Italian quarrel* also emerged in the nineteenth century as another name for any of the crimes or misdeeds with which the Borgias had been associated or accused – including murder, poisoning, corruption, and betrayal.

7. NORWEGIAN STEAM

Dating from just after the Second World War, *Norwegian steam* is an American expression meaning 'manpower' or 'hard, physical work'. It is thought to have first appeared in American naval slang before being picked up more widely elsewhere, and refers to the characteristically impressive strength of the Norwegian sailors and labourers who emigrated to America in the 1940s.

8. PORTUGUESE PARLIAMENT

Portuguese parliament is an old English naval expression referring either to a noisy argument or to a rowdy meeting in which all those present speak over one another and fail to listen to each other's opinions. Dating from the late nineteenth century, as a naval expression it is likely based on nothing more than Victorian English sailors' reactions to their apparently hot-headed and impassioned Portuguese counterparts.

9. SPANISH TRUMPETER

Trumpeter has been a slang name for a mule or an old out-of-condition horse since the seventeenth century, along with a number of other equally evocative names like *wheezer, roarer, whistler,* and *piper* (as in BY THE PIPER!). Likewise a *Spanish trumpeter* – dating from the eighteenth century – is another name for a donkey, deriving from nothing more than a fairly cringeworthy pun imagining 'Don Key' as a Spanish name.

10. WHEN GREEK MEETS GREEK

According to an old English proverb, *when Greek meets Greek, then comes the tug of war.* The saying is derived from *The Rival Queens, or The Death of Alexander the Great,* a 1677 work by the Elizabethan playwright Nathaniel Lee which dramatizes the rivalry between Alexander's first and second wives, Roxana and Statira. In one scene, one of

Alexander's generals dispiritedly points out that while he wastes time squabbling with his lovers, his father Philip of Macedon would have been fighting battles against the other leaders of Greece all for the better of his kingdom: 'When Greeks join'd Greeks,' he explains, 'then was the tug of war.' The line soon became proverbial in English, used to point out that if an argument or battle is fought between two equally matched or equally powerful sides, it is likely to be a lengthy and arduous encounter.

XXI

TEN ANIMAL PHRASES

The ten phrases listed here all make reference to some kind of animal, ranging from swans and geese to monkeys and parrots, and from A WOLF IN SHEEP'S CLOTHING to THE ELEPHANT IN THE ROOM. A full list of phrases like these would also include a number of unusual and inventive similes, like *as bald as a coot,* a small water rail with a noticeably featherless shield above its bill; *as fit as a butcher's dog,* which would be especially well fed; *as happy as a clam at high tide,* when clams are out of the reach of predatory birds; *as dead as a dodo,* in use since the late 1800s and partly inspired by the dodo in *Alice's Adventures in Wonderland*; and *as busy as a bee,* first mentioned in Chaucer's *Canterbury Tales* as far back as the fourteenth century.

1. 800-POUND GORILLA

Describing someone or something as an *800-pound gorilla* implies that it is so aggressively or overwhelmingly powerful that it leaves little room for anything or anyone else. Particularly used in reference to the domineering or monopolizing effect of vast corporations and organizations, the phrase first appeared in American slang as recently as the 1980s and was apparently inspired by an old joke: 'Where does an 800 lb gorilla sit? Anywhere it wants to.'

2. ALL YOUR SWANS ARE GEESE

The sixteenth-century expression *all your swans are geese* either implies that all of someone's stories are boastful and inflated or have been proven false, or else that all your hopes and dreams have fallen short and come to nothing. Likewise *to turn geese into swans* means 'to exaggerate' or alternatively 'to make the most of a bad situation', while an inverted *all your geese are swans* is used to suggest that children will always be seen as flawless in their parents' eyes. In all these cases, the implication is simply that swans are considered more valuable and elegant than the more foolish and raucous geese – in fact geese are further maligned in a whole host of other English words and phrases like *goose-cap*, 'a fool' (late 1500s); *goose egg*, 'zero' (1800s); *goose-headed*, 'stupid, foolish' (mid-1800s); and *goose tracks*, 'unreadable handwriting' (nineteenth century).

3. BRANDY IS LATIN FOR GOOSE

'Brandy' is not the Latin word for goose of course, but *anser* is; and it is this fairly obscure bit of trivia that is at the root of this equally obscure and tenuous pun, used in English from the 1500s to 1800s as both a test of a gentleman's education and a call for another drink. According to most accounts of how the phrase developed, it was once common for upper-class gentlemen to quiz their fellow diners after a particularly rich meal of goose with the question, 'What is the Latin for goose?' The correct answer is *anser*, hence the pun, but instead the reply would customarily be a shout of 'brandy!', as any self-respecting gentleman should be aware that a glass of brandy would rightly follow a rich meal just as naturally as an 'answer' follows a question.

4. *To* BRING HADDOCK TO PADDOCK

Dating from the sixteenth century, *to have brought haddock to paddock* means 'to have lost everything' or 'to have spent all of your money'. *Haddock* has long been an English slang name for a purse, derived from a story in the Gospel of Matthew in which St Peter miraculously pulls a coin from a fish's mouth. *Paddock* is an old English dialect name for a frog or toad, perhaps included here for no other reason than that it rhymes with *haddock*, but altogether the phrase clearly implies reducing something of value to something entirely worthless.

5. A CAT MAY LOOK AT A KING

A cat may look at a king is an old English proverb dating from the sixteenth century that wisely acknowledges that even the lowliest or most inferior of people still have rights, even in the presence of their superior. The origin of the phrase is unknown, and it has been suggested that it was invented by the English playwright John Heywood in whose anthology, *The Proverbs, Epigrams and Miscellanies of John Heywood*, it first appeared in 1562. In his collection of *English Proverbs with Moral Reflexions* in 1713, however, the scholar Oswald Dykes offered a very different view, mirroring the religious tension of the time: 'kings do not . . . call cats to an account for their looks,' he wrote, '. . . But there are many cats of this kind which are too much made of, indulg'd and encourag'd, 'till they fly at last in the face of Sacred Majesty. In this sense, it is a true-blue Protestant proverb.'

6. ELEPHANT IN THE ROOM

The elephant in the room is an uncomfortable issue obviously in need of discussion but which remains (often just as obviously) unsaid, usually because it is easier to ignore than to resolve. The phrase is of American origin and apparently dates from the 1930s, but nothing of any certainty is known of its history. One explanation claims that it is somehow derived from *The Stolen White Elephant*, a parody of detective fiction written by Mark Twain in 1882. But whether this tale of an African elephant that disappears while in quarantine in New Jersey – that is, something enormous that cannot be seen – genuinely inspired the phrase is debatable.

7. PARROT AND MONKEY TIME

Parrot and monkey time is an obscure but no less useful phrase referring to a vicious argument or squabble. Quite why parrots and monkeys should be proverbial adversaries is unknown, but the association appears to be a long-standing one – in an 1899 collection of short stories the French humorist Alphonse Allais included a fable called 'Le Singe et le Perroquet', 'The Ape and the Parrot', which he claimed was based on an old Persian folktale. Allais' story is not the origin of *parrot and monkey time*, however, as it apparently originated in America in the mid-1800s and is thought to have been inspired by an old joke that was so popular at the time that it was even printed in the *New York Times* in 1885. According to the tale, a man who owned both a monkey and a parrot as pets came home one day to find the monkey had adorned itself with red and green feathers, and that the parrot was nowhere to be seen. After some time, the bird emerged unsteadily from a corner of the room, plucked bald save for a single feather in its tail, and hopped up onto its perch. After taking a moment to make itself look as best it could, the parrot finally turned to its owner and exclaimed, 'Oh, we've had a hell of a time.'

8. PIG IN A POKE

A *pig in a poke* is a foolish deal or purchase, especially one that is accepted without question by the buyer. In this context a *poke* is an old-fashioned word for a cloth sack, and the phrase literally refers to someone buying a pig unseen without checking its quality, or if indeed it is a pig at all – the purchaser might return home only TO LET THE CAT OUT OF THE BAG. Remarkably, *pig in a poke* has its origins as far back as the thirteenth century, when *when a man gives you a pig, open the pouch* was listed in a Middle English collection of adages and sayings written in 1275.

9. *To* PUT AN APE IN SOMEONE'S HOOD

Apes are the subject of a great many English sayings and expressions, including *to make someone your ape*, meaning 'to dupe' or 'get the better of someone'; *an ape may chance to sit among the doctors*, an old eighteenth-century proverb; and *to say an ape's paternoster*, a seventeenth-century phrase meaning 'to chatter your teeth'. *To put an ape in someone's hood* is an even earlier expression, first recorded in Chaucer's *Canterbury Tales* in the late 1300s. It is usually said simply to mean 'to fool someone', but an alternative theory claims that because the Latin for 'hood' (*cucullus*) was so similar to the Latin for 'cuckold' (the husband of an unfaithful wife, *cuculus*), this might actually have meant 'to cheat on another man's wife'. What is more, babies at the time would typically be carried in hood-like pouches tied around their mother's chest, and so *putting an ape in another man's hood* might even have implied secretly fathering a child with another man's wife, which he would then rear as his own.

10. WOLF IN SHEEP'S CLOTHING

The image of a *wolf in sheep's clothing* – a familiar metaphor for someone disguising their treachery or dangerousness behind an unassuming demeanour – is a particularly ancient one, thought to derive from an old fable in which a wolf dresses in a fleece to hide among a flock of sheep and steal an easy meal, only to be picked out by the farmer and killed for his supper. This tale is often credited to the Ancient Greek writer Aesop, but no exact version of it appears in his work. Whatever its true origins, the story was apparently well known by the time the New Testament was written, as the Gospel of Matthew famously contains a warning against 'false prophets, which come to you in sheep's clothing, but inwardly . . . are ravening wolves'.

XXII

TEN ANATOMICAL PHRASES

Phrases making some kind of reference to a part (or parts) of the body are particularly common in English, and even the short list of ten here covers every part of the body from the nose and the tongue to the liver and the spleen, and ranges from Ancient Greece through to the twentieth century. A full list of bodily expressions like these would include such familiar terms as *a stiff upper lip* and *an arm and a leg* alongside some very peculiar expressions indeed – as well as PLENTY OF GUTS BUT NO BOWELS, *there's no difference of bloods in a basin* was a Tudor expression meant to imply that all men are equal; to be *all of a kidney* was an old way of saying 'all of the same mind'; and in the eighteenth century, a pair of friends who had grown inseparably close were sometimes said to have *tied their navels together.*

1. *To* CUT TO THE QUICK

The earliest use of *quick* in the English language dates back more than a thousand years to when the Old English word *cwice* was used to mean 'alive' or 'animate'. The modern use of *quick* to mean 'lively' or 'fast moving' eventually developed from there, as did the more old-fashioned uses of *quick* to mean 'capable of sensation', 'capable of feeling pain' and ultimately 'raw or tender flesh'. It is this less familiar sense that is retained in *cut to the quick* – here *quick* refers to the highly sensitive flesh protected beneath the fingernails and toenails, which is particularly painful if damaged. To be *cut to the quick* ultimately means to be hurt deeply, while something able *to cut to the quick* is proverbially very heartless or cruel.

2. FROG IN THE THROAT

Various folk etymologies often try to connect the phrase *frog in your throat* either to the block or 'frog' at the end of a violin bow which 'stops' the sound, or else to an unusual medieval cure for a sore throat in which a live frog would supposedly be kept in the mouth until it died. The real derivation, however, is much less remarkable, as apparently *frog in your throat* simply refers to a hoarse person's 'croaky' voice. It dates from as recently as the nineteenth century, with the earliest written record found in an advisory book for boys called *How to Be a Man*, written by an American clergyman named Harvey Newcomb and published in 1847. Alongside rules like 'avoid tight-dressing as you would a black snake', 'it is better to read the Bible alone than to spend time over a poor book', and a two-and-a-half page essay ironically explaining how to 'avoid prolixity', the book advises that all young men should 'learn to say NO. If you find any difficulty in uttering it . . . if you find a "frog in your throat" which obstructs your utterance – go by yourself and practise saying no, NO, NO!'

3. *To* HANG YOUR LIVER ON (SOMETHING)

To hang your liver on something is an old dialect expression meaning 'to desire' or 'to crave deeply'. Dating from the nineteenth century, if not earlier, the phrase probably alluded to the long-standing belief that the liver was one of the bodily organs capable of controlling a person's deepest emotions and characteristics, and in particular their courage or audacity. References to this ancient misconception date back as far as the fourteenth century in English and are the origin of a number of other expressions like *lily-livered* or *white-livered*, meaning 'cowardly'. Likewise *to wash the milk off your liver* was an old seventeenth-century English expression meaning 'to become brave' or 'to embolden'.

4. KINGS HAVE LONG ARMS

The English proverb *kings* (or *governments*) *have long arms* dates back to the sixteenth century, although it has its origins in an Ancient Greek saying, *rulers' hands reach a long way*, which dates back more than 2,000 years. The implication is clear – the most powerful people are also those able to wield the greatest influence over the greatest number of people – but it is often also used in reverse, warning those who consider themselves outside the authority of others that they are not, and hence that it is impossible for criminals to evade capture forever.

5. NEAREST THE HEART, NEAREST THE LIPS

What is nearest the heart is nearest the lips is an old Scottish or Irish proverb dating from the sixteenth century. It refers to what might otherwise be called a 'Freudian slip', in this case referring to someone accidentally and tellingly using one person's name instead of another, with the implication that the name they mistakenly use is that of their sweetheart. The proverb has been found in a number of different variations over the centuries, including *nearest the heart, nearest the mow*, an old Scots dialect name for the mouth, and *nearest the heart comes out first,* an American version dating from the nineteenth century.

6. NOSE TO THE GRINDSTONE

Meaning 'working hard' or 'without pause', *nose to the grindstone* dates from the sixteenth century in English and was first recorded in writing as far back as 1533. One popular theory of its origin claims that it refers to industrious millers in the Middle Ages who would apparently press their noses against their millstones so as to ensure that they were not overheating and burning the wheat. As ingenious an explanation as this is, there is no evidence to support it and the fact that this expression has never once been found as *nose to the millstone* casts yet more doubt on it. A more plausible idea is that it refers to a knife-grinder diligently sharpening blades on a grindstone, but why this should become so famously associated with ceaseless hard work remains a mystery.

7. OVER THE LEFT SHOULDER

The left side has long been considered the improper or inauspicious opposite of the right, and an aversion to anything concerning the left (like the wrong side of bed) can be traced back to Ancient Greece and Rome. This association is presumably the origin of the old expression *over the left shoulder,* which has been used in English since the fifteenth century to refer to anything being said or done improperly or ironically. By the Victorian era, *over the left shoulder* even appears to have given rise to a gesture which, like *tongue-in-cheek,* would have been made to indicate that something being said should be taken sarcastically or sceptically. As Charles Dickens explains in *The Pickwick Papers*: 'each gentleman pointed with his right thumb over his left shoulder. This action, imperfectly described in words by the very feeble term of "over the left", when performed by any number of ladies or gentlemen who are accustomed to act in unison has a very graceful and airy effect; its expression is one of light and playful sarcasm.'

8. PLENTY OF GUTS BUT NO BOWELS

While the liver was once considered the seat of a person's resolve or fortitude (as in TO HANG YOUR LIVER ON), the bowels were seen as the source of compassion and empathy. Quite where this association comes from is debatable, but it can be traced back as far as the fourteenth century in English with John Wycliffe's translation of the Bible even making reference to 'the bowels of Jesus' in 1382. The eighteenth-century expression *plenty of guts but no bowels* was ultimately used to describe someone who, although courageous, is particularly unfeeling and pitiless.

9. TONGUE-IN-CHEEK

To do something *tongue-in-cheek* has meant 'ironically' or 'insincerely' in English since the late eighteenth century. Although it is often said to derive from the tongue physically distorting or obstructing a person's words, the phrase alludes to an old gesture, popular in Georgian and Victorian England, in which the tongue was pushed into the cheek while someone else was talking as a signal to others that what was being said was untrue.

10. *To* VENT YOUR SPLEEN

The figurative use of the word *vent* to mean 'to express your emotions' or 'to make your feelings clear' dates from the early 1600s, while the earliest reference to *venting the spleen* comes from a Restoration drama called *The Distracted State* written by the playwright John Tatham in 1641: 'Away with him!' one character demands of another, 'Did you e'er hear a spleen better vented?' The phrase derives from the ancient belief that the spleen was responsible for a person's ill-tempered or melancholic feelings – *to bear upon the spleen* similarly was an Elizabethan expression meaning 'to bear resentment'.

XXIII

TEN COLOURFUL PHRASES

Colours are another common source of phrases and idiomatic expressions in English, many of which make reference to the long-held associations between certain colours and characteristics; blue, for instance, has long been considered the colour of nobility (BLUE BLOOD), while purple is traditionally the colour of royalty (BORN IN THE PURPLE). Associations like these, however, tend not to pass readily from one language to the next. Blue is also the colour of gloominess or depression in English, but is the colour of drunkenness in German and Russian, whilst a Spanish *príncipe azul* or 'blue prince' is equivalent to an English 'Prince Charming'. Similarly, English speakers might consider yellow to be the colour of cowardice, but in German it is associated with enviousness and in French *rire jaune*, 'to laugh yellow', means 'to laugh insincerely'.

1. BLUE BLOOD

The idea that royal dynasties have *blue blood* dates from as recently as the nineteenth century in English, but has its origins in eighteenth-century Spain where the identical term *sangre azul* first emerged. Quite why aristocratic families are said to have *blue blood*, however, is unclear. It might allude to pale blue veins easily visible through fair skin, as members of the wealthiest families would never have to work outside in the heat of the sun and so would remain relatively untanned, but given its Spanish origins another likely suggestion is that it is somehow meant to refer to a family whose bloodline has never been tainted by invading Moorish blood.

2. BLUE CHIP

In gambling terms, *chips* was originally a slang term for the money wagered in a game of cards before references to different coloured counters or tiles used in place of cash began to appear in the 1850s; the earliest specific mention to *poker chips* comes from an 1864 anthology of sports and games. Blue-coloured chips were customarily those of highest value, and hence the phrase *blue chip* soon came to refer to anything of superior quality. This long-standing association found its way onto the stock market as far back as the 1870s, when the companies and stocks with the highest market values were first labelled *blue chips.*

3. A BOLT FROM THE BLUE

Dating from the early 1800s, something that comes as a complete surprise is proverbially said to be like *a bolt from the blue.* The *bolt* in question is a thunderbolt and the *blue* is a clear blue sky – hence something as surprising as a *bolt from the blue* is said to be as unexpected as a strike of lightning from a cloudless sky.

4. *To be* BORN IN THE PURPLE

Around 3,500 years ago, the people of the ancient Phoenician city of Tyre, now in modern-day Lebanon, began to obtain a rich purple dye from the shells of sea snails that lived off the city's Mediterranean coast. Enormous numbers of the snails – all of which had to be taken from their shells by hand before their dye-producing glands were removed, rinsed and dried in the sun – were required to produce only tiny amounts of the dye, and consequently the manufacture of so-called 'Tyrian purple' was a lengthy and costly process. Only the richest and most privileged families could afford it and in order to ensure its high status, its production and distribution eventually fell under tight legal control. Purple was reserved as the colour of royalty and privilege, and this tradition lasted long into the Greek, Roman and Byzantine eras, where any child born one day to accede to the throne was known as a *porphyrogenite*, literally 'born in purple'. The colour continues to have associations with royalty to this day, and *to be born in the purple* has been used to mean 'born into royalty' or 'into good circumstances' in English since the seventeenth century.

5. BROWN STUDY

A *brown study* is a melancholy, meditative mood or a period of absent-mindedness, especially one accompanied by deep musing thoughts or daydreams. Rarely used in modern English, the expression dates back to the mid-sixteenth century when it first appeared in a 'discourse for all young gentlemen' called *A Manifest Detection of the Most Vyle and Detestable Use of Diceplay*, which wisely advised that a 'lack of company will soon lead a man into brown study'. Quite why the colour brown should be associated with moodiness or inattentiveness is unclear, although it likely derives from an old use of *brown* to mean 'gloomy' or 'dusky'. An alternative suggestion that *brown* should in fact be *brow* (as in a 'furrowed brow') seems less plausible in comparison.

6. *To be* IN THE PINK

The word *pink* has one of the most surprisingly complicated histories in the entire English language, largely because it has such a vast array of different meanings, almost all of which have entirely unrelated etymologies. Historically, a *pink* could be a small sailboat (1400s); a minnow (1400s), or young salmon (1600s); an eyelet in a piece of fabric (1500s); a type of flower (1500s); a hole cut or stabbed into something, particularly with a dagger (1600s); a dandy or smartly attired person (1600s); a tiny fragment (1600s); a chaffinch (1800s); a short metallic sound or chirp (1800s); and even in early 1900s America a private detective, so-called because they worked for Chicago's Pinkerton Detective Agency. Even more confusingly, the colour *pink* originally referred to a murky greenish-yellow, and what we now know as *pink* today did not acquire its name until as recently as the 1600s; before then, anything pale red in colour would simply have been described as *rose* or *rosy-coloured.*

In the pink, meaning 'in good health' or 'the best possible condition', dates from the 1700s. Although it is tempting to presume that it derives from some reference to a person's rosy complexion or their blushing cheeks, the phrase comes from another old-fashioned use of *pink* to mean 'the best of something', or 'a prime example', a sense first recorded in Shakespeare's *Romeo and Juliet* ('I am the very pink of courtesy', II. iv). In this context, it derives from flowers of the *Dianthus* family better known as *pinks* (because of their 'pinked' edges, not their colour), which were among the most prized flowers in Elizabethan England.

7. RED-LETTER DAY

Red-letter day was originally a general term for any major Christian festival or saint's day, so-called as such days were customarily noted in church calendars in red ink. In this context the phrase dates from the mid-1600s (although the actual practice of writing important dates in red is considerably older), but by the 1800s it had come to refer more generally to any significant or celebratory day. The opposite of a *red-letter day* is a *black-letter day*, which also derives from the coloured inks of old church calendars, and which has been used of any inauspicious or ill-fated time of year since the early 1700s.

8. RED TAPE

The political phrase *red tape* literally refers to the red ribbons that have long been used to secure legal documents and official papers, references to which date from the 1600s. Proving that meddlesome, overbearing bureaucracy is nothing new, as a byword for a disproportionately strict adherence to rules and regulations *red tape* dates from the early 1700s when an English politician named John Hervey, Lord Privy Seal under Prime Minister Robert Walpole, sneeringly wrote of 'Red tape and wisdom at the Council' in a 1736 satirical poem entitled 'Poetical Epistle to the Queen'.

9. *To* SCREAM BLUE MURDER

A popular expletive in medieval France was *mort Dieu!*, literally 'God's death!', which was borrowed into English in the 1500s. By the mid-1600s this had morphed into *morbleu* in both French and English, with *bleu*, the French for 'blue', used as a rhyming euphemism for *Dieu.* This idea of a 'blue death' eventually inspired the English phrase *to scream* or *to cry blue murder*, which first appeared in the early nineteenth century to mean 'to make a loud noise or commotion', often with the implication that doing so is unnecessary or overdramatic.

10. *To be* TICKLED PINK

It was not until the sixteenth century that *tickle* began to be used to refer to the act of intentionally making someone laugh, as on its earliest appearance in the language in the 1300s it originally meant simply 'to thrill' or 'to please'. It is this original meaning of *tickle* that is maintained in expressions like *tickled pink*, which dates from as surprisingly recently as the early 1900s and refers to a person being so pleased or amused with something that they flush pink.

XXIV

TEN METEOROLOGICAL PHRASES

'Everybody talks about the weather,' the American novelist Charles Dudley Warner once commented, 'but nobody does anything about it.' The ten phrases listed here comprise a mixture of weather-related metaphors and figurative expressions (GREAT WINDS BLOW ON HIGH HILLS), as well as expressions used to describe the weather itself (QUEEN'S WEATHER) and various old omens and portents from which bad weather can apparently be foretold (THE CAT HAS A GALE OF WIND IN HER TAIL).

1. THE CAT HAS A GALE OF WIND IN HER TAIL

A long-held belief among sailors and seafarers was that the ship's cat was able to foretell the approach of bad weather. If the cat appeared unsettled or more playful than usual, she would be said to *have a gale of wind in her tail*, apparently predicting the approach of a storm; in fact the small wavelets on the surface of an otherwise calm sea that often precede a storm are known as *cat's paws*. The saying *a gale of wind in her tail* dates from the late eighteenth century in English, and although it may seem like superstitious folklore it is possible that the cat's fur would have been able to detect the slight increases in atmospheric electricity that occur before thunderstorms.

2. A FOG CANNOT BE DISPELLED WITH A FAN

The old adage that *a fog cannot be dispelled with a fan* implies that someone's means of doing something is ineffective and likely to fail, or else that if some great effort is to be made then the outcome needs to be assuredly worth it. The oldest record of this saying in English comes from an 1818 translation of *Narrative of My Captivity in Japan*, the memoirs of an acclaimed Russian sea captain named Vasily Golovnin who was held prisoner for three years by Japanese authorities during an exploratory voyage off the east coast of Russia in 1811. Golovnin writes that while trying to negotiate his and his crew's release, he read a letter from his Japanese interpreter in which he 'reminded us of the Japanese proverb: "A fog cannot be dispelled with a fan"'. He goes on to explain that, 'the coasts of Japan are frequently enveloped in fog. From the age of six, the Japanese . . . carry fans during the summer months. These circumstances have of course given rise to the proverb.'

3. GREAT WINDS BLOW ON HIGH HILLS

Recorded as far back as the thirteenth century, *great winds blow on high hills* or *on the highest towers* is an old English proverb implying that it is the most prominent people who routinely face the greatest amount of criticism and scorn. It is apparently inspired by the Latin saying *feriuntque summos fulmina montes*, 'lightning strikes the mountain tops', taken from one of the *Odes* written by the Roman poet Horace in the first century BC.

4. *To* KNOW ENOUGH TO COME IN OUT OF THE RAIN

To know or *to have wit enough to come in out of the rain* is an old sixteenth-century expression meaning 'to have barely adequate intelligence', usually with the implication that someone knows only the most basic of facts but lacks any other knowledge. More often than not, however, the phrase is used in the negative – *to not know enough to come in out of the rain* – to imply a complete lack of common sense.

5. QUEEN'S WEATHER

From the day of her coronation on 28 June 1838 through to the day of her funeral on 2 February 1901, Queen Victoria was known across Britain and the British Empire for always seeming to bring fine weather with her on the days of her public appearances and official engagements and visits. The earliest use of the phrase *Queen's weather* to describe a period of sunny weather comes from an 1851 edition of Charles Dickens' journal *Household Words*, although his account seems to suggest that the phrase was already fairly well established by then: 'The sky was cloudless; a brilliant sun gave to it that cheering character which – from the good fortune Her Majesty experiences whenever she travels, or appears publicly – has passed into a proverb, as "The Queen's Weather".' Although much less familiar today, in the nineteenth and early twentieth centuries *Queen's weather* was a well-known expression not just in British and Irish English, but also in Canadian, Australian and New Zealand English.

6. *To* REAP THE WHIRLWIND

To reap the whirlwind is an unusual expression adopted in English from a verse in the biblical Book of Hosea: 'For they have sown the wind, and they shall reap the whirlwind' (8:7). Its earliest record in English comes from John Wycliffe's Bible in the late fourteenth century, but by the 1500s the phrase had become an idiomatic expression in its own right, essentially meaning 'to sow the seeds of your own downfall' or 'to suffer the consequences'. Although not a well-known phrase today, *to reap the whirlwind* was famously used in 1940 in a rousing wartime speech given by Sir Arthur 'Bomber' Harris, then Air Officer Commanding-in-Chief of the RAF. Following the devastating air raids on London and other cities across Europe that became known as the Blitz, Harris famously commented that, 'The Nazis entered this war under the rather childish delusion that they were going to bomb everyone else, and nobody was going to bomb them . . . [and now they have] put their rather naïve theory into operation. They sowed the wind, and now they are going to reap the whirlwind.'

7. As RIGHT AS RAIN

An array of seemingly random objects can be used to complete the simile *as right as . . .*, including *ninepence, nails, a trivet, a ram's horn* and, since the nineteenth century at least, *rain*. Why any of these words should be chosen ahead of any others is open to question, and it is certainly possible that the only real reason for their appearance here is that they are all fairly familiar everyday things – and there are few things more everyday than rain to British English speakers. One alternative explanation of *as right as rain*, however, claims that *right* here might mean 'straight' or 'level' rather than 'correct', suggesting that it in fact refers to the straight lines made by sheets of heavy rainfall.

8. A STORM IN A TEACUP

The notion that a problem that only affects a small area

(or that appears to be a much larger problem than it truly is) is like a 'storm' contained inside something dates back as far as the 1600s in English when on its first appearance just such a commotion was described as *a storm in a cream bowl.* Several equally curious versions of the phrase followed, including *a storm in a wash-hand basin, a storm in a wine glass, a storm in a coffee-pot, a storm in a chamber-pot* and even *a storm in a slop-basin* until the very first *storm in a teacup* appeared in 1854 in the title of a popular West End farce, which no doubt helped to establish this as the most common version of the phrase today. Regardless of its wording, the phrase is clearly intended to be a metaphor for a small-scale or containable commotion, but that did not stop a popular folktale emerging in the early nineteenth century that purported to trace *a storm in a wash-hand basin* back to the tale of a young Scottish woman accused of witchcraft in the late 1700s. According to the story, the woman placed a small shallow dish inside a larger bowl of water so that it floated on top, and then began chanting an increasingly forceful magic spell until the water in the basin churned and rolled and sank the dish; later that day, a ship was lost at sea along with the entire crew, among them several men with whom the woman had apparently had a long-standing disagreement. As intriguing a tale as this is however, it is of course only local legend.

9. TELL ME IT SNOWS!

English is home to a number of weird phrases essentially meaning 'that goes without saying', most of which are typically used as sarcastic replies to someone who has stated the obvious. Among them is the old English dialect expression *we can guess eggs when we see shells,* meaning 'the evidence is clear'; *to walk round the church to see the steeple* means 'to take a long time to uncover something obvious'; and *to seek water in the sea* means 'to commit to doing something utterly pointless'. Dating from the sixteenth century, *tell me it snows!* is another early example of this kind of expression, the implication being that if it were snowing, you would clearly not need to be told (although maybe that goes without saying).

10. THE WIND KEEPS NOT IN ONE QUARTER

If you are told that *the wind keeps not in one quarter* then you are being advised that you cannot expect circumstances to remain unchanged forever. If on the other hand you are told that *the wind sits in that quarter*, then proverbially the way things appear to be going is clear and cannot be changed. Both of these are nautical expressions dating from the sixteenth century, and in both cases the *quarter* is a so-called 'quarter point' or 'quarter wind', an old name for one of the smaller subdivisions of the compass that is used to describe the direction of the wind at sea.

XXV

TEN GODLY PHRASES

The proverbial *Gods* listed here have control over everyone's fate (THERE BUT FOR THE GRACE OF GOD), are able to dole out divine reward or retribution (GOD HELPS THOSE WHO HELP THEMSELVES), are unstoppably or unquestionably powerful (ACT OF GOD, DEUS EX MACHINA), and know all that is unknown or unknowable (GOD'S ALGORITHM, THE GOD PARTICLE). This is far from a purely religious list, however, as, proving that *God* is indeed omnipresent, the entries take in subjects as diverse as the law, mathematics, anthropology, particle physics, Ancient Greek drama – and lice-infested sheep.

1. ACT OF GOD

The earliest reference to an *act of God* in English dates from the early 1600s. As a purely legal term, it refers to any occurrence considered entirely beyond human control and to which no legal responsibility can therefore be assigned. Examples of *acts of God* include sudden and unpreventable events and natural disasters like floods, storms and earthquakes, which are not only unforeseen but entirely unforeseeable. The initial inquiry into the sinking of the *Titanic* in 1912 deemed it an *act of God*, controversially exonerating the ship's captain and the White Star shipping line from any criminal negligence.

2. DEUS EX MACHINA

In general terms, a *deus ex machina* – the 'god from the machine' – is someone or something that appears just in time to help rescue or resolve a difficult situation. The phrase is typically used in literary contexts to refer to the swift (and often unrealistic) resolution of a plot or story, thanks to the sudden (and often contrived) appearance of some divine saviour or rescuer. In this sense, the phrase dates back to the seventeenth century in English, but has its roots in the stage dramas of Ancient Greece wherein the 'machine' in question was originally a pulley-like device used to suspend actors playing gods and goddesses above the stage. Such characters would often be introduced towards the end of performances in order to tie up all the loose ends in the plot and bring the story to a close.

3. GOD BLESS THE DUKE OF ARGYLL!

The nineteenth-century Scottish saying *God bless the Duke of Argyll!* apparently derives from the fact that the duke's lands were once so bare that he was forced to erect dozens of wooden posts all across it so that his sheep had somewhere on which to scratch their backs. The sheep would typically carry lice, ticks and other parasites in their fleece, many of which would be passed on to their shepherds. With little else to relieve the itching, the shepherds too would use the duke's scratching posts, exclaiming *God bless the Duke of Argyll!* in relief. The phrase soon caught on as a means of drawing attention to anyone seen to be fidgeting or scratching awkwardly.

4. GOD HELPS THOSE WHO HELP THEMSELVES

The popular maxim *God helps those who help themselves* is

often mistakenly presumed to be a biblical quotation but no such verse exists, and indeed much of the Bible is spent maintaining that God helps those who are *unable* to help themselves. Instead the phrase comes from the writings of a seventeenth-century English politician called Algernon Sidney, although it is possible that it was already in popular use, or else that Sidney took inspiration from some much earlier equivalent: one of Aesop's fables tells of a wagoner who is divinely helped to haul his cart from a ditch only after he has tried to move it himself, while the Greek tragedian Euripides once wrote, 'First try yourself, and after call in God, for it is to the worker that God lends aid.'

5. GOD OF THE GAPS

In general, the expression *God of the gaps* refers to the use of God – or more broadly, religious belief – as a means of accounting for the mysteries still not yet fully explained by science; God is effectively seen to fill in the gaps in our knowledge and understanding of the world around us. Although the phrase was not recorded in the language until the 1950s, the idea behind it dates back to the late nineteenth century and *The Ascent of Man*, a series of lectures delivered by the Scottish evangelist Henry Drummond in 1893 in which he spoke of 'reverent minds who ceaselessly scan the fields of nature and the books of science in search of gaps – gaps which they will fill up with God'.

6. *The* GOD PARTICLE

In 2013, the British theoretical physicist Peter Higgs, alongside Belgian physicist François Englert, was awarded the Nobel Prize in Physics for his work on the Higgs boson, an elementary subatomic particle. Although the science behind Higgs' and his fellow physicists' model is predictably complex, in layman's terms the Higgs boson is a particle located inside the already minute individual components of the nucleus of an atom whose presence accounts for how everything in the universe comes to have mass. The extraordinary importance of the Higgs boson – the discovery of which, after more than forty years of research, was tentatively announced in March 2013 – has led to it being nicknamed *the God particle*, a turn of phrase first used as the title of a 1993 popular science book by the American physicist (and fellow Nobel laureate) Leon Lederman. The name is largely rejected by physicists, however, who see it as wrongly introducing religion into the realm of science or else of overstating or sensationalizing its importance. Lederman himself claims the phrase was originally a joke invented by his co-writer and editor Dick Teresi, and apparently prefers the nickname 'the goddamn particle' due to its maddening elusiveness.

7. GOD'S ALGORITHM

In mathematics, the term *God's algorithm* essentially refers to any solution to a problem that uses the fewest number of components or moves. The phrase itself dates from the early 1980s and first appeared among mathematical discussions of the quickest way in which to solve a Rubik's cube. After considerable research, mathematicians proved that the puzzle required no more than twenty different moves, a figure that was ultimately nicknamed *God's number*.

8. GOD'S (OWN) COUNTRY

A number of locations around the world have claimed the popular slogan *God's country* as their own, including Australia, New Zealand, the United States, Ireland, England, and in particular Yorkshire. However, the earliest record of the phrase outside purely religious contexts comes from a translation of a French travelogue called *A Voyage To Ethiopia* written by a seventeenth-century explorer named Charles Jacques Poncet and first published in English in 1709. Poncet describes travelling alongside the Blue Nile through 'the Kingdom of Sennar', 'a plentiful country' that the local inhabitants had named '*Beladalla*, that is to say, "God's country"' – the first known written reference to *God's country* ultimately referred to a desert region of what is today Sudan.

9. THERE BUT FOR THE GRACE OF GOD

The familiar expression *there but for the grace of God (go I)* basically implies that your fate is not in your own hands, but it is often used more specifically when someone is seen to suffer a misfortune that could easily have befallen yourself. It is popularly claimed to have been coined by John Bradford, an English Protestant reformer and a former prebendary of St Paul's Cathedral, who was imprisoned in the Tower of London in 1553 soon after the Catholic Queen Mary Tudor ascended to the throne. Knowing full well that he would never be released, Bradford supposedly saw a line of prisoners being led from the Tower to be executed one morning and remarked, 'There but for the grace of God, goes John Bradford.' After two years' imprisonment, Bradford was finally tried, found guilty of heresy on 1 July 1555, and burnt at the stake in Smithfield in central London.

10. WHOM THE GODS WOULD DESTROY

Whom the Gods would destroy they first make mad is an old adage used of those whose apparently reckless actions or decision-making seem destined to bring about their downfall. It has its origins in Ancient Greece and was first recorded in the works of the playwright Euripides in the fifth century BC, long before its first appearance in English in the mid-1600s. Although several different versions exist, this wording is perhaps the most common and was coined by the American writer Henry Wadsworth Longfellow in his 1875 work 'The Masque of Pandora'.

XXVI

TEN DEVILISH PHRASES

For centuries the Devil has been called on as the personification of deception (THE DEVIL SICK WOULD BE A MONK), malfunction (THE DEVIL IN THE HOROLOGE), danger (THE DEVIL AND THE DEEP BLUE SEA), belligerence (THE DEVIL AND HIS DAM) and unrest (THE DEVIL AMONG THE TAILORS), whose name alone is often enough to tempt misfortune (SPEAK OF THE DEVIL). But we are a heathen bunch – the Devil has more than twice as many proverbs and sayings to his name in English as God.

1. AS THE DEVIL LOVES HOLY WATER

According to Christian tradition, holy water has long been said to be able to drive off the Devil, and so saying that you love someone or something as much *as the Devil loves holy water* unsurprisingly implies that you do not love it at all. Dating from the sixteenth century, this is just one of a handful of similarly ironic expressions used in the language, alongside *as a dog loves a whip* (early 1600s), *as a cat loves mustard* (mid-1600s), and even *as pigs love marjoram,* a common expression in Ancient Rome.

2. BETWEEN THE DEVIL AND THE DEEP BLUE SEA

Essentially meaning 'in a dilemma' or 'trapped between two equally undesirable alternatives', the familiar expression *between the Devil and the deep blue sea* dates back to early 1600s English, but was likely in use long before then. Its exact origin is unknown, although it is often said to derive from a tale from Greek legend recounted in Homer's *Odyssey* in which the hero Odysseus was forced to sail his ship BETWEEN SCYLLA AND CHARYBDIS, a great sea monster and a vast destructive whirlpool. Alternatively, the phrase could allude to a ship's so-called 'devil seam', the longest of all the seams between the planks forming a ship's hull, which typically lies just on the waterline. This seam would have to be kept unfailingly watertight and so would require almost constant upkeep at sea. The unlucky crewmember given the job of repairing it would be lowered over the side of the ship, which would have to be weighted down on the opposite side to tilt the 'devil' out of the water, leaving him literally hanging *between the devil and the deep blue sea.*

3. THE DEVIL AMONG THE TAILORS

The Devil among the tailors is both a nineteenth-century expression for a row or noisy disagreement, and the name of an old bar game in which players attempt to knock over a group of wooden skittles with a ball tethered to a crossbar fixed above. In both cases, the phrase derives from the title of an eighteenth-century stage play called *The Tailors: A Tragedy for Warm Weather* that was revived at what is now London's Haymarket Theatre in 1805. Many local tailors took offence at the play's satirical portrayal of their industry and protested in their hundreds in the streets outside. The few constables who were present were quickly overwhelmed and ultimately a group of Life Guards, mounted troops of the king's Household Cavalry, were called in to help disperse the crowds. The phrase *the Devil among the tailors* soon came to refer to any similarly riotous disturbance, whilst the bar game took its name from the image of the ball (or 'the Devil') knocking its way through the skittles much like the Guards battled their way through the crowds.

4. THE DEVIL AND HIS DAM

Dam is an old Middle English name for a female animal, and in particular one with young, which in the fourteenth century came to be used as an insult for an unpleasant, bad-tempered woman. The phrase *the Devil and his dam,* which dates from the late 1300s, ultimately refers to the Devil and either his wife or mother, and is often used to imply that behind any awful or ferocious man there is usually an equally ferocious woman.

5. THE DEVIL CATCH THE HINDMOST

The Devil catch the hindmost is an old proverb often taken to mean 'those who lag behind will suffer the consequences', or else 'concern yourself only with your own affairs', thereby leaving any who lag behind you literally to 'go to Hell'. Dating from the seventeenth century in English, the saying's exact origin is unknown, but one popular legend claims that it derives from an old school of black magic in Toledo in central Spain whose students would apparently be made to run through a tunnel once their studies were complete. The last to come through would be captured by the Devil and turned into an imp.

6. THE DEVIL IN THE HOROLOGE

A *horologe* is an old-fashioned English name for a clock dating from the fourteenth century, while the long-forgotten phrase *the Devil in the horologe* is essentially an old equivalent of what would today be called a 'gremlin' or a 'glitch', namely something that causes a fault in an otherwise organized system. Dating from the early 1500s, the phrase seems to have all but disappeared from the language by the turn of the seventeenth century, and remains little known today.

7. THE DEVIL RIDES ON A FIDDLESTICK

The Devil rides on a fiddlestick is an old sixteenth-century expression referring to a noisy commotion or uproar; its earliest written use comes from Shakespeare's *Henry IV: Part 1* (II. v), but it is likely that it was already an established saying in English long before then. What it actually implies is unclear – a *fiddlestick* is the bow used to play a fiddle, and so it could simply be intended to refer to the awful sound a badly tuned or badly played instrument makes, but the use of *fiddlesticks!* as another word for 'nonsense!' could imply that the entire phrase is simply a nonsensical formation.

8. THE DEVIL SICK WOULD BE A MONK

The old proverb *the Devil sick would be a monk* refers to someone who, when in difficulty, makes many virtuous promises and resolutions that, as soon as the difficulty has passed, they quickly forget and return to their normal ways – the implication being that even the Devil can act as righteously as a monk to better serve himself when times are hard. As it is, the English version of this proverb comes from a 1694 translation of a work by the French Renaissance writer Rabelais, who in turn took the saying from an even older Italian proverb *passato el pericolo, gabbato el santo,* literally meaning 'when danger has passed, we mock our saint'.

9. *To* HOLD A CANDLE TO THE DEVIL

Holding a candle to the Devil means 'serving an evil person' or 'assisting someone's wrongdoings', and is often incorrectly presumed to derive from the image of a helper or co-conspirator literally 'holding a candle' for their superior while they carry out some nefarious deed after dark. In fact it derives from a fifteenth-century expression, *to set* or *proffer a candle for the Devil*, which meant to honour him in much the same way as worshipped saints have candles lit for them in shrines.

10. *To* WHIP THE DEVIL AROUND THE STUMP

Dating from the early eighteenth century, *whipping the Devil round the stump* is an American expression variously used to mean 'procrastinating', 'getting out of trouble', 'shirking responsibility' or 'resolving a problem' by some convoluted or roundabout means, and in particular by fabricating some outlandish excuse. Quite how the phrase came into being is unknown. Perhaps it is a reference to some long-forgotten game, or even some old punishment? Perhaps it is related to being *up the stump* ('confused') or *on the stump* ('preaching', 'soapboxing')? Or perhaps *whipping around the stump* is simply a variation of *beating about the bush*? Whatever its origin, the phrase apparently first appeared in local use in Virginia and North Carolina in the 1700s.

XXVII

TEN FOOLS

If there is one area where the English language comes into its own, it is insults. Old dictionaries and glossaries of English slang contain a whole host of weird and wonderful insults, like *slug-a-bed* or *morning-killer,* both nicknames for a lazy idler or wastrel. A *knuckylbonyard* or a *hog-in-armour* is a clumsy person. A vain or foppish young man can be called a *spangle-baby,* a *musk-cod,* a *monkeyroney* or a *prick-me-dainty.* A shabby or promiscuous woman can be called a *driggle-draggle,* a *mopsy,* a *rubbacrock,* a *slammakin* or a *sozzle.* And a fool or a dunderhead – alongside the ten expressions listed here – can also be called a *sap-head,* a *nodgecock,* a *fopdoodle,* a *pigwidgeon,* a *doddypoll,* a *jobbernowl* and, if they look as foolish as they are, a *look-like-a-goose.*

1. COD'S HEAD AND SHOULDERS

Calling someone a *cod's head* has been an insult in English since the mid-1500s. It is just one example of a host of similar expressions – like *hammer-head* (1530s), *ass-head* (mid-1500s), *beetle-head* (mid-1500s), *ox-head* (early 1600s) and *cabbage-head* (mid-1600s) – that compare a fool's head to that of some random animal or object. By the nineteenth century *cod's head* had expanded into the much more emphatic *cod's head and shoulders,* taken from the name of a recipe published in Mrs Beeton's *Book of Household Management* in 1861.

2. ESSEX CALF

Essex has long been famous for its fine-quality cattle and an *Essex calf* was originally precisely that. In the seventeenth and eighteenth centuries, however, this name came to be used more contemptuously to refer to the county's supposedly rustic and dim-witted locals, especially compared to the urbane Londoners living only a few miles away, and by the Victorian era *Essex calf* had established itself as a general name for any slow or foolish person.

3. GOD'S APE

Often in the sense of mindlessly mimicking or 'aping' someone else's actions, apes have long been associated with foolishness or gullibility in the English language, with expressions like *to make someone your ape* or TO PUT AN APE IN SOMEONE'S HOOD dating back to the Middle Ages. As well as being an old name for the Devil – in the sense of him mimicking God's work but making a mess of it – *God's ape* was also a fifteenth-century name for 'a born fool', namely someone naturally predestined to be stupid.

4. HORRID HORN

Horrid horn is an old English slang name for a lazy simpleton or dimwit that dates from around the mid-nineteenth century. It is thought to be a corruption of an earlier Irish English word *omadhaun*, which was in turn adapted from the Gaelic word for 'fool', *amadán*. All three are almost unique to the British Isles but oddly, due to an influx of Irish immigrants in the 1700s and 1800s, *omadhaun* is still used today in the local slang of Newfoundland on the east coast of Canada.

5. JACK ADAMS

Alongside *Tom Farthing, Johnny Raw, Joe Soap, Ralph Spooner, Tom Towly* and *Tom Cony, Jack Adams* is one of an array of actual 'names' that have been applied to fools in English slang. It dates from the seventeenth century and is apparently derived from a genuine John or Jack Adams who lived in Clerkenwell in London during the reign of Charles II. The butt of numerous local tales of his stupidity, Adams apparently became something of a local celebrity in the mid-1600s and eventually turned his hand to astrology and fortune-telling – a nineteenth-century history of London said of him that 'you got a better fortune . . . for five guineas than for five shillings', while a 1774 *Biographical History of England* called him 'a blind buzzard that pretended to have the eyes of an eagle'.

6. JACK OF LENT

In the 1600s, *jack-a-lent* was the name of a popular children's game in which a thin wooden figure of a man, known as a 'Jack of Lent', was hung up as a target and pelted with sticks and rocks. Similar to guys made for Bonfire Night, Jack of Lents were made for Ash Wednesday and, although built around a wooden skeleton and bulked out with hay and grass, were kept intentionally slim to symbolize the fasting that would take place during Lent; on Easter Sunday, whatever remained of the Jack was burnt. The practice dates back to Tudor times with the first written reference to a *Jack of Lent* dating from 1604, but over time the name became attached to anyone who is the target of a joke, and ultimately to any foolish or insignificant person.

7. PILOT OFFICER PRUNE

Pilot Officer Percy Prune was the star of a series of informative RAF cartoons created by the British artist William John Hooper, known as 'Raff', in 1941. A bumbling and inattentive pilot, *Pilot Officer Prune* soon became a nickname for any similarly incompetent character in Air Force slang during the Second World War, and eventually any equally foolish or easily confused person.

8. RIGHT CHARLIE

Charlie has an array of odd meanings and uses in the English language, including 'a small triangular beard' (such as that seen in portraits of Charles I), 'a nightwatchman', 'a male fox' and, originating in First World War military slang, 'a soldier's backpack'. Its use as another name for a fool, particularly in the phrase *a right Charlie,* dates from the 1940s and seems also to have originated in soldiers' slang but it likely has its roots in the rhyming slang expression *Charlie Smirke* (the name of a famous jockey of the 1920s–30s), meaning 'berk'.

9. SIMPLE SIMON

The earliest mention of *Simple Simon* in English comes from 'Simple Simon's Misfortunes and his Wife Margery's Cruelty', an Elizabethan comic ballad (in which Simon is not-so-comically poisoned by his wife) dating from the 1680s. Whether this misfortunate Simon is the same *Simple Simon* who appears in the famous nursery rhyme is unknown, but either way the name has been used as that of a fool in English since the mid-eighteenth century.

10. WISE MEN OF GOTHAM

They might sound like a band of Batman's companions but *the wise men of Gotham* are nothing of the sort. *Gothamites* or *Gothamists* are proverbial fools and this phrase – as well as several others along similar lines referring to a group of nincompoops – derives from an English village named Gotham whose inhabitants for some long-forgotten reason have been associated with foolishness and slow-wittedness in English folklore since the fifteenth century. Precisely where this proverbially foolish Gotham is, however, is unclear. The most obvious contender is the village of Gotham in Nottinghamshire, but a nineteenth-century *Slang Dictionary of the Turf* claims instead that it was 'Gotham-hall' in Essex, some of whose inhabitants were even immortalized in an old children's song: 'Three wise men of Gotham / went to sea in a bowl; / If their bowl had been stronger, / My song would have been longer.' Confusing things further, over time the name *Gotham* came to be applied to various other towns and cities across England that were apparently the butt of similar jokes, including Newcastle upon Tyne where the name soon lost its negative connotations and became simply a nickname for the city itself; a local folksong called 'Kiver Awa' proclaims, 'Heav'n prosper thee, Gotham! thou famous old town, / Of the Tyne the chief glory and pride.' Written in 1804, *Kiver Awa'* predates the first record of New York City being called Gotham by three years, apparently making Newcastle the original Gotham City.

XXVIII

TEN CHARACTERS AND CHARACTERISTICS

From old women to handsome young men, and from baldness to freckles to bad breath, the ten phrases listed here are all synonyms and euphemisms for different types of people, and different physical characteristics and traits. Although many of these are flippant slang expressions that fall short of being fully acknowledged in the language, that is not to say that they are any less interesting than any of the other entries, as the intriguing stories behind phrases like the ATHANASIAN WENCH and the MARQUIS OF GRANBY quickly prove.

1. APE LEADER (IN HELL)

Since Tudor times references have been made in English to 'old maids' and unmarried women 'leading apes in Hell', a tiresome task considered the eternal punishment of women who die having chosen not to have children – or as one Victorian dictionary put it, 'for neglecting to increase and multiply'. Where this peculiar punishment comes from is unknown, but by the eighteenth century the image of an *ape leader* had become an odd slang name for any unmarried woman, and especially one whose younger sister had married before her and so, by Georgian standards at least, seemed destined to a life alone.

2. ATHANASIAN WENCH

St Athanasius of Alexandria was a fourth-century theologian known for writing (or at least inspiring) an ancient Christian declaration known as the Athanasian Creed. In its original Latin, the forty-four-line Creed opens *Quicunque vult salvus esse, ante omnia opus est, ut teneat catholicam fidem,* roughly meaning 'Whoever wants to be saved must, before all else, keep the Catholic faith'. No doubt much to the horror of the Christian scholars who abided by it (as well as to St Athanasius himself) in the eighteenth and nineteenth centuries the opening words of the Creed, 'whoever wants to', were taken entirely out of context and inspired an old slang term for a promiscuous woman – or as one nineteenth-century *Dictionary of the Vulgar Tongue* defined it, an *Athanasian wench* was 'a forward girl, ready to oblige every man that shall ask her'.

3. CHRISTENED BY A BAKER

Saying that someone appears to have been *christened by a baker* is an old eighteenth- and nineteenth-century way of saying that they have freckles, the brown spots on their white skin apparently looking like the brown flecks of bran in the baker's flour or bread. Saying that someone appears to have been *christened in the pump water,* meanwhile, is an even older reference to a person's flushed complexion dating back to the seventeenth century when pump water would often be so shockingly cold that it would flush a person's skin bright pink.

4. DELO NAMMOW

Delo nammow is a nineteenth-century example of so-called 'back slang', a method of forming new and inventive slang expressions that originated among stallholders in Victorian

London, in which the letters of a word or the words of a phrase are reversed; a *delo nammow* ultimately is an 'old woman'. An 'old man' likewise would be a *delo nam*, while an 'old maid' was a *delo diam*. Back slang did not stop there, however, as it was used for everything from the names of numbers (*exxes*, 'six'; *neves*, 'seven') to foods (*kayrop*, *'pork'*; *retsio*, 'oyster'), drinks (*reeb*, 'beer'; *yardnarb*, 'brandy'), coinage (*yenep*, 'penny'; *flatch yenep*, 'halfpenny') and other everyday objects (*eefink*, 'knife'; *sresworts*, 'trousers'; *esclop* 'police'), as well as full-blown phrases like *eevach a kool*, to 'have a look', and *pew the elop*, a reversal of 'up the pole', a slang phrase meaning 'pregnant'.

5. DUKE OF LIMBS

Duke of Limbs is a nickname for a tall person, invented in the 1700s as a humorous 'title' bestowed on any particularly lanky or gangly man. Two similar nicknames, *Jack of Legs* and *Long Meg* – referring to any noticeably tall man or woman respectively – each derive from characters from English folklore. The Robin Hood-like Jack O'Legs was a legendary giant whose tale of stealing flour from wealthy millers to give out to the poor dates from the thirteenth century, while Long Meg of Westminster was a London woman so strikingly tall that she apparently managed to pass herself off as a man, enlisted in the English Army, and fought against France and Italy in clashes across Europe in the mid-1500s.

6. A DYING DUCK IN A THUNDERSTORM

Dating from the late 1700s, someone said to look like *a duck in thunder* or *a dying duck in a thunderstorm* appears utterly hopeless or depressed, with their eyes glumly rolled back – the same miserable expression supposedly shown by ducks in bad weather. Conversely, a period of heavy rain has been known as *fine weather for ducks* or a *nice day for the ducks* since the early sixteenth century.

7. GENTLEMAN OF THE THREE OUTS

A *gentleman of the three outs* is a man 'without money, without wit, and without manners'. Dating from the late eighteenth century, this popular expression went on to inspire a host of later versions that are just as inventive, and just as desperate. A *gentleman of the four outs* for instance was all three of the above, as well as 'without credit'. Someone unlucky enough to be *of the five outs* was 'out of money, out of clothes, out at the heels, out at the toes, and out of credit'. And a *gentleman of the three ins* was 'in debt, in danger, and in poverty', or else 'in jail, indicted, and in danger of being hanged'.

8. LEAVE-YER-OMER

To lower-class women in Victorian England, a *leave-yer-omer* was a dashing young man – someone you would literally 'leave your home for'. A beautiful young woman, meanwhile, might be called *white magic*, in the sense of something able to bewitch a man, or else a *bit o' jam* or a *bit of raspberry*, both derived from the London rhyming slang 'jam tart', meaning 'sweetheart'. Similarly a *treacle-man* was a good-looking young man either employed as a door-to-door salesman and able to charm the lady of the house into buying his wares, or a particularly handsome member of a criminal gang who would use his looks to beguile the housekeeper while the rest of his gang sneaked inside. And a *masterpiece of nightwork* was an especially handsome or beautiful criminal or 'unfortunate' on the streets of nineteenth-century London.

9. LEND US YOUR BREATH TO KILL JUMBO

The word *jumbo* has been applied to any oversized or unwieldy person in English since the early nineteenth century, but it is only since the late 1800s that the term has become much better established thanks to its use as the name of an enormous elephant housed at London Zoo from 1865 to 1881. Born in what is now Mali sometime in the early 1860s, Jumbo reportedly weighed more than 5,000 kg and stood almost 4 m (13 ft) tall. Unsurprisingly he proved to be an equally enormous attraction at London Zoo, until he was sold for $10,000 (equivalent to more than $200,000 today) to the American showman P. T. Barnum in November 1881. *Lend us your breath to kill Jumbo* was a popular London catchphrase of the time used to draw attention to someone's terrible breath.

10. MARQUIS OF GRANBY

It might sound like some kind of ostentatious compliment, but calling or comparing a man to the *Marquis of Granby* is in fact an early-nineteenth-century means of pointing out his baldness. The nickname derives from the real Marquis of Granby, John Manners, who served as a lieutenant general of the British Army during the Seven Years' War. According to legend, the marquis gallantly led a British cavalry charge against French troops at the Battle of Warburg in Germany in 1760 but lost his hat and his wig in the process. Undeterred, he fought on bald-headed and helped lead a union of British and Hanoverian troops to victory.

XXIX

TEN PHRASES DERIVED FROM REAL PEOPLE

Unlike those referring to gods, goddesses and various characters from folklore and literature, the ten phrases listed here all make reference to some real-life famous (or infamous) figure. This short list alone ranges from Ancient Rome through the Elizabethan era to the golden age of Hollywood, and includes as diverse a bunch of characters as an Archbishop of Canterbury, a seventeenth-century schoolteacher, a murder victim, an Irish field marshal, a Georgian actor and an infectious cook.

1. ACCORDING TO COCKER

Like ACCORDING TO HOYLE, something done *according to Cocker* is done correctly and appropriately, or in accordance with the basic rules. The phrase dates from the late eighteenth century but refers back to a seventeenth-century British engraver and schoolmaster named Edward Cocker, who spent much of the final years of his life compiling a vast mathematical textbook known as his *Arithmetick*. Cocker was published posthumously in 1677 so sadly did not live to see how hugely popular and influential his textbook became, thanks to his innovative use of real-life mathematical problems that schoolchildren found easy to relate to. One typical question asks, 'I demand how many furlongs, poles, inches and barley-corns will reach from

London to York, it being accounted 151 miles.' The book ran to more than one hundred editions, and from its publication was used all across Britain as the standard textbook for arithmetic teaching right up to the early 1800s.

2. ALL SIR GARNET

Field Marshal Garnet Wolseley was an Irish-born Commander-in-Chief of the British Armed Forces and one of the most respected and experienced British Army leaders of the nineteenth century. Born in Dublin in 1833, his fifty-year military career began when he was just eighteen years old and went on to include service in almost every corner of the world, from the Siege of Sevastopol to the Indian Mutiny; from the Opium Wars with China to Canada's Red River Rebellion; and from campaigns in Ghana, Sudan and Egypt to the Anglo–Zulu War of 1879. Wolseley's impeccable military record and his reputation for absolute efficiency led to anything in perfect order being known as *all Sir Garnet* from the late nineteenth century onwards.

3. *To* BREAK PRISCIAN'S HEAD

Priscian was a sixth-century Roman grammarian who is celebrated among Latin scholars for his *Institutiones Grammaticae*, a vast explanatory textbook of the language that was widely used by students throughout the Middle Ages. The expression *to break* or *scratch Priscian's head* is almost as obscure and as rarely encountered today as Priscian's work, but from the sixteenth century onwards it remained a familiar way of referring to making a grammatical error.

4. *To* DINE WITH DUKE HUMPHREY

The Elizabethan expression *to dine with Duke Humphrey*

means not to dine at all; it means to go without food entirely, either by fasting or dieting, or through a total lack of money or means. The Duke Humphrey in question is Humphrey of Lancaster, Duke of Gloucester, youngest son of Henry IV and the youngest brother of Henry V. On his death in 1447, Humphrey was buried in St Albans Cathedral, but that did not stop Londoners mistakenly believing his tomb to lie in St Paul's Cathedral (not that which stands today, but the Old St Paul's destroyed by the Great Fire of 1666) beneath a monument that was actually dedicated to Sir John Beauchamp, a fourteenth-century knight of Edward III. Regardless, the aisle in front of Beauchamp's monument became known as 'Duke Humphrey's Walk' and according to different accounts of the story was either frequented by thieves and beggars or by fasting clerics, who would pace up and down it in contemplation while others ate their meals. Phrases like *to dine with Duke Humphrey*, *to have Duke Humphrey as your host* and even *to eat Duke Humphrey's picnic* from the sixteenth century onwards all came to refer to going without food.

5. *The* FULL MONTY

Other than that it appears to have originated in the north of England in the mid-to-late 1900s, the origin of *the full monty*, meaning 'the whole thing', remains a complete mystery. Different accounts of its history range from the British Army leader Field Marshal Montgomery to a gambler's or card player's 'full monte', but perhaps the most likely explanation is that it refers to the English retail entrepreneur Sir Montague Burton who founded the gents' clothing chain Burton in 1904. Ironically for a phrase which – thanks to the success of Peter Cattaneo's

1997 film – is forever associated with taking clothes off, the original *full Monty* is presumed to have been a full three-piece suit, comprising trousers, jacket and waistcoat.

6. *To be* IN LIKE FLYNN

In the 1940s and 1950s *to be in like Flynn* meant 'to be immediately or easily successful', particularly with reference to impressing someone of the opposite sex. Although the true origin of the phrase is debatable, the most likely explanation is that the eponymous *Flynn* is Errol Flynn, the Australian-born film star who became famous in the mid-1900s for his lead roles in films like *Captain Blood* (1935), *The Adventures of Robin Hood* (1938) and *The Private Lives of Elizabeth and Essex* (1939). Off screen, Flynn gained a notorious and long-lasting reputation as a heavy drinker and womanizer which, coupled with his on-screen persona, is the likely origin of *in like Flynn.* The phrase remained in use mainly in American and Australian slang until as recently as the 1970s and 80s, several years after Flynn's sudden death in 1959.

7. *To see the* JOE MILLER

Joe Miller was a popular eighteenth-century English theatrical actor who appeared on the London stage from 1709 right up to his death in 1738. Although he acted in a variety of different roles, Miller was best known as a comedian and ultimately gave his name to a posthumous collection of jokes and anecdotes, *Joe Miller's Jests,* published in 1739. To a modern audience Miller's 'jests' might not seem up to much ('A lady being asked how she liked a gentleman's singing, who had a very stinking breath, the words are good, said she, but the air is intolerable') but the book nevertheless proved hugely popular in its time, to the extent that a *Joe Miller* or *Joe Millerism* became a common slang term for a joke in eighteenth- and nineteenth-century England. Likewise, *seeing* (or *not seeing*) *the Joe Miller* meant 'to see the joke' or 'funny side' of something.

8. MORTON'S FORK

John Morton was Archbishop of Canterbury under Henry VII from 1486 until his death in 1500. During this time he was put in charge of national taxation and began raising cash to fund Henry's Royal Army by imposing a series of harshly enforced loans nationwide. According to popular history, Morton devised a cunning way of assessing a person's wealth by determining that those who seemed to be living lavishly were quite clearly wealthy and so could afford to pay tax, while those seen to be living frugally were presumably saving their money – and so could also afford to pay tax. Whether or not Morton was truly responsible for such a devious rule is questionable, but either way his name soon became attached to any 'no-win' situation; *Morton's fork* refers to a dilemma in which both of two possible options or outcomes are detrimental to those involved.

9. SWEET FANNY ADAMS

On 24 August 1867 an eight-year-old girl named Fanny Adams was walking with two friends in Alton, Hampshire, when she was abducted by a local solicitor's clerk named Frederick Baker who carried her to a nearby field, murdered her and horrifically butchered her body. Baker – who wrote in his diary for the day, 'killed a young girl. It was fine and hot' – was arrested that evening and within a matter of months had been found guilty and executed.

Understandably the crime horrified Victorian England and, as the full grotesque details of the murder appeared in the press, the case soon became known all across the country. As time went on, however, Adams' death became the butt of a number of grim jokes, most notably among Royal Navy sailors who would joke that the tinned meat in their daily food ration was of such poor quality that it likely contained her butchered remains. Despite its crudeness, the joke soon led the name *Fanny Adams* to be attached to anything of generally poor quality. *Sweet Fanny Adams* or *SFA* is still used to mean 'utter rubbish' or 'nothing at all' today.

10. TYPHOID MARY

A *typhoid Mary* is someone or something found to be the source of an outbreak of infection or disease, or figuratively someone who does not fit in or subverts an otherwise accepted opinion. The original *typhoid Mary* was an Irish-born American immigrant named Mary Mallon who in the early 1900s became the first person known to have brought typhoid fever to the United States from Europe. Mallon herself remained asymptomatic and so never suffered any ill-effects, but she nevertheless infected some fifty people across New York City as she moved from place to place working as a cook. In the days before the exact cause of the disease was known, the only way of addressing Mallon's contagiousness was to quarantine her, and sadly she spent the last twenty-two years of her life, from 1915 to 1938, in hospitalized isolation.

XXX

TEN PHRASES DERIVED FROM HISTORICAL EVENTS

The Watergate affair of 1972 not only changed the history of American politics but introduced a new scandal-coining suffix to the language. Since then journalists have reported on everything from *Billygate* (a scandal involving Jimmy Carter's younger brother Billy) to *Zippergate* (Bill Clinton's affair with White House intern Monica Lewinsky) and even *Gategate* (the debacle following an alleged quarrel between Tory minister Andrew Mitchell and police at the gates of Downing Street in 2013). Ten expressions similarly inspired by real historical events are listed here.

1. THE CACKLING GEESE SAVED ROME

Phrases like *the cackling geese saved Rome, the geese that saved the Capitol* and *the cackling of a goose saved a city* are all used idiomatically in English to refer to an early warning or to someone seen as being overly watchful or prepared; a *cackling goose,* meanwhile, is another name for a saviour or protector. All these expressions derive from an attempted attack on a Roman garrison by a detachment of Gallic troops during the Siege of Rome in 390 BC. According to the tale, the invading Gauls managed to scale Rome's Capitoline Hill unnoticed but, on climbing over the garrison's walls, the first man disturbed a flock of geese whose cackling alerted the Roman troops inside. Marcus Manlius, the general in charge of the garrison, promptly hurled the invader back over the wall and the attack was halted.

2. DON'T BE LIKE THE SADDLER OF BAWTRY

Telling someone not to be *like the saddler of Bawtry* is an eighteenth-century means of telling them to finish their drink. The phrase derives from an old Yorkshire tradition in which criminals sentenced to be hanged at York gallows would stop off on their way there at a nearby tavern for one final drink. According to history, a saddler from the nearby village of Bawtry near Doncaster refused the offer and was taken directly to the gallows. Had he accepted the drink, however, a horseman carrying his last-minute reprieve from a local justice of the peace would have arrived in time to spare his life.

3. *To* EAT CROW

To eat crow is a nineteenth-century American expression meaning 'to be forced to do something humiliating or unpleasant'. Although it is often said that the phrase refers simply to the bad-tasting meat of birds like crows and ravens, one popular tale claims that it derives from a chance meeting between an American and a British soldier during the War of 1812. The British trooper supposedly happened across his American counterpart in a field, where he had been out hunting crows for sport. As the two sides were currently in a short-lived truce, the two men began talking casually and the British solider asked to try out the American's rifle. Predictably, as soon as he handed his gun over the British soldier turned it on the

American and, to humiliate him further, forced him at gunpoint to take a bite out of one of the crows he had shot. A popular addition to the tale, however, claims that as soon as the American was handed back his gun, he quickly turned it on the British soldier and forced him to do exactly the same.

4. HEADS WILL ROLL

Popular history maintains that the expression *heads will roll* – meaning 'those responsible will be punished' – has its origins in the French Revolution and the mass execution of the moneyed aristocracy on the guillotine. The Revolution lasted for ten years from the Storming of the Bastille in 1789 through to Napoleon rising to absolute power in 1799, during which time a staggering number of people were executed. The so-called 'Reign of Terror' alone (1792–93) saw almost 17,000 people guillotined, and the bloody reputation of the Revolution and its 'national razor' no doubt inspired the menacing warning that *heads will roll.* It was not until 1930, however, that the phrase first appeared in print – in an account of a speech given by Adolf Hitler at the trial of three Nazi soldiers who had been accused of plotting a coup and charged with high treason. Speaking in person at Germany's Supreme Court in Leipzig, Hitler rallied to the soldiers' defence and claimed that his Nazi Party had no plans to overthrow Germany's democratically elected government. As the legality of his party was called into question, he added ominously, 'I may assure you, if our movement is victorious . . . heads will roll.'

5. NEWCASTLE PROGRAMME

The Newcastle Programme was a series of political reforms outlined at a meeting of the National Liberal

Federation, an assembly of Liberal Party associations from across Britain, in Newcastle upon Tyne in 1891. The Programme promised an array of developments and improvements, including the introduction of universal male suffrage, employers' liability for industrial accidents, a reform of the House of Lords, shorter parliamentary terms and home rule for Ireland, a cause that Liberal leader William Gladstone had already been championing for some time. The following year the Liberals won the election, relying heavily on the Irish Nationalist vote, and an eighty-two-year-old Gladstone began his record fourth term as Prime Minister. However he soon found his attempts to pass an Irish Home Rule Bill scuppered by the mainly Conservative-controlled House of Lords and, proving that politicians failing to keep election promises is by no means a modern problem, over the years that followed his party failed to implement many of the other reforms that they had promised, and Gladstone eventually stepped down in 1894. In the 1890s and early 1900s the *Newcastle programme* ultimately became a popular satirical name for broken promises, or for a promise that in practice proves impossible to keep.

6. NIGHT OF THE LONG KNIVES

Since the early 1900s, *night of the long knives* has been used metaphorically to refer to any ruthless shake-up or reorganization, especially one involving high-ranking individuals being removed from office. It was famously used to refer to a series of bloody political murders carried out across Nazi Germany on 29–30 June 1934, but the phrase itself was originally coined as far back as 1136 by the English historian Geoffrey of Monmouth, who used it to describe the massacre of a number of native

British chieftains at the hands of Hengist, a Saxon invader, in the fifth century AD. Although several different accounts of the massacre exist (and while some historians doubt it ever took place at all), Monmouth's account claims that Hengist and his brother Horsa arrived from Saxony in the 440s and quickly befriended Vortigern, King of the Britons, who was so impressed by the pair that he granted them their own lands in exchange for their assistance in fighting against the Picts and Gaels. Soon, however, Hengist and Horsa began manipulating Vortigern to increase their influence and eventually revolted against him, claiming the Kingdoms of Kent and Essex as their own. Finally at a banquet on Salisbury Plain celebrating the signing of a peace treaty Hengist and his men slaughtered the unarmed British lords, leaving the country in disarray.

7. NOT A WORD OF PENZANCE

In August 1595, seven years after the Spanish Armada and at the height of the First Anglo–Spanish War, Spain launched a series of devastating attacks against the far south-west of England. The so-called Battle of Cornwall lasted just two days, during which time hundreds of Spanish troops invaded the county's south coast, sinking several English supply ships, burning hundreds of buildings to the ground, and stealing a number of cannon and other important arms. Amid tales of almost all the local Cornish militiamen deserting their posts and fleeing for their lives, the town of Penzance was singled out for its cowardice, having apparently offered no assistance to the nearby village of Mousehole as it was burnt to the ground. Soon *not a word of Penzance* had become a popular expression across southern England referring to someone who offers no help, especially when it is most needed.

8. *To* READ THE RIOT ACT

The Riot Act was an Act of Parliament that came into force across Britain in 1715 and was designed to prevent social disorder and civil unrest. The Act made it illegal for groups of twelve or more individuals, who 'unlawfully, riotously, and tumultuously assemble together', to refuse to disband within an hour of being cautioned. Once a complaint had been made, a local justice of the peace would approach the crowd and read aloud a lengthy proclamation outlined word-for-word in the Act: 'Our Sovereign Lord the King chargeth . . . all persons being assembled immediately to disperse themselves and peaceably to depart'. The group then had one hour to disperse or else be 'guilty of a felony'. As such, *to read the riot act* originally meant precisely that, but by the late 1700s it had come to mean simply 'to reprimand' or 'to become enraged'.

9. *A* WHIFF OF GRAPESHOT

Metaphorically a *whiff of grapeshot* is the smallest amount of force or opposition needed to control a situation or to subdue unrest. The phrase derives from an account by the nineteenth-century Scottish historian Thomas Carlyle of the Battle of 13 Vendémiaire, a clash between Royalist anti-revolutionary forces and French Republican troops on the streets of Paris in 1795. Named after the date in the French Revolutionary calendar on which it took place (equivalent to 5 October), the battle saw the Republicans under the command of then *général* Napoleon Bonaparte quickly quash the uprising after just two hours of fighting despite being outnumbered six to one. The Royalist movement suffered a huge setback, and Napoleon was quickly portrayed as a national hero.

10. *The* WRECK OF THE HESPERUS

Saying that something or someone looks like *the wreck of the Hesperus* has been used since the early 1900s to imply that they appear dishevelled, untidy or utterly worn out. The phrase is taken from the title of an 1840 poem by the American writer Henry Wadsworth Longfellow telling the tale of an arrogant sea captain who takes his daughter out sailing on his ship the *Hesperus.* Despite warnings from his crew that a storm is approaching the captain boasts that his ship can withstand anything – but he is soon proven wrong and the ship is wrecked, killing everyone on board.

Whether or not Longfellow's poem was inspired by a real-life shipwreck has been the subject of debate for decades. One account claims that he wrote it after the sinking of the steamboat *Lexington* off the coast of New England in January 1840, with the loss of all but four of its 143 passengers, while another legend even claims that Longfellow had written the poem already and had been scheduled to travel on the *Lexington* but was delayed in New York and missed it. The true story, however, comes from Longfellow's own journals, in which he wrote of 'news of shipwrecks horrible, on the coast', on 17 December 1837. 'There is a reef called Norman's Woe,' off the coast of Massachusetts, he continued, 'where many of these took place; among others the schooner Hesperus.'

XXXI

TEN PHRASES DERIVED FROM LEGEND AND MYTHOLOGY

The myths of Greece and Rome and other tales from ancient history might seem like an obscure subject, but their characters and events have inspired an array of surprisingly familiar phrases and expressions. Anything arduous or time-consuming might be called a *Herculean task.* A metaphorical 'can of worms' could just as easily be a *Pandora's box.* And anyone particularly successful might be said to have a *Midas touch,* while their one downfall could be their *Achilles heel.*

1. ALTHAEA'S BRAND

Althaea was a queen of Greek legend who was warned by the Fates after the birth of her son Meleager that he would only live as long as an iron brand burning in the fireplace remained intact. Terrified of losing one of her children so quickly, Althaea doused the fire, retrieved the brand and locked it away never to be used, and Meleager grew to be a fine young prince and an exceptional hunter. While out hunting one day, Meleager slayed an enormous boar and gave its skin to his lover, Atalanta, as a gift. His brothers and uncles were appalled that such a prized trophy should be given to a woman and when a bitter quarrel broke out among them Meleager flew into a violent rage and killed them all. Althaea was horrified to discover what her son had done, and on hearing the news took the brand from its hiding place and threw it onto the fire, killing Meleager and finally fulfilling the Fates' prophecy. *Althaea's brand* has since become synonymous with any problem or issue that, although temporarily put aside, will eventually come into effect and have to be addressed.

2. APPLE OF DISCORD

An *apple of discord* is anything that causes upset among friends or colleagues. First recorded in English in the sixteenth century, the phrase derives from the tale of a lavish wedding banquet thrown by Zeus to which all the gods and goddesses of Greece were invited except for the goddess of chaos and discord, Eris, whom Zeus feared would cause trouble among the guests. When she found that she had been excluded, Eris stormed into the banquet hall and threw an apple onto the table bearing the Greek word *kallisti*, 'for the fairest'. Hera, Athena and Aphrodite each presumed themselves to be the fairest at the table and, each claiming the apple as their own, immediately began a lengthy and bitter squabble that even Zeus was unable to resolve.

3. BETWEEN SCYLLA AND CHARYBDIS

In Homer's *Odyssey*, the hero Odysseus is forced to sail his ship through a narrow sea strait on one side of which stands a giant sea monster called *Scylla* and on the other an enormous whirlpool named *Charybdis*. In attempting to avoid one danger the ship would be forced towards the other, making any safe passage between the two impossible. Odysseus eventually risks sailing past Scylla, deciding that sacrificing a few crew members to the monster is relatively more favourable than risking the loss of the entire ship. His terrible predicament soon led *Scylla and Charybdis* to enter the language as simply another variation of the *rock and a hard place* or DEVIL AND THE DEEP BLUE SEA idiom, referring to an impossible choice between two equally unpleasant alternatives.

4. GORDIAN KNOT

According to legend, Gordius was a king of Phrygia, an ancient kingdom now located in central Turkey. Born a peasant, he was chosen as king by an oracle who declared that the next person to ride an ox-cart into the city of Telmessos would become king. As a symbol of his gratitude, Gordius had his ox-cart tied to a post in a temple using an intricate and apparently utterly undoable knot, and there it remained for hundreds of years until Alexander the Great arrived in the city in the fourth century BC. Alexander was told that whoever was able to loosen the knot would come to rule all Asia; he promptly sliced it in half with his sword. The image of the *Gordian knot* has been synonymous with anything impossibly complex since the fourteenth century in English, whilst *cutting the Gordian knot* has come to imply solving a problem by force rather than following the usual rules or conditions.

5. IXION'S WHEEL

Anything said to be like *Ixion's wheel* is a continual or recurring torment, or a proverbial 'vicious circle'. It is named after a legendary king of Thessaly called Ixion, who is infamous in Greek mythology for being the first human to kill a member of his family. According to one account, when Ixion's father-in-law came to collect a payment he had promised on marrying his daughter, Ixion threw him into a pit of burning leaves. Horrified by what he had done, Ixion fled into exile but was rescued by Zeus, who took pity on him and offered him the chance to dine with the gods on Mount Olympus. Instead of being grateful, however, Ixion used the meal to try and seduce Zeus's consort, Hera, for which Zeus banished him to Tartarus, a torturous dungeon in the Greek Underworld reserved only for those guilty of the worst crimes. There, Ixion was tied forever to a burning and revolving wheel as punishment.

6. NO STONE UNTURNED

Dating from the mid-1500s in English, *to leave no stone unturned* means 'to do everything possible', usually in order to find or recover something. It is popularly said to derive from the tale of an ancient king of Samos named Polycrates, who helped the Greeks to defeat Xerxes and his Persian Empire in battle in 479 BC. On realizing that the battle was lost, one of Xerxes' generals, Mandonius, buried a hoard of treasure on the battlefield, which Polycrates was determined to retrieve. He purchased the field and began digging, but after several weeks had still found nothing. In desperation, he turned to the Oracle at Delphi, who advised him simply to 'turn every stone' – the more systematic approach eventually proved successful and Polycrates unearthed the general's treasure.

7. OEDIPUS COMPLEX

The term *Oedipus complex* was coined by Sigmund Freud in the late 1800s. It refers to the subconscious attraction a young boy or man feels towards his mother, and his opposing subconscious desire to exclude his father; although Freud originally intended the term to be used of both male and female children, the equivalent female term – describing a daughter's attraction towards her father and her hostility towards her mother – is usually called the *Electra complex.* Either way, both terms derive from characters in Greek mythology: the tragic hero Oedipus, having been abandoned as a child, unwittingly returned to his homeland of Thebes and happened to kill his father in an argument before unknowingly marrying his mother, Jocasta. Likewise, Electra was the daughter of Agamemnon and Clytemnestra, rulers of Mycenae, but when Clytemnestra had her husband killed so that she could marry her lover Aegisthus, Electra and her brother Orestes murdered them both.

8. PROCRUSTEAN BED

Used in English since the eighteenth century, the unusual expression *Procrustean bed* describes anything that brutally enforces bland consistency in something that would otherwise be diverse. It derives from the story of Procrustes, one of the sons of the Greek sea god Poseidon, who was also a robber and a serial murderer. He lived on one of the main roads leading out of Athens, where he owned a guesthouse used by weary passers-by on their way out of the city. Once inside, however, Procrustes (whose name literally means 'he who stretches') would strap his unwitting guests to an iron bed; anyone deemed too short for it would be broken, beaten and wrenched until they fit, while those too tall would literally be cut down to size. Procrustes' crimes were eventually uncovered by the Greek hero Theseus, who killed him by 'fitting' him into his own gruesome bed.

9. RHADAMANTHINE JUDGE

In Greek mythology, Rhadamanthus was a son of Zeus who was renowned as a lawmaker and a strictly principled judge. After his death he is said to have been sent to the paradise of the Elysian Fields, from where he was selected to become one of the three judges of souls entering the Underworld. The earliest references to Rhadamanthus in English date from the sixteenth century when his name was used as a byword for any equally stern ruler or master, while a *Rhadamanthine judge* is one who is utterly incorruptible and uncompromising.

10. SISYPHEAN TASK

The adjective *Sisyphean* has been used in English since the seventeenth century to describe anything unrewarding or unrelenting, while a *Sisyphean task* is simply another name for a fruitless yet unending chore. Both terms derive from the Ancient Greek legend of Sisyphus, a king of Corinth whose life was marked by his constant deceitfulness and greed. He would routinely rob and even murder guests to his home, and spent much of his life trying to usurp his brother and rival king Salmoneus, even seducing his own niece in an attempt to father a purebred son to dethrone him. Eventually, Zeus heard of Sisyphus's terrible acts and demanded that he be chained up in the Underworld by Thanatos, the Greek equivalent of Death; but even then Sisyphus first tricked Death into testing out his chains on himself and then fled, leaving Thanatos imprisoned in his own jail. For all of his crimes, Sisyphus was finally sentenced to the torturous realm of Tartarus, where he was told he could only guarantee his release by rolling an immense boulder to the top of a hill. Before his task could be completed the boulder would always slip from his grasp or, once at the top, would tumble down the opposite side of the hill, leaving him to toil forever without reward.

XXXII

TEN PHRASES DERIVED FROM WEAPONS AND THE MILITARY

Military terminology is a particularly fruitful field for the invention of new phrases and expressions, with the last century alone giving us *friendly fire* (1918), *reaction force* (1923), *regime change* (1925), *precision bombing* (1934), *ground zero* (1946), *staging post* (1952), *brinkmanship* (1956), *deep-cover* (1963) and *situation room* (1967). The first *weapon of mass destruction*, meanwhile, was described in an article in *The Times* as early as 1937.

1. BASKET CASE

In modern English, a *basket case* is someone incapable of functioning in a certain situation, often simply through nervousness or stress. In this metaphorical sense the expression dates from the mid-1960s, but on its first appearance in the 1910s it bore a much darker meaning when a *basket case* was a horrifically wounded soldier who had lost all his limbs in battle and so had to be carried on a stretcher. In this context, *basket case* was originally coined by troops serving in the First World War.

2. *To* BITE THE BULLET

Biting the bullet, thereby accepting or enduring an unpleasant task, is usually said to refer to a practice once common in military field hospitals of giving an injured soldier a bullet to bite down on while some grisly medical procedure was carried out without anaesthesia. While it is true that in the absence of painkillers everything from leather straps to wooden spoons were once placed in patients' mouths in an attempt to stifle their cries, the use of something as hazardously small (and relatively soft) as a bullet seems unlikely. However, as an eighteenth-century *Dictionary of the Vulgar Tongue* confirms, 'It is a point of honour in some regiments . . . never to cry out . . . whilst under the discipline of the cat of nine tails, to avoid which, they chew a bullet.'

3. *To* BURN YOUR BOATS

To burn your boats means 'to ruin any chance of going back' or 'to reach the point of no return'. It derives from an ancient military tactic in which the leader of an invading force, having arrived by sea in some new or hostile land, would immediately demand that his forces destroy their own ships. Doing so would cut off any chance of them returning home, thereby motivating them to continue their campaign and spur them on to victory in any ensuing battles. As odd a tactic as this might seem, it is not without precedent and is known to have been used by the Spanish conquistador Hernán Cortés during the conquest of Mexico in the early 1500s.

4. FIELD DAY

Field day dates back to the mid-1700s in English, when the term was originally used purely in military contexts to refer to a date on which troops would take part in field exercises or other outdoor manoeuvres. This exclusively military meaning lasted long into the nineteenth century, when the term began to be used more loosely of any event that takes place out of doors, including a hunting party (1770s), an athletics tournament or sports day (1820s) and a scientific field study (1820s), until finally in the mid-1800s *field day* came to refer simply to any enjoyable or exciting activity.

5. *To be* HOISTED BY YOUR OWN PETARD

A *petard* is a rudimentary explosive device, little more than a small box filled with gunpowder, that would once have been used to blast open a hole in a wall or gateway. As such devices tended to be fairly unpredictable, soldiers being blown up by their own bombs was by no means unheard of and so being *hoisted by their own petard* – a Shakespearean invention first used in *Hamlet* (III. iv) – came to mean 'becoming the victim of your own malicious intentions'. The word *petard* itself was borrowed into English from French in the sixteenth century and, in the sense of a small explosion, is descended from an old French word, *pet,* meaning 'fart'.

6. LIKE WOOD, LIKE ARROWS

Like wood, like arrows was a seventeenth-century English proverb implying that children tend to take after their parents. The implication here is that no matter how skilled an archer may be an arrow can only ever be expected to be as good as the wood from which it is made, and likewise children from an unruly household cannot be expected to behave any better than the rest of their family.

7. RANK AND FILE

The phrase *rank and file* has been used to describe an orderly line-by-line arrangement of something since the seventeenth century, and the ordinary members (as opposed to the leaders) of an organization or group since the early nineteenth century. Originally, however, it was a military expression, referring to the orderly lines into which soldiers are made to stand during drills and exercises, in which case it dates back as far as the late 1500s.

8. *To* SHOOT YOUR BOLT

If you have *shot your bolt* then you are said to have used up all your available resources too quickly, often with the added implication that they cannot be easily replaced; a thirteenth-century English proverb similarly warned that *a fool's bolt is soon shot.* In both of these contexts – and several others like it – a *bolt* is another name for an arrow, and in particular the arrow shot from a crossbow, which once used in the heat of battle cannot be recovered. Likewise *bolt upright,* literally meaning 'straight as an arrow', dates from the fourteenth century.

9. THROUGH THE GRAPEVINE

To hear something *on* or *through the grapevine* has meant 'to hear something unofficially' or 'through gossip' since the American Civil War era in the mid-1800s. The *grapevine* in question was originally the so-called 'grapevine telegraph', a type of communications cable that would once have been strung from tree to tree across a battlefield like a vine, so that information and intelligence could be passed from the front line back to those in command more quickly than in person. The cables were often of such poor quality that the messages became distorted and confused, and so hearing something *through the grapevine* became especially synonymous with hearing something unreliably.

10. UNDER WHICH KING, BEZONIAN?

Bezonian is a long-forgotten word for a new military recruit that is derived from the Italian word for 'need', *bisogno,* implying that an inexperienced soldier would require almost constant assistance or advice. The equally obscure expression *under which king, bezonian?* is a quote from Shakespeare's *Henry IV: Part 2* (V. iii), in which it is used as a challenge to an unfamiliar soldier to quickly reveal which of the play's two warring kings he supports. Since then, it has come to be used more loosely in English as a means of pushing someone to make a selection between two or more options.

XXXIII

TEN PHRASES DERIVED FROM THE NAVY

Like the military, the language of the Navy and of ships and sailing in general is a particularly fertile field for English expressions thanks to its lengthy history, its rich vocabulary and even richer slang. In fact the seafaring contribution to the language is so great that it is often wrongly touted as the origin of words and phrases whose true histories lie elsewhere. TO LET THE CAT OUT OF THE BAG, for instance, does *not* refer to a sailor unleashing the cat-o'-nine-tails. The first *posh* people were *not* ocean-liner passengers who had *p*ortside cabins on the *o*utward journey and *s*tarboard on the *h*omeward journey. SQUARE MEALS have nothing to do with the specialized square trays once used by the Royal Navy. And, despite being a brilliantly imaginative explanation, a pregnant woman going into labour after being shocked by cannon fire at sea would *not* give birth to a *son of a gun.*

1. *To the* BITTER END

To the bitter end has been used to mean 'to the extreme' or 'to the very end of a lengthy process' since the mid-nineteenth century. Popular opinion sometimes claims that *bitter* here means 'acrid' or 'unpleasant', in the sense that after a long and drawn-out procedure *the bitter end* is a fairly unpleasant place to be, but the phrase actually refers to a stump or post on the deck of a ship known as a *bitt,* around which loose ropes and chains would be wound when not in use. The *bitter* was the end of a rope that remained permanently fastened around the bitt, and so if a rope were unravelled *to the bitter end* then it had reached its full length.

2. BY AND LARGE

In nautical contexts the words *by* and *large* have far more precise meanings than they do in everyday English. *By* essentially means 'in the direction of the wind', and so a ship said to be sailing *by the wind* is heading straight into it. *Large,* conversely, means that the wind is blowing from behind the ship's current direction. Put together, *by and large* literally meant 'in all conditions', regardless of the direction of the wind. From here, the phrase slipped into common use in the early eighteenth century and has been used ever since to mean 'anyhow' or 'in general'.

3. CLEAN BILL OF HEALTH

The earliest reference to a *bill of health* in English dates from the early seventeenth century, when the term originally described an official certificate given to any ship that had stopped in a place where the crew were liable to pick up some kind of communicable disease. A *clean bill of health* would be issued if there were no signs of disease on board; the opposite was a *foul bill of health;* and a *suspected bill of health* warned that although no sign of disease had been spotted among the crew, it was possible that one might develop later. Whatever the result, the ship's captain would be made to show the most recent *bill of health* when entering any subsequent port on their journey. By the nineteenth century, having a *clean bill of health* had come to refer to anyone in fine condition or with an unblemished record.

4. *To* CUT AND RUN

In English slang, *to cut and run* has been used to mean 'to make a quick escape' since the early 1800s, but the phrase itself dates back to the early 1700s (if not earlier) when it was originally used to refer to a ship needing to leave its mooring or exit port hastily. In such cases, the crew would have had no alternative but literally to *cut* the ship's anchor loose rather than go through the lengthy and arduous task of hauling it up from the seabed, and *run*, 'to set sail ahead of the wind'.

5. *The* CUT OF YOUR JIB

A *jib* is a small triangular sail set between the foremost mast of a ship and the *jib-boom*, a long bar projecting forward from the ship's prow. Among sailors, it was widely known that different cultures and nationalities had their own different shape and style of jib and, as it was always positioned alone at the front of a ship, it could very quickly be used to identify her origin or nationality. By the nineteenth century, noticing *the cut* (i.e. appearance) *of someone's jib* ultimately became a popular expression referring to a person's general appearance or character.

6. *A* DIFFERENT TACK

Expressions like *to be on the right* (or *wrong*) *tack*, meaning 'to have the right (or wrong) purpose', and *to change tack*, meaning 'to try a different approach', all derive from a sixteenth-century nautical term for a rope or chain used to secure the corners of a sail in place. This *tack* would often have to be altered depending on the direction of the wind or the ship, and so *to change tack* and *to use a different tack* both came to refer to any general change of approach or course of action.

7. FLOTSAM AND JETSAM

Individually, *flotsam* and *jetsam* are two clearly defined terms from maritime law. *Flotsam*, which dates from the early 1600s, is descended from the same root as *float* and so refers to the debris of a ship or its cargo that can be seen floating on the surface of the sea after a shipwreck. *Jetsam* dates from the late 1400s and, as a corruption of *jettison*, refers to anything intentionally thrown from a ship in order to lighten its load. Despite their differences of meaning, the two terms have become so well associated with one another that *flotsam and jetsam* has been used loosely to mean 'odds and ends' or 'bits and bobs' since the mid-nineteenth century.

8. PANIC STATIONS

Given that it tends only to be used fairly light-heartedly or ironically today, it might be surprising to find that *panic stations* was originally a genuine command in the Royal Navy which, when declared in an emergency, ordered all members of a ship's crew to remain on high alert; of identical origin is *action stations*, which ordered the crew to be prepared to do battle. In this context, both *panic stations* and *action stations* date from as recently as the early 1900s and were first used during the First World War.

9. *To* SHOW A LEG

To show a leg has been used to mean 'to get out of bed' or simply 'to make an appearance' since the mid-nineteenth century. It is often claimed to date back to a time when sailors were permitted to bring their wives or girlfriends on long voyages, who would typically remain in bed while their husbands or partners were busy working. If a member of the crew were unaccounted for, the sleeping quarters would be searched and anyone remaining under the covers would be obliged *to show a leg* to prove that there was not a hairy-legged man skiving in bed. As ingenious a story as this is, however, the more likely explanation is that *show a leg* began simply as a wake-up call on board ships, used to rouse the crew from their beds.

10. TRUE COLOURS

To show your true colours has been used to mean 'to show your true character or intentions' since the mid-1500s in English, while *to see someone's true colours* has meant 'to see someone as they truly are' since the early 1600s. In both cases, the *colours* in question are those of the ensign or flag of a particular maritime regiment or country, as in times of warfare a ship wishing to deceive the opposition might cunningly fly their opponent's flag in order to stave off an attack, or else sail close enough to be within fighting range before switching to its *true colours* and launching an assault. Sailing *under false colours*, as it was known, went against the Royal Navy's code of conduct, the Articles of War, but this practice is nevertheless known to have been used by many English ships during the Napoleonic Wars.

XXXIV

TEN PHRASES DERIVED FROM CRIMES AND CRIMINALS

Criminals' slang is one of the richest and most inventive in the whole history of the language. An 1859 American *Rogue's Lexicon*, for instance, includes such terms as *turkey merchants*, 'purchasers of stolen silk'; *rumble the flats*, 'playing cards'; *ambidexter*, 'a lawyer who takes fees from both parties in a suit'; and *stubble your red rag*, 'hold your tongue'. A British dictionary of *Vulgar Words* from 1865, meanwhile, lists such entries as *shivering jemmy*, 'a beggar who deliberately wears little clothing on a cold day', to elicit more sympathy; *moll-tooler*, 'a female pickpocket'; *dead-lurk*, 'to burgle a house while its occupants are at church'; and *scaldrum dodge*, begging after intentionally 'burning the body with a mixture of acids and gunpowder', so as to pass as the unfortunate injured victim of a house fire or battle.

1. *To* ACKNOWLEDGE THE CORN

In nineteenth-century America, *acknowledging the corn* became a popular expression meaning 'to admit to a crime', or more specifically, 'to admit to *part of* a crime' while simultaneously denying any involvement in anything else. Although the origin of the phrase is unclear, popular history suggests that it refers to a court case in the early 1800s in which a thief who had been accused of stealing four horses and a supply of corn to feed them acknowledged stealing the corn, but did not admit to taking the horses: stealing livestock amounted to grand larceny in most American states at the time and was punishable by death.

2. BLUE PIGEON

Dating from the early eighteenth century, *blue pigeon* is an old English nickname for the lead used to construct roofs, alluding to the similarity between the colour of the sheets and the colour of the plumage of birds like wood pigeons and rock doves. The phrase originated in criminals' slang and is the root of a number of similar English sayings and expressions like *to fly the blue pigeon,* meaning 'to steal lead from a roof', and *blue pigeon-flyer,* 'a thief expert in stealing lead', both of which date from the late 1700s.

3. BUCKLEY'S CHANCE

Born in Cheshire in 1780, William Buckley was an English soldier found guilty of possessing stolen goods in London sometime around the turn of the century and sentenced to transportation for a period of fourteen years. Leaving England in 1803, Buckley arrived in Australia several months later where he was immediately given the task of helping to build a new settlement on a narrow spur of land on Port Phillip Bay, opposite what is now Melbourne. The construction soon hit upon a number of problems, most notably a lack of fresh water and poor-quality soil, and it was eventually decided that the entire site should be relocated to Van Diemen's Land (now Tasmania). During the move Buckley and a handful of accomplices took the opportunity to escape and, stealing a rowing boat under cover of darkness, sailed across the bay to the mainland and went their separate ways. What happened to his colleagues is unknown, and after several weeks Buckley was presumed dead. In fact he had stumbled across a group of Aboriginal people whom he quickly befriended, and incredibly remained with them for the next thirty-two years. When he was eventually discovered in 1835, Buckley's remarkable story of fortuitousness and survival made him a national celebrity and to this day *Buckley's chance* is 'a near impossibility' in Australian English, while *to not have a Buckley's* is another way of saying 'to have no chance at all'.

4. *To be* CAUGHT RED-HANDED

The idea that a visibly guilty person has *red hands* dates back as far as the fifteenth century, when it was originally a specific term in Scottish law: a *red-hand* criminal, or one *caught* or *taken with red hand,* was one who had been apprehended with clear evidence of his crime still apparent, whereas a criminal *caught without red hand* did not. Either way, the image is obviously that of a murderer or poacher being caught quite literally with blood on his hands. The earliest reference to someone being *caught red-handed* comes from Sir Walter Scott's classic novel *Ivanhoe* in 1819.

5. COCK LANE GHOST

The story of the *Cock Lane ghost* was one of the most famous scandals of eighteenth-century England, which proved so notorious that the phrase itself slipped into the language as another name for a fraudulent scheme or hoax. Cock Lane is in Smithfield, central London, and it was here in the early 1760s that the haunting was supposed to have taken place. According to reports, a young couple named William and Fanny Kent began renting a room at 25 Cock Lane from a local landlord named Richard Parsons. Soon afterwards, Richard's daughter Betty began to hear odd scratching noises and knocks all around the house and claimed to have seen a ghost. Richard maintained that the ghost must be that of William's deceased first wife, Elizabeth, and blamed his presence in the house for all of the weird occurrences. He evicted the couple and the noises soon subsided, but when Fanny also died just a few weeks later they immediately resumed. A séance was held at which Fanny's ghost confirmed her presence and accused William of poisoning her with arsenic. By now news of the Cock Lane ghost had spread all across London and once the press took hold of the story, scores of people began turning up at the house, queuing for hours out in the street hoping to see any sign of supernatural activity. The suspicion of murder led to a full criminal investigation (by a committee whose members included Dr Samuel Johnson) and after several weeks' inquiry the entire story was revealed to have been concocted by Richard Parsons. His daughter Betty had been making the noises herself, using a small piece of wood sewn into the lining of her clothes, while Richard, it transpired, had borrowed a considerable amount of money from William which he had no means and apparently no intention of repaying. When the two men had finally fallen out, he set about elaborately framing him for his wives' deaths. The Parsons, along with their housemaid who was also in on the scam, were all prosecuted and Richard Parsons was sentenced to two years in prison.

6. HIGHER THAN GILDEROY'S KITE

Higher than Gilderoy's kite is an old English colloquialism meaning 'extremely high' or 'so high as to be barely visible', while *to be hanged higher than Gilderoy's kite* means 'to be punished more severely than anyone else'. The eponymous Gilderoy was a seventeenth-century Scottish robber who operated in Perthshire in the 1620s and 30s. Although much of his life has since become legend, tales abound of Gilderoy's preposterously bold crimes including stories of him robbing Oliver Cromwell and even picking Cardinal Richelieu's pocket in front of the king, and when he and his gang were finally arrested and given a prison sentence they celebrated their release by tracking down the judge who had sentenced them and murdering him. Eventually, Gilderoy was apprehended again and sentenced to death. Scottish law at the time ruled that 'the higher the crime, the higher the gallows' and so Gilderoy was hanged 9 m (30 ft) in the air, where his body was said to have blown around in the breeze like a kite.

7. 'HOW'S THAT?' SAID DUFTON

In the nineteenth century, *'How's that?' said Dufton* was a northern British saying used when some difficulty or setback is unexpectedly encountered. According to folklore, it derives from the story of a local thief named Dufton who was known for stealing grain from silos by boring a hole in the floor and then holding a sack beneath it while the grain poured through. Eventually, one Cumberland miller grew wise to Dufton's trick and fastened sheets of iron across the floor of his mill, and when Dufton found it impossible to drill through, he evidently exclaimed *'How's that?'*.

8. *To* LET THE CAT OUT OF THE BAG

Letting the cat out of the bag apparently derives from an old con once used by dishonest farmers and tradesmen selling pigs at market. Customers coming to market would be able to take a pig home with them in a cloth bag or sack (a PIG IN A POKE) but at the last minute the farmer would secretly swap the pig for a cat. If he were not wise enough to check his purchase there and then, the buyer would be left to return home only to *let the cat out of the bag* and discover that he had been swindled. Whether this practice ever actually took place or not is debatable, but either way *letting the cat out of the bag* has been used to mean 'to reveal a secret' in English since the 1700s.

9. A MISS IS AS GOOD AS A MILE

Implying that missing your target regardless of the margin is still a failure, phrases like *a miss is as good as an ell* (a length of fabric, equal to 45 in/1.15 m) and *an inch of a miss is as good as a span* (the width of a hand) date from the seventeenth century. The only version of the phrase still in use today is *as good as a mile,* which is said to have originated among London criminals in the mid-1700s who joked that if they were being shot at by someone they had just robbed, they would be able to run a mile in the time it would take their victim to reload their gun.

10. *To* THROW OVER THE BRIDGE

Dating from the mid-nineteenth century, *to throw (someone) over the bridge* is an old slang expression meaning 'to double-cross' or 'to betray someone's confidence'. It derives from Victorian criminal slang, and alludes to the image of two men conspiring against a third whom they would overpower and hurl off a bridge. Whether this technique was ever carried out or not is unclear, but by the late 1800s the phrase had slipped into gamblers' jargon to refer to two players ganging up against a third, from where its more general meaning eventually derived.

XXXV

TEN PHRASES DERIVED FROM HUNTING

To be IN THE PINK, meaning 'in good health' or 'good condition', is often said to derive from the scarlet jackets worn by foxhunters that have been known as *pinks* since the late eighteenth century. In fact, *in the pink* dates back to Elizabethan times, while huntsmen's jackets – often also mistakenly claimed to be named after an English tailor named Thomas Pink – simply take their name from their bright red colour. Ten expressions that do derive from hunting are listed here.

1. *To* BARK UP THE WRONG TREE

Barking up the wrong tree dates from 1832 when it first appeared in a work by the American writer James Kirke Paulding. Whether Paulding himself coined the phrase or not is unclear, but it seems certain that it originated in American English before crossing the Atlantic sometime towards the turn of the century. Whatever its origin, *barking up the wrong tree* clearly refers to hunting hounds, having become confused by a scent, barking at the foot of a tree in which they mistakenly think their quarry is hiding.

2. *To* BEAT ABOUT THE BUSH

To beat about the bush is a familiar idiomatic expression meaning 'to stall' or 'procrastinate', concerning yourself with unnecessary details rather than coming straight to the point. It dates from the fifteenth century, when it first appeared in a Middle English poem in which its literal meaning was made clear: 'But as it hath be sayde full long agoo, / Some bete the bush and some the byrdes take'. The *beating* is that of bird-scarers, who would thrash bushes in order to rouse the birds inside into the air, where they would then be caught in the hunters' nets: hence *beating about the bush* was an outlying action that led up to the main event.

3. *To be* HIT UNDER THE WING

Dating from the mid-1800s, someone who has been *hit under the wing* is drunk, often with the implication that they are so drunk that they cannot walk in a straight line. The phrase alludes to the shooting of grouse and other game birds, in which a bird that has been *hit under the wing* – not shot cleanly enough to bring it down immediately – would often continue in an unsteady, meandering flight.

4. *At* ONE FELL SWOOP

In the case of *one fell swoop*, the word *fell* has nothing to do with falling but is an old adjective meaning 'fierce' or 'cruel'. *Swoop* is another form of *stoop*, the swift falling catch of a bird of prey. Altogether, *at one fell swoop* has been used to mean 'all at once' or 'in a single stroke', like the sudden pounce of a falconer's hawk, since the early seventeenth century.

5. OPEN SEASON

In hunting terms, *open season* is an annual period during which all restrictions on hunting a particular species or in a particular area are lifted. The phrase is an American invention dating from the mid-nineteenth century, but by the early 1900s it had gained an unusual figurative meaning in reference to a time when criticism or condemnation of something appears unfairly or ruthlessly unrestricted; in more recent years it is especially used in reference to celebrities or political figures who suddenly find themselves the focus of unwanted or intrusive public attention.

6. *At* RANDOM

Today, doing something *at random* means 'haphazardly' or 'without planning', but originally it meant 'at full speed', and is derived from an Old French word, *rendon*, meaning 'haste' or 'impetuousness'. The term first arrived in English in the fourteenth century, when *at random* appeared both in military contexts, to refer to an individual soldier running at full speed into a group of opponents, and in hunting contexts, to refer to a hawk flying at full speed into a flock of birds. As there was no way of predicting which opponent the soldier would kill, or which bird the falcon would catch, the modern sense of *random* to mean 'haphazardness' or 'aimlessness' ultimately developed in the mid-sixteenth century.

7. RED HERRING

A *red herring* is a dried smoked herring that naturally turns a dark reddish-brown colour as it is cured. In this literal context the term dates back as far as the fourteenth century, but the use of *red herring* to refer to a deliberately misleading clue, or to anything that is intended to distract from a real issue or investigation, dates from as recently as the early 1800s. The connection between the two was long believed to be that criminals escaping from police dogs would drag red herrings along the ground behind them to mask their scent, but there is no evidence to suggest this ever took place. The strong-smelling herrings were, however, used as early as the sixteenth century to lay a fake trail, which was then used to train foxhounds to follow a scent. As the Elizabethan writer Thomas Nashe explained in 1599, 'to draw on hounds to a sent [*sic*], to a redde herring skinne there is nothing comparable'.

8. *To* RUN RINGS AROUND

Running rings around someone has meant 'outwitting' or 'outperforming' since the early nineteenth century; a later American version, *running circles around*, dates from the 1890s. In both cases, the *rings* or *circles* in question are those made by hares, foxes and other equally swift creatures desperately trying to escape a hunter's hounds; if the quarry managed to escape, it would be said to have *run rings around* the dogs.

9. STALKING HORSE

Since the late sixteenth century, the term *stalking horse* has been used to refer to anything used to conceal someone's genuine intentions. It is used particularly in politics, referring to a decoy electoral candidate put forward for no other reason than to instigate an election and give a stronger candidate someone to compete against. The original *stalking horse*, however, was precisely that: in Tudor England, hunters would often conceal themselves behind a specially trained horse that had been taught to approach deer and other characteristically skittish game slowly, allowing them to come within striking distance without disturbing it.

10. STOOL PIGEON

The earliest record of a *stool pigeon* dates from 1812, when it appeared in a *History of Animals: Designed for the Instruction and Amusement of Persons of Both Sexes* written by the American writer (and lexicographer) Noah Webster. In the book, Webster describes how hunters would catch birds using 'a pigeon . . . tied to a moveable stool'. This 'decoy or stool pigeon', he explains, is then 'made to flutter', which would typically attract pigeons and other birds down to a nearby scattering of wheat or grain, where they could then be shot or trapped. Derived from this original hunters' term, by the early 1800s *stool pigeon* had become a popular metaphor in American English for anything or anyone used as a decoy or bait.

XXXVI

TEN PHRASES DERIVED FROM GAMES AND GAMBLING

Card games and similar pastimes are so widely known that a full list of gambling expressions used in everyday English would include such familiar terms as *to be dealt a bad hand, to hedge your bets, to stake a claim, to hit the jackpot, to have the cards stacked against you, to come up trumps, to up the ante, to keep your cards close to your chest* and *to lay your cards on the table.* The intriguing stories behind several equally familiar gamblers' expressions are listed here alongside a handful of much more obscure turns of phrase.

1. ACCORDING TO HOYLE

Like ACCORDING TO COCKER, anything done *according to Hoyle* is done in accordance with the strictest or most authoritative rules. The phrase dates from the mid-eighteenth century and derives from the works of an English writer and scholar named Edmond Hoyle who, in the 1740s and 50s, compiled a number of groundbreaking titles outlining the full rules of a variety of games and pastimes. The earliest of Hoyle's rule books, *A Short Treatise on the Game of Whist,* appeared in 1741 and was quickly followed by titles devoted to backgammon, piquet, brag, chess and even probability theory, all of which soon established his rules as the benchmark for English gameplay. In recognition of his contribution, in 1979 Hoyle became one of the first inductees into America's Poker Hall of Fame, 210 years after his death – and regardless of the fact that poker did not even exist in his lifetime.

2. ACE IN THE HOLE

Like having an *ace up your sleeve*, having an *ace in the hole* is nineteenth-century American slang meaning 'to have a secret advantage'. Both terms clearly have their origins in card games but *an ace in the hole* derives specifically from stud poker, in which each player is dealt a so-called 'hole card' at the start of each hand, which remains face down during play. Their remaining cards are dealt face up and bets are made based purely on the cards that can be seen. If a player unknowingly happens to have an *ace in the hole*, then they clearly have an unseen advantage.

3. *To* BRAG IT OUT WITH A TEN

To brag it out with a card of ten is thought to be an old naval expression dating back to the sixteenth century. In its simplest sense it means merely 'to brag' or 'to boast', but it can also be used much more specifically to refer to someone putting on a brave face in an attempt to cover their doubtfulness, or else entering into a conflict without being confident of the outcome. In either case, it derives from any one of a number of different card games dating from the time in which a ten would have been a valuable card but was by no means enough to guarantee a win. A player would have to *brag it out with a ten*, and hope that with a little luck it would be enough to win the game.

4. CLOSE, BUT NO CIGAR

In nineteenth-century America, cigars were often included among the prizes that players could win at sideshow games and carnivals. Anyone coming close to winning but falling short would literally be close, but not close enough to take home a cigar. Unfortunately, written evidence of the phrase *close, but no cigar* from the time is lacking, but it had nevertheless become an established expression by the 1920s and 30s.

5. *To* DRAW A BLANK

To draw a blank dates from the nineteenth century in English and can variously be used to mean 'to fail', 'to look for unsuccessfully' or 'to be unable to recall'. It alludes to the drawing of blank tickets in a lottery or raffle, which according to some accounts dates back to Tudor England and a series of lotteries organized by Elizabeth I to raise funds for the 'strength of the Realm and towards further public works'. Tickets for the lotteries cost a staggering ten shillings each in 1567, equivalent to more than £80 today, and despite the expense even those contestants whose names were picked out of the 'lot-pot' were still not guaranteed a win: two tickets were drawn simultaneously from two pots, one containing tickets bearing players' names, and the other a mixture of tickets bearing the names of various prizes along with a number of 'blanks'. If your name was drawn with a 'blank', you would win nothing.

6. *To* FOLLOW SUIT

In reference to card games, *following suit* has been used since the seventeenth century in English to refer to a player being obliged to play a card of identical suit to the so-called 'leading card', which establishes the suit used in the remainder of the game. The figurative use of *to follow suit* to mean 'to imitate' or 'emulate what someone else has done' developed in the nineteenth century, and was first recorded in Herman Melville's *Moby-Dick* in 1851.

7. *The* HARD WAY

Doing something *the hard way* is an early 1900s expression used to describe doing something in the most difficult manner possible, often at great expense to oneself or via some lengthy or arduous process. The phrase itself is believed to have originated in the game of craps, a gamblers' dice game that developed in the southern United States in the latter half of the nineteenth century. Although the rules of craps are somewhat complex, in basic terms a player betting on the outcome of two rolled dice *the hard way* means that the only outcome in which they would win would be a pair: so if they bet on 'six the hard way', then they would have to roll a pair of threes, and would lose on any combination of five and one, or two and four; indeed *to roll the hard six* is American slang meaning 'to take a risk'.

8. *To be* LEFT IN THE LURCH

Meaning 'to be left in a difficult position' with little chance of assistance or escape, *to be left in the lurch* dates back as far as the sixteenth century. Popular history often wrongly associates being *left in the lurch* with being 'left in the lych', the gateway at the entrance to a churchyard, and so mistakenly associates the phrase with jilted brides, or even coffins on their way into funerals. In fact *lurch* is the English form of an old French word, *lourche,* the name of a long-forgotten board game thought to have been similar to backgammon. Whatever its rules might have been, it was apparently possible for players of *lourche* to find themselves in some intractable position during play from which it was especially difficult for them to go on and win the game, and it was this impossible situation that originally became known as *the lurch*.

9. MONTE CARLO FALLACY

Also known as *the gambler's fallacy*, or *the maturity of chances* in probability theory, *the Monte Carlo fallacy* is the mistaken belief that a random chain of events is somehow able to influence the probability of events to come. For instance, imagine that someone tossing a coin ten times in a row finds that in all ten cases it lands on tails. This might make it seem that heads is now 'overdue', making it seem more likely to come up next, even though the probability of *either* heads or tails remains exactly the same each time. The same phenomenon describes why some people might feel that they are 'due' good fortune after a string of losses or failures, or conversely that a series of successes or good times somehow increases the likelihood of a misfortune in the future. First described in the 1950s, this fallacy takes its name from an incident at a Monte Carlo casino in 1913 when during a game of roulette the ball landed on black a staggering twenty-six times in a row, leading a number of gamblers to lose vast sums of money under the misconception that red was now somehow more likely to come up.

10. *To* PASS THE BUCK

Passing the buck has been used to mean 'shifting responsibility or blame' in English since the early 1900s. It derives from the counter or *buck* used in a game of poker which is passed from player to player at the start of each hand to indicate whose turn it is to deal; a player wishing to transfer his or her responsibility of dealing to another player would ultimately *pass the buck.* Quite how this counter came to be known as a *buck*, however, is unknown.

XXXVII

TEN PHRASES DERIVED FROM THEATRE AND PERFORMANCE

The stage is the origin of a host of English expressions, including such obvious examples as *curtain call, to be upstaged, to take your cue, to wait in the wings* and *to ham something up.* Bad actors have been known as *hams* since the late 1800s, and although some explanations claim the term derives from 'amateur' or even 'Hamlet', the most likely explanation is that *ham* comes from an earlier American expression, *hamfatter,* which originally referred to an incompetent performer who would overzealously apply too much greasepaint make-up, which at the time was made from a base of pig fat.

1. BLUE FIRE

In Victorian theatres, an explosive mixture of sulphur, copper and potassium compounds was used to produce an eerie blue light on stage known colloquially as *blue fire.* Deeper or darker shades of blue could be produced by increasing the quantity of copper in the mixture, which would then be ignited, usually below stage, so that the light emitted would shine upwards and illuminate a mysterious or supernatural character above. In the days before coloured lighting was readily available in theatres, the astounding effect of *blue fire* became widely known and the phrase soon entered English as another name for anything sensational.

2. CHARLES HIS FRIEND

In theatrical circles *Charles his friend* is a general name for any secondary or relatively unimportant male character in a play. By definition this role is often reduced to merely being the 'friend' or companion of the lead character in a play, and so is required to do little else than feed him lines or give him someone to talk to or play off – like Hamlet's relatively uninteresting companion Horatio. The term itself dates from the early nineteenth century, and apparently derives from the character list or *dramatis personae* of some unknown play, in which a 'Charles, his friend' would have appeared.

3. CLOAK AND DAGGER

In the late 1700s, dramas of intrigue and espionage became so popular in European theatre that the mysterious and often duplicitous characters they featured – typically disguised in capes, and often armed with swords or knives – soon gave their name to the entire genre. Known in French as *de cape et d'épée* stories and in Spanish as *de capa y espada,* these literal 'cloak and sword' stories eventually made their way into English in the early nineteenth century, and within a matter of decades the term had come to refer generally to anything done in a mysterious or clandestine manner.

4. *To* CRACK THE MONICA

As another word for someone's name or signature, *moniker* first appeared in the nineteenth century. Its origin is debatable, with various accounts suggesting that it is an alteration of 'monogram', a combination of 'monogram' and 'signature', or else that it derives from 'monarch', in the sense that a person's name is just as important as the reigning king or queen. Whatever its history, in the late 1800s *moniker* became *monica* in theatrical jargon, and through some equally mysterious development eventually came to refer to a bell in Victorian slang; as a 1909 dictionary of the *Passing English of the Victorian Era* explains, in music halls 'the chairman . . . had before him a table bell, which he sounded after certain ways, one of which informed the audience applauding a singer who had retired that he or she would appear again'. Soon, *to crack the monica* came simply to mean 'to ring the bell' in English slang, before the term vanished from the language sometime around the First World War.

5. HAMLET WITHOUT THE PRINCE

Shakespeare wrote his great masterpiece *Hamlet* sometime around 1600, with the earliest text published in the autumn of 1603. Since then, it has gone on to be recognized as perhaps the greatest English-language play ever written, while its notoriously troubled and multifaceted title character, a young Prince of Denmark who avenges his father's murder, is widely considered the high point of any stage actor's career. A performance of *Hamlet without the Prince* however would be entirely pointless, and so the phrase has been used since the early nineteenth century to refer to any event that goes ahead without its leader or central figure, and often suffers as a consequence.

6. *The* MAN OUTSIDE HOYTS

In Australia in the early 1900s, the original *man outside Hoyts* was Charles Fredricksen, the doorman or *commissionaire* of Hoyts De Luxe Theatre (and later cinema) in the centre of Melbourne. Opened in 1914, Hoyts became one of the city's biggest attractions in the twenties and thirties and made Fredricksen one of its most notable characters. Soon, references to *the man outside Hoyts* began appearing in local slang, and he became a general term for anyone whose name was unknown; he was a proverbial scapegoat, blamed for anything for which the real culprit could not be identified; saying that something came from *the man outside Hoyts* meant that its true origin was a mystery or a secret; and anyone *dressed like the man outside Hoyts* was showily or unnecessarily overdressed for an occasion. The expression remains in use in Australian slang today, while Hoyts has gone on to become one of the country's largest cinema chains.

7. *To* PLAY TO THE GALLERY

Often used today in reference to politicians canvassing for support, someone accused of *playing to the gallery* would be performing or behaving in such a way as to appeal to the widest audience possible. The phrase dates from the mid-nineteenth century and derives from the long-held understanding that different sections of a theatre's audience have different tastes and sensibilities: those sat in the stalls tended to be wealthier and had relatively more sophisticated tastes compared to those sat in the gallery, the theatre's cheapest and uppermost tier, who tended to appreciate bawdier and more raucous material.

8. *To* SEE THE ELEPHANT

In nineteenth-century America, *to have seen the elephant* was a popular idiomatic expression used in a number of different contexts. On its first appearance in the language in the 1830s, it appears to have meant 'to have seen it all' or 'to have seen something extraordinary'. During the California Gold Rush in 1848, *to see* or *seek out the elephant* meant 'to go in search of adventure', but before long *to have seen the elephant* came to mean 'to have experienced life', both good and bad, often with the implication of being disappointed or jaded. Likewise, Civil War soldiers who had served in battle and had experienced the horrors of war first-hand would say that they too had *seen the elephant.* Regardless of its meaning, the phrase likely derived from the circuses and shows that would have travelled across America in the nineteenth century. As an elephant would literally be the show's biggest attraction, it would typically be kept for the finale and so audiences who had *seen the elephant* had not only seen something extraordinary, but had seen everything before it too.

9. *To* STEAL (SOMEONE'S) THUNDER

Stealing someone's thunder is a familiar expression used to refer to 'getting in there first', pilfering or plagiarising another person's ideas, often with the implication of then passing them off as your own. It dates from the late nineteenth century, but has its origins in the early 1700s when a London theatrical writer named John Dennis invented a new method of creating the sound of thunder on stage, which was required for a performance of his new play *Appius and Virginia.* What Dennis's method actually entailed is unknown, but when his poorly received play closed shortly after opening in 1704, he soon heard exactly the same sound being produced nearby in a performance of *Macbeth.* According to some contemporary accounts, Dennis was furious that someone had literally *stolen his thunder* and exclaimed, 'Damn them! They will not let my play run, but they steal my thunder!'

10. WHEN WILL THE GHOST WALK?

In the early nineteenth century, the cast of a particular production of *Hamlet* had apparently not received their wages for several weeks. Soon the situation became so desperate that the actor playing the ghost of Hamlet's father – who, in the play's opening scene, mysteriously appears walking around the grounds of his castle – refused to go on until he and his fellow actors had been paid. The protest brought the production to a halt and it was not until some days later, when all of the outstanding wages had been paid out, that 'the ghost walked' once more. Whether genuine or not, this popular anecdote is nevertheless the origin of a clutch of Victorian theatrical expressions, all referring to receiving a wage – asking *when will the ghost walk?* simply meant asking 'when will we be paid?'

XXXVIII

TEN PHRASES DERIVED FROM SPORTS AND GAMES

Sports and games are a rich source of English phrases and expressions thanks to their widespread familiarity and popularity. For instance, even on its own boxing is the origin of *to fight your corner, below the belt, out for the count, to take it on the chin, to pull* or *roll with the punches, to be on the ropes, to throw in the towel* and *when the gloves are off* – but not TO DROP YOUR GLOVES.

1. ALL OVER BAR THE SHOUTING

All over bar the shouting means 'all but decided' or 'almost over'. Although some explanations suggest that it might originally have derived from accounts of closely fought political battles, arguably the more likely idea is that it refers to the cheering (or jeering) of the winner of a sporting contest or race. In fact its earliest appearance in the language comes from an 1842 edition of *Life Sportsman* magazine, in which it was specifically used to refer to the raucous finish of a horse race.

2. AT THE DROP OF A HAT

Doing something *at the drop of a hat* has meant 'instantaneously' or 'at the slightest provocation' since the early 1800s. Although its true origin is unknown, the phrase is often claimed to derive from the American West in which fights between rivals would be started by some third party literally 'dropping his hat', but there is little evidence to suggest this was the case. A more plausible suggestion is that it alludes to a starter lowering or 'dropping' his hat to signal the start of a race, or else comes from the days of bare-knuckle boxing in which participants would show their readiness to begin by *rolling up their sleeves* and removing their hats. Either way, doing something *at the drop of a hat* seems certain to have a sporting or competitive history.

3. BACK TO SQUARE ONE

Meaning simply 'back to the start', the earliest record of *back to square one* comes from the mid-1950s, although (depending on which explanation is to be believed) it is likely considerably older. The most straightforward idea is that the phrase derives from simple counting games like hopscotch or snakes and ladders. A more complicated (yet no less plausible) explanation is that it comes from radio commentaries of football matches in the days before widespread television coverage. In the absence of footage of the game, BBC radio commentators divided the playing field up into a series of eight rectangles, allowing listeners at home – who would be provided with diagrams of the pitch in the press – to follow the game as the ball was kicked from section to section. This technique is known to have been used as far back as 1927, but unfortunately none of the original recordings of these commentaries uses the phrase *back to square one* to mean 'returning to the beginning' as we would today. Whether they are the origin of the phrase or not is therefore debatable, but it is likely that they at least inspired it.

4. (*Not*) BY A LONG CHALK

To win *by a long chalk* is a nineteenth-century expression meaning 'by some great distance'; conversely *not by a long chalk* essentially means 'by no means', or 'not yet'. In both of these contexts, *chalk* is an old sixteenth–seventeenth-century word for a point scored in indoor games and pub games like darts, skittles and billiards, where players' scores would literally be chalked up on walls or table tops. *A long chalk*, ultimately, was a substantial difference between two players' scores.

5. *To* DROP YOUR GLOVES

To drop your gloves is a fairly recent North American coinage typically used to mean 'to fight' or 'argue'. It might sound like a boxing expression but the phrase derives from ice hockey, in which players routinely become involved in brawls on the ice during play and typically remove their gloves before fighting. The phrase itself dates from the late 1960s, and in more recent years has come to be used more figuratively to mean 'to remove a hindrance', or simply 'to make something easier'.

6. POINT BLANK

Although it is often used more loosely to mean 'at close range', *point blank* specifically refers to the maximum distance at which a projectile can be aimed directly at a target without it falling short, or without the firer having to compensate by adjusting the angle of the shot. The term is believed to be of French origin, in which case the *blank* was probably originally the *blanc* ('white') centre of an archery target; an archer standing at a distance would have to arc his arrow into the air in order to reach it, whereas one standing at *point blank* range could aim squarely at the white bull's-eye to hit it accurately.

7. *To* START FROM SCRATCH

In sporting contexts, *scratch* is an old name for a line drawn onto the ground and used as a marker or boundary for play. The earliest *scratch* in this context dates from as far back as 1778 when it originally referred to the 'crease' behind which a batsman stands in cricket, but by the nineteenth century the term had come to be used much more generally to refer to any starting point or position in an array of different sports and games. The modern use of *to start from scratch* to mean 'from the very beginning' comes from the nineteenth-century popularity of handicap races, in which poorer-quality competitors would deliberately be given a head start or similar advantage over their stronger opponents, who would in turn be deliberately disadvantaged; any player starting from a normal starting position would be said *to start from scratch.*

8. *To* TAKE AN EARLY BATH

Meaning essentially 'to be forced to make a premature departure', the phrase *to take an early bath* (or *an early shower*) is a British sporting euphemism dating from the mid-1940s. Derived originally from football, the phrase is particularly used in reference to players who are dismissed or removed from play before the end of the game, and are left merely to return to the changing rooms for 'an early bath'. In recent years, however, it has come to be used more loosely of anyone or anything who fails to see something through to its conclusion.

9. *To* STEP UP TO THE PLATE

The *plate* in *to step up to the plate* is the home plate of a baseball field, marking the position on the diamond-shaped field on which the batter stands to play; once one batter has had his turn, the next must *step up to the plate* for his. In this original context the phrase dates back to the 1870s, but by the early 1900s it had gained its modern figurative meaning of 'to take action' or 'to take responsibility for something', particularly in times of crisis. *To cover all the bases,* another expression from baseball meaning 'to prepare for every eventuality', dates from the 1940s.

10. *To* WIN HANDS DOWN

The expression *to win with hands down,* meaning 'to win easily' or 'without doubt', is said to derive from horse racing, in which jockeys who were assured of victory in a race would lower their hands, relaxing the reins and allowing their horse to slow down as they approached the finish line. In this sense, the earliest record of *winning hands down* dates from as far back as the 1830s, although it is likely the phrase – and indeed the practice it refers to – is even older than that.

XXXIX

TEN PHRASES DERIVED FROM SCIENCE AND TECHNOLOGY

From algebra to aerodynamics, the ten expressions listed here all have scientific, technological and mathematical origins. Such terms seem rarely to drop into everyday use in English, but the relatively recent development of computing and the Internet is a different story. Alongside a whole new vocabulary of technical jargon like *modem*, *multitask* and *broadband*, modern computing and social media have given the language terms like *dot-com*, *podcast*, *hashtag* and *crowdsourcing*, and have altered the meanings of existing words like *follower*, *firewall*, *bookmark*, *wallpaper*, *troll*, *guestbook*, *surf* and *shoot-'em-up* – used of computer games since the 1980s, but originally coined in the 1950s to refer to formulaic Hollywood Westerns.

1. 404 NOT FOUND

The number 404 is the standard error code returned by an Internet server when it cannot connect to a website; in its place, a *404 not found* error message is displayed on screen. The familiarity of the message among computer users eventually led *404 not found* – or simply *404* – to enter into American slang in the early 2000s as simply another way of saying 'absent' or 'unaccounted for'. Likewise, a webpage said to have been *404ed* has been blocked or taken down.

2. ACID TEST

The term *acid test* has been used figuratively in English since the mid-nineteenth century to refer to any particularly rigorous examination, and especially one used to determine authenticity or value. It has its roots several centuries earlier, however, when chemists and metallurgists first began to use acid to test for the presence of gold and other precious metals. Gold – alongside silver and platinum – is one of the noble metals, and so is naturally resistant to most acids. In an *acid test,* a small sample of material would be taken (often by rubbing a small scratch onto a rough black stone, known as the 'touchstone'), which would then be submerged in nitric acid or any similarly corrosive compound. The acid would destroy the surrounding material leaving only the undamaged gold behind, from which the purity and value of the sample in question could be determined.

3. BLUE MOON

Since the mid-1800s, anything that occurs *once in a blue moon* has been said to occur only occasionally, if ever, as a proverbial *blue moon* is a fanciful name for any rare or unlikely occurrence. In astronomy, however, the term *blue moon* is sometimes used to refer to the second of two full moons that fall within the same month. As its name suggests, this phenomenon is a particularly rare occurrence brought about as a result of our calendar months being slightly longer on average than the twenty-nine-and-a-half days it takes for the moon to pass through one lunar cycle or 'lunation', the period from one new moon to the next. Twelve of these cycles total 354 days, making our year eleven days too long to accommodate them, and so over time these extra days accumulate until two full moons happen to fall within the same month. These 'extra' moons have been known as *blue moons* since the early 1900s, having apparently taken their name from the proverbially rare *blue moons* described since the nineteenth century.

4. DOG DAYS

The term *dog days* is a rough translation of the earlier Latin phrase *caniculares dies*, used in Ancient Rome to refer to a particular time of year when Sirius (the 'Dog Star', the brightest star in the constellation Canis Major) appeared to rise and set at the same time as the sun. By chance, these so-called 'canicular' days happened to fall at the height of summer in the Northern Hemisphere, and so the Romans mistakenly concluded that Sirius somehow managed to contribute to and intensify the heat of the sun. Since the sixteenth century in English these *dog days* have been synonymous with any lengthy or exceptional period of warm weather, and figuratively any period of laziness or good times.

5. ELEPHANT ON THE MOON

Sir Paul Neile was a renowned seventeenth-century astronomer and politician, and one of the twelve founder members of London's Royal Society. Sometime in the mid-1600s, Neile stunned his fellow scientists when he announced that during an observation of the moon he had dimly managed to make out the outline of an elephant living on its surface. What it eventually transpired Neile had observed, however, was the unfocused outline of a mouse that had somehow found its way inside his telescope. Whether there is any truth in this tale of one of England's foremost scientists being duped into believing something so ludicrous is questionable, but nevertheless Neile's *elephant on the moon* soon became associated with any great discovery or belief that is eventually proven to be untrue.

6. HINDSIGHT IS 20/20

The idea of perfect *20/20 vision* dates back to the mid-nineteenth century when the Snellen chart – the familiar eye chart of eleven rows of increasingly smaller letters – was invented as a means of assessing a person's eyesight by the Dutch ophthalmologist Hermann Snellen. Figures like *20/20* are properly known as 'Snellen fractions', ratios between the size of the smallest readable letters on the chart and the distance at which they can be read: a person with 'nominal' or *20/20 vision* should be able to read the entire chart from a distance of 20 ft (6.1 m), while the row of letters twice the size of the smallest should still be readable at a distance of 40 ft (12.2 m). A person whose eyesight is only half as clear as 20/20 (namely 20/40) would only be able to see these larger letters at a distance of 20 ft, while the smallest letters would be unreadable. Although the science behind Snellen's test is unsurprisingly quite complicated (and even the 'letters' on the chart are not actually classed as letters but 'optotypes', symbols whose precise height and breadth are very specifically dictated), the term *20/20 vision* came to be commonly used to describe perfect eyesight in the late 1800s and has remained in use ever since. The humorous expression *hindsight is 20/20*, implying that it is easy to see why mistakes were made in the past, dates from the 1960s.

7. *To the* NTH DEGREE

In algebra, *n* is often used in place of *x* to refer to any unknown or unspecified quantity, and ultimately the adjective *nth* has been used since the mid-eighteenth century to designate anything that appears at position *n* in a series, just as ordinal numbers like *fourth* and *fifth* are used to designate the numerical positions 4 and 5. Taking something *to the nth degree* dates from the mid-1800s and figuratively implies taking it to some utterly unfathomable or unquantifiable extent.

8. OLD NEWTON GOT HIM

Dating from the early 1920s, saying that *old Newton got him* was once a common phrase among members of the Royal Air Force used to imply that the person in question has been killed in a plane crash. A characteristically tactless wartime expression, the phrase alludes to Sir Isaac Newton's famous formulation of the laws of gravitation in the seventeenth century, thereby blaming gravity for causing the deaths of aircraft pilots.

9. *To* PUSH THE ENVELOPE

Used to mean 'extending beyond current limitations', *pushing the envelope* is a surprisingly modern expression dating back no further than the 1970s. Far from having anything to do with sending or opening your mail, the *envelope* in question is a fairly obscure term from aeronautical science, referring collectively to all the factors and variables – like speed and load – that limit the performance of an aircraft. This so-called 'flight envelope' is said to be 'pushed' when an aircraft is flown outside its usual capabilities, and forced to exceed its expected performance.

10. *As* SURE AS EGGS IS EGGS

Meaning 'absolutely certain', *as sure as eggs is eggs* first appeared in the language in the seventeenth century. The fact that it is deliberately ungrammatical (*eggs is eggs* not *eggs are eggs*) hints at its fairly unusual origins – it has nothing to do with food but is instead a corruption of the logical and mathematical formula $x = x$ or x *is* x, expressing in algebraic terms an absolute equivalency.

XL

TEN PHRASES DERIVED FROM POLITICS

Besides those derived from various political incidents and anecdotes, the soundbite-fuelled speeches and catch-phrases of politicians have long provided the English language with an array of phrases and expressions. Alongside Churchill's JAW-JAW NOT WAR-WAR, Macmillan's YOU'VE NEVER HAD IT SO GOOD and Pierre Trudeau's WALK IN THE SNOW, the rule that *power corrupts, absolute power corrupts absolutely* was first used by the nineteenth-century British politician Lord Acton; Margaret Thatcher's famous statement that *the lady's not for turning* was made during the Conservative Party conference in 1980; and in a speech to the Republican National Convention in New Orleans in 1988, George Bush's famous promise to introduce 'no new taxes' popularized the emphatic expression *read my lips.*

1. ALL ON ONE SIDE, LIKE A BRIDGNORTH ELECTION

As a simile of one-sidedness or lopsidedness, *all on one side like . . .* can be completed with a handful of often fairly peculiar suffixes. A common saying in Ireland is *all on one side like the town of Fermoy*, which notably stands on just one side of the River Blackwater in County Cork; the equivalent in Scotland is *like Gourock*, which occupies only one side of the Firth of Clyde. It was common in the

1700s and 1800s to say *all on one side like Lord Thomond's cocks*, referring to an infamous error made by the keeper of a flock of prize fighting cockerels bred by James O'Brien, an eighteenth-century Marquess of Thomond. On the eve of a major cockfight, the keeper transferred the best of Lord Thomond's cockerels into a room of their own away from the others in the collection, under the misconception that they would not fight each other as they were 'all on the same side' – he was, of course, proven wrong. *Like a Bridgnorth election* is another eighteenth–nineteenth century expression, referring to the fact that the parliamentary constituency of Bridgnorth in Shropshire elected successive members of the same family, the Whitmores, without exception at almost every election from 1624 to 1870.

2. *That's* ANOTHER COUNTY HEARD FROM

Inspired by the collection and announcement of county-by-county election results, in American English *that's another county heard from* has become a popular slang expression used in response to someone unwantedly or unexpectedly joining in a conversation and offering their opinion, or else as a response to someone who has remained silent for a long time before suddenly speaking up. Dating from the early 1900s, by the 1930s this notion of drawing attention to some sudden and unwelcome outburst was taken one step further in Canadian slang, when *that's another county heard from* came to be used as a response to someone suddenly burping or breaking wind.

3. *To* CLIMB ON THE BANDWAGON

To climb or *jump on the bandwagon* has been used in English since the early 1900s to refer to someone belatedly joining a successful enterprise or showing their support for a particular project or opinion. It was first used in America, and derives from the American custom of celebrating victory or raising support in electoral campaigns with raucous processions of wagons and floats that parade through city streets. Such parades typically feature live music, which would originally have been played by a band housed on a special mobile 'band-wagon'. Literally *climbing on the bandwagon* meant joining in the victor's celebrations, but only once victory had been assured.

4. COALITION OF THE WILLING

The term *coalition of the willing*, referring to a group of like-minded collaborators, was coined in the mid-1990s and is usually credited to the US President Bill Clinton who famously used it to describe an American-led alliance of nations that enacted sanctions against North Korea in response to their nuclear weapons programme in 1994. This original *coalition of the willing* was formed amid widespread criticism of the United Nations' peacekeeping capabilities, after it failed to stop the genocides in Rwanda in 1994 and Srebrenica in 1995, and ultimately the term itself came to refer to any international intervention that falls outside of a UN framework. It has since been applied to several military campaigns in recent years, including those in Afghanistan, Iraq and Libya.

5. IF YOU CAN'T STAND THE HEAT, GET OUT OF THE KITCHEN

US President Harry S. Truman is known to have been an uncompromising and straight-talking leader whose career, in the days before political spin and PR, was peppered with a number of frank and belligerently witty soundbites. Among his many famous lines, Truman explained that, 'I never gave anybody Hell. I just told the truth and they think it's Hell.' He claimed Richard Nixon was one of only two people he had ever met that he hated, bluntly calling him a 'no-good lying bastard', who was capable of 'talking out of both sides of his mouth at the same time, and lying out of both'. He apparently hated 'The Star-Spangled Banner', did not believe in 'shooting anything that cannot shoot back', and called General Douglas MacArthur's famous 'old soldiers never die' speech 'a damn bunch of bullshit'; when asked why he later relieved General MacArthur of command at the height of the Korean War, Truman replied, 'I didn't fire him because he was a dumb son of a bitch, although he was, but that's not against the law for generals. If it was, half to three-quarters of them would be in jail.' In comparison to quotes like these, *if you can't stand the heat, get out of the kitchen* – a maxim Truman coined whilst serving as Senator of Missouri in 1942 – seems fairly tame.

6. JAW-JAW NOT WAR-WAR

The idea that negotiation is preferable to confrontation was neatly summed up by Winston Churchill in a speech at the White House on 26 June 1954, when he famously declared that 'to jaw-jaw is always better than to war-war'; Churchill's precise words, spoken in the aftermath of the Korean War of 1950–53, are in fact unknown as the luncheon at which he was speaking was closed to the press. Whatever its original wording might have been, Churchill's statement was soon picked up and echoed by other public figures, notably the later British Prime Minister Harold Macmillan who used it in a speech of

1958, and it has since become a popular maxim of diplomacy and anti-war activism.

7. LAISSEZ FAIRE

Adopted into the language in the nineteenth century, the French expression *laissez faire* (literally 'let do') is often used today to describe a lenient or apathetic attitude, particularly with connotations of laziness or weariness. Originally, however, it was a political term used to refer to a government's policy of not restricting or interfering with the work of individual businesses. In this context, *laissez faire* is believed to have originated in a meeting between a French finance minister, Jean-Baptiste Colbert, and an alliance of French merchants and businessmen led by an unknown Monsieur Le Grande in the late seventeenth century. According to the tale, Colbert asked Le Grande how he thought the state could best help French businessmen like him, to which he apparently answered, '*Laissez-nous faire*', or 'let us get on with it'. In economic contexts, the phrase *laissez faire* is still used today to refer to an entirely free market, devoid of outside interference or restrictions.

8. A RIDDLE WRAPPED IN AN ENIGMA

Describing anything mysterious as *a riddle wrapped in an enigma* is a familiar expression famously lifted from a wartime speech given by Winston Churchill. Churchill's exact words were 'a riddle, wrapped in a mystery, inside an enigma', which he used in a BBC radio broadcast on 1 October 1939 to describe what he saw as Russia's inscrutable reaction to the outbreak of the Second World War, and their equally unknowable response to the threat of a German invasion. Churchill went on to explain that 'perhaps there is a key. That key is Russian national interest.'

9. A WALK IN THE SNOW

A charismatic 'philosopher politician', Pierre Trudeau served two terms as Prime Minister of Canada, a total of fifteen years in power, between 1968 and 1984. Known for his frankness and eccentricity, Trudeau dated Barbra Streisand in the early years of his premiership, was famously photographed sliding down a bannister, took judo lessons with his sons and always wore a red rose in his lapel because it 'made him happy'. This openness coupled with his vision for a fully united, bilingual Canada, made him a popular and refreshing politician, and sparked a 'Trudeaumania' in Canada in the late sixties and seventies. Towards the end of his second term, however, Trudeau's popularity was waning, and on 29 February 1984 he finally announced his resignation. In typically characterful style, at a press conference Trudeau recounted that he had made the decision to retire following a long midnight walk in a snowstorm, during which he looked for 'any signs of my destiny in the sky', but 'there were none – there were just snowflakes'. A *walk in the snow* has since become a popular Canadian English expression for any period of deep reflection or contemplation.

10. YOU'VE NEVER HAD IT SO GOOD

Today often used humorously (or ironically) to point out someone's good fortune (or lack of it), to British English speakers *you've never had it so good* is an expression inextricably associated with the post-war Prime Minister Harold Macmillan, who famously used it in a speech to

Conservative Party members in Bedford in 1957. Speaking about Britain's mounting economic prosperity in the decade after the Second World War, Macmillan's actual words were, 'Indeed let us be frank about it – most of our people have never had it so good', but over time his quote has simplified to the snappier motto still used today.

XLI

TEN PHRASES DERIVED FROM THE BIBLE

Although various fragments of the Bible were translated into English during the Old English period, the earliest full translation was undertaken by the scholar John Wycliffe in the early 1380s. Wycliffe's Bible stuck closely to the Latin texts from which it was translated and so, although popular, proved tricky to read and paved the way for a series of increasingly modernized and ever more accessible editions. In the 1520s, William Tyndale's Bible took advantage of the recently invented printing press and made the Bible accessible to all (for which Tyndale was burnt at the stake in 1536); The Great Bible, commissioned by Henry VIII in 1538, was the first fully authorized English version; and the King James Bible, commissioned by James I and completed in 1611, remained the standard Bible across England and beyond in the centuries that followed. Indeed many of the biblical expressions listed here and elsewhere in the language retain the old-fashioned wordings found in the King James Bible.

1. *To* CAST PEARLS BEFORE SWINE

Figuratively, *to cast pearls before swine* means 'to give something of great value to someone incapable of appreciating it'. This phrase, albeit in various different versions and phrasings, has been used as a saying in English since the fourteenth century and is lifted directly from Jesus's Sermon on the Mount, recorded in the Gospel of Matthew (7:6): 'Give not that which is holy unto the dogs, neither cast ye your pearls before swine, lest they trample them under their feet, and turn again and rend you.' The full quotation ends with a dire warning that such unwise acts as *casting pearls before swine* could lead to your eventual downfall.

2. *The* DAUGHTER OF THE HORSELEECH

Among the most unusual expressions to have been taken from the Bible is *the daughter of the horseleech,* a proverbial name for any greedy, spoilt or demanding person, or else anyone who undermines someone else's good humour. Taken from the Book of Proverbs (30:15), in which it is explained that 'the horseleach hath two daughters, crying Give, give!', the phrase was misconstrued when first adopted into English in the sixteenth century as these 'daughters' are not people but rather the leech's two suckers, one at either end of its body.

3. *At the* ELEVENTH HOUR

The eleventh hour has been synonymous with the latest possible moment since the mid-nineteenth century. The phrase is taken from the Parable of the Workers recalled in the Gospel of Matthew (20:1–16). Also known as the 'Parable of the Gracious Employer', the story tells of a man who hires a number of labourers to work in his vineyard for the day. 'At the third hour', he returns to the marketplace and hires more labourers, then again 'at the sixth and ninth hour', and again finally at 'about the eleventh hour', until he has amassed a full workforce.

Despite starting at different times, and despite those who started earlier working through the heat of the day, all the labourers receive the same daily wage. The story might seem more than a little unfair to modern minds, but the parable is generally understood to show that all God's followers will receive the same reward no matter when they choose to convert.

4. *The* GOLDEN BOWL IS BROKEN

Once a familiar image in English literature used by writers including Henry James, Edgar Allen Poe and Herman Melville, to modern speakers today the *golden bowl* is a much less familiar point of reference, not aided by the fact that it is taken from a relatively obscure part of the Bible. It comes from Ecclesiastes (12:6), which along with the Psalms, Proverbs and Song of Songs comprises the largely poetic central section of the Old Testament focusing on imparting wisdom and advice. In it, a preacher recites a poem, 'Remember now thy Creator', highlighting the shortness and fragility of life and warning against vanity, procrastination and loss of faith. The *golden bowl* is mentioned in a list of metaphors representing injury or death – 'Or ever the silver cord be loosed, or the golden bowl be broken, or the pitcher be broken at the fountain, or the wheel broken at the cistern' – and ultimately the image of a 'broken golden bowl' came to be used as a metaphor for any destructive, life-changing or fatal misfortune.

5. *The* LAND OF NOD

In the Book of Genesis (4:16), Cain is exiled to the *land of Nod* by God after he murders his younger brother Abel; Cain is the first human born in the Bible, and Abel the first to die. Little is said in Genesis of where the *land of Nod* actually lies other than that it is 'east of Eden', which has led some biblical scholars to suggest that, rather than being a place name, the *land of Nod* might be a metaphor for exile or banishment. Whatever its original meaning, in modern English the *land of Nod* has since become synonymous with falling asleep. In this context – first used by Jonathan Swift as early as 1738 – the phrase is a pun on *nod*, meaning 'to drop' or 'lower the head'.

6. PRIDE GOES BEFORE A FALL

The famous warning that *pride goes before a fall* is an alteration of the original biblical verse, 'Pride goeth before destruction, and an haughty spirit before a fall.' It is just one of a number of expressions adopted from the Old Testament Book of Proverbs (16:18), alongside *a soft answer turneth away wrath* (15:1); *spare the rod and spoil the child* (13:24, 'He that spareth his rod hateth his son: but he that loveth him chasteneth him betimes'); *the wicked flee though no man pursues* (28:1); and even *as a dog returns to his vomit, a fool returns to his folly* (26:11).

7. *By the* SKIN OF YOUR TEETH

The Old Testament Book of Job recalls the title character's persecution at the hands of several tormentors, after which he discusses with his friends why he has been allowed to suffer having apparently done nothing wrong. In a conversation with one of his friends, Job recounts all the misfortunes that have befallen him before finally stating, 'My bone cleaveth to my skin and to my flesh, and I am escaped with the skin of my teeth' (19:20). Biblical scholars often query *the skin of my teeth* as it does not quite fit the context of Job's story, thereby casting doubt on the reliability of its original translation, but despite their uncertainty it has become familiar as a figure of speech in its own right used since the seventeenth century in English to mean 'by the slightest margin' or 'only just'.

8. TELL IT NOT IN GATH

According to the Second Book of Samuel (1:19–20), on hearing of the deaths of King Saul and his son Jonathan in battle against the Philistines, King David immediately proclaimed, 'How are the mighty fallen! Tell it not in Gath, publish it not on the streets of Askelon.' Gath and Askelon were two of the five major Philistine city-states, known as the 'Pentapolis', which were considered enemies of the Kingdom of Israel. Any news there of the death of Israel's King Saul and his heir Jonathan – who was one of David's closest friends – could have provoked further unrest and so David's declaration wisely warned against letting his enemies hear the news. Although somewhat outdated today, *tell it not in Gath* has been used since the early eighteenth century in English to mean essentially 'this goes no further'.

9. THERE IS NOTHING NEW UNDER THE SUN

A familiar expression of world-weariness, the old proverb *there is nothing new under the sun* is often wrongly attributed to Shakespeare, who used a similar idea – 'If there be nothing new, but that which is / Hath been before' – as the opening line of Sonnet 59. In fact, the phrase is taken from the opening of the Old Testament Book of Ecclesiastes (1:9): 'that which is done is that which shall be done: and there is no new thing under the sun'.

10. *The* WRITING ON THE WALL

The writing on the wall has been a proverbial omen of misfortune since the eighteenth century, while saying that the *writing is on the wall* for someone or something has since become a means of drawing attention to its impending downfall. The phrase is derived from the Old Testament story of Belshazzar's Feast, recounted in the Book of Daniel (5:1–31), in which the Babylonian king Belshazzar hosts a grand banquet for a thousand of his lords. In front of his guests, the king takes the golden cups and goblets that his father Nebuchadnezzar had earlier stolen from the Temple of Jerusalem and ignominiously uses them to serve wine. Suddenly a ghostly, disembodied hand appears and writes on the wall behind him the words *mene mene tekel upharsin.* Unable to interpret the text himself (the words are literally a list of different Hebrew measurements), the king calls for the prophet Daniel who quickly deduces that the message implies that Belshazzar's kingdom is soon to be 'numbered, weighed, and divided'; that night, Belshazzar is killed and Babylon falls to the invading Persians.

XLII

TEN ADVERTISING SLOGANS

Having a FROG IN THE THROAT is often mistakenly said to have been coined in an American advertisement for a brand of cough lozenges in the late 1800s and early 1900s. In fact, the lozenges were simply known as 'Frog In Your Throat?' sweets, and were manufactured in New York by the self-titled Frog In Your Throat Company.

1. ALL SINGING, ALL DANCING

Describing something as *all singing and all dancing* typically implies that it has an array of extra features and functions, which was certainly the case when the phrase first appeared as the advertising slogan for the MGM musical *The Broadway Melody* in 1929. Directed by silent-film impresario Harry Beaumont, the film was Hollywood's first all-talking musical and featured one of cinema's first full Technicolor sequences. However, just as the phrase *all singing, all dancing* has come to often imply that these extra features are ironically far from useful or impressive, despite all its razzle-dazzle *The Broadway Melody* has since come to be considered one of the poorest of the major Hollywood musicals and one of the worst films ever to win the Best Picture Oscar, thanks to its melodramatic and heavily clichéd storyline.

2. ALWAYS A BRIDESMAID, NEVER A BRIDE

Featuring a chorus of 'Ding, dong, wedding bells / Only ring for other gals', 'Why Am I Always a Bridesmaid, and Never a Blushing Bride?' was a popular song in Edwardian music halls. Written by songwriter Fred W. Leigh (better known for the London standard 'My Old Man Said Follow the Van'), in the mid-1920s the song's image of a dejected young woman agonizing over the prospect of a life alone was picked up by Listerine, who used it as part of a hugely successful advertising campaign aimed at selling mouthwash to single women. Featuring photographs of doleful young women under the tagline 'Often a bridesmaid but never a bride', by modern standards the 1920s Listerine campaign is startlingly outdated – one advert features the caption 'Edna's case was really a pathetic one. Like every woman, her primary ambition was to marry . . . And as her birthdays crept gradually toward that tragic thirty-mark, marriage seemed farther from her life than ever' – but nonetheless it helped to establish this very familiar expression in the language.

3. THE CUSTOMER IS ALWAYS RIGHT

The notion that *the customer is always right* is usually credited to one of three world-renowned entrepreneurs. Probably the earliest person to use the phrase (or at least something like it) was the Swiss-born hotelier César Ritz, whose maxim that *le client n'a jamais tort*, 'the customer is never wrong', was employed at the opening of his Hôtel Ritz in Paris as early as 1898. The first record of the phrase as it is, however, dates from 1905 and a profile in the *Boston Globe* of Chicago department-store owner Marshall Field, whose self-titled company grew to become one of the city's biggest retailers in the early 1900s. That Field used the slogan *the customer is always right* in his store is certain, but it seems likely that the phrase was actually coined by a member of his staff who went on to become a retail giant in his own right: Harry Gordon Selfridge joined Field's company as a stock boy in 1876 and over the next twenty-five years rose to become assistant manager. Having amassed a vast personal fortune, and having married into one of Chicago's wealthiest families, Selfridge left for London in 1901 and spent an astonishing £400,000 (equivalent to tens of millions today) developing the Oxford Street department store that still stands today. His slogan that *the customer is always right* began appearing in Selfridge's advertisements and in-store promotions soon after it opened in 1909.

4. DIAMONDS ARE FOREVER

Since 1948, the De Beers diamond company has used the slogan 'A diamond is forever' in almost all its advertisements. In 1956 a slightly altered version of the already well-known slogan was used as the title of Ian Fleming's fourth James Bond novel, *Diamonds Are Forever,* which Fleming was inspired to write after reading an article about African diamond smugglers in *The Times,* and following a meeting with Sir Percy Sillitoe, a former head of MI5 who at the time was working with De Beers in South Africa. The novel was adapted for the cinema in 1971, becoming the seventh film in the Bond franchise and the sixth to star Sean Connery.

5. EVERY PICTURE TELLS A STORY

In the early 1900s advertisements began appearing in British newspapers for 'Doan's Backache Kidney Pills', a new over-the-counter medication that promised to cure an array of different conditions including backache, rheumatism, diabetes, dizziness, 'congestion of the kidneys' and even 'gravel'. The advertisements – the earliest of which dates back to 1904 – typically featured an image of a gruff-looking gentleman or a young woman climbing a staircase, both pictured painfully clutching their lower backs. Alongside the images read the caption *every picture tells a story*, which as later advertisements in the campaign explained, was 'a story of weak, aching backs and inactive kidneys'. The slogan ran for over a decade, and eventually the phrase dropped into everyday use in English referring to any image that proves particularly telling or memorable.

6. FLAVOUR OF THE MONTH

Anything described as a *flavour of the month* is currently and often temporarily popular. The phrase originated in 1930s America, where it began as a gimmick among ice-cream sellers and manufacturers. Its earliest record dates from 1935 and an article proclaiming that the Golden State Ice Cream Company in San Jose, California, was offering 'fresh peach' as 'August's flavor of the month'. The promotion seems to have been quickly picked up by other retailers and within months similar campaigns were appearing all across America. By the 1960s, the phrase had slipped into everyday use to describe any short-lived craze or flash in the pan.

7. FOUR MORE YEARS

According to the American Constitution, all presidents of the United States are to be elected for a term of precisely four years, after which any president wishing to remain in office is required to run for election once more. In 1900, the incumbent Republican president William McKinley secured a narrow electoral victory over the Democratic candidate William Jennings Bryan using the slogan 'Four More Years of the Full Dinner Pail!', designed to appeal to working-class, blue-collar voters and emphasizing the prosperity his leadership had enjoyed. The motto 'Four More Years' was picked up again in the 1972 election by Richard Nixon, whose Democrat opponent George McGovern punningly campaigned under the slogan 'No More Years'. Nevertheless, Nixon won the election in a landslide, astonishingly securing victory in forty-nine states; only Massachusetts and the District of Columbia voted for McGovern. More recently, the slogan *four more years* became fully established in the language on 7 November 2012 when the newly re-elected President Barack Obama tweeted via the official US Presidential Twitter account a photograph of him embracing his wife Michelle. The accompanying tweet read simply 'Four more years', and within hours had been shared more than 500,000 times on Twitter.

8. A PICTURE IS WORTH A THOUSAND WORDS

The old adage that *a picture is worth a thousand words* first appeared in America in the early 1900s. Although later explanations of its origin claim that it might have originally been an old Chinese proverb, its earliest recorded use nevertheless comes from an advertisement for a local American newspaper supplement, the *San Antonio Light*, in 1918: 'One of the Nation's Greatest Editors Says: One Picture is Worth a Thousand Words'. An even earlier version, 'One Look is Worth A Thousand Words', appeared in an advert for an Ohio tyre supplier in 1913.

9. WHERE'S THE BEEF?

In January 1984, the American hamburger chain Wendy's began an advertising campaign in which a crotchety old woman, played by octogenarian actress Clara Peller, was served a tiny hamburger inside an oversized bread bun, prompting her to demand 'Where's the beef?!' The slogan became an instant catchphrase across America and was soon printed on all manner of tie-in merchandise, while Peller even went on to release her own novelty single. Soon anything lacking substance or flair would be met with shouts of 'Where's the beef?!', and even Vice President Walter Mondale used the phrase during a live television debate in response to the policies championed by his opponent in the 1984 election, Gary Hart. The phrase has remained in use in American slang ever since, and was revived by Wendy's for another ad campaign in 2011.

10. YOU'VE COME A LONG WAY, BABY

In 1968, the Virginia Slims brand of cigarette was introduced in America. Aimed squarely at women smokers and intended to tap into the feminist and women's liberation movements of the time, the brand was advertised under the slogan *you've come a long way, baby* and was accompanied both in print and on television by images highlighting the progression of women through the twentieth century. The campaign proved hugely successful and continued to run throughout the 1970s and 80s, while its accompanying slogan was soon adopted by other social movements and became a catchphrase for any sign of improvement or progression.

XLIII

TEN SUPERSTITIOUS PHRASES

The ten phrases listed here all make mention of or derive from some kind of superstitious belief or folklore. Although the superstitions themselves might seem ungrounded, the phrases that they have inspired have all slipped into common use in the language, albeit often in figurative or – as in HAIR OF THE DOG and SEVEN-YEAR ITCH – entirely unrelated contexts.

1. *The* BLEEDING OF A DEAD MAN

It was once widely believed that in the presence of its killer, the body of a murder victim would begin to bleed again. Even the slightest movement or change in the appearance of a corpse – such as the twitching of a muscle or the smallest movement of an eye or mouth – was said to be a sign that the murderer was present. In the Middle Ages, this superstitious 'proof' was often used against those accused of witchcraft and was even maintained by James I who wrote in 1597 that, 'if the dead carcase be at any time thereafter handled by the murtherer, it will gush out of bloud, as if the blud were crying to the Heaven for revenge'. Ultimately, *the bleeding of a dead man* became synonymous in English with any sign or proof of guilt.

2. *The* HAIR OF THE DOG

The hair of the dog has been used to refer to an alcoholic drink used as a cure for a hangover in English since the sixteenth century. Surprisingly, there is some (albeit highly dubious) proof that this old remedy might have some truth to it, as the symptoms of a hangover can occasionally be caused by an increase in methanol and formaldehyde in the body, both of which are more readily processed by ethanol (alcohol) than by the body's own enzymes. There is no truth at all, however, behind the expression's original meaning; it was once supposed that in order to cure rabies, the infected bite should literally be bandaged with *the hair of the dog that bit you.*

3. *To* KNOCK ON WOOD

Knocking on wood, or else merely saying *knock on wood!* or *touch wood!*, is a long-standing superstition in Western folklore that purportedly guarantees good fortune and protects against future misfortune or disaster. This belief is thought to date back to pre-Christian Europe, when trees and their timbers were believed to house benevolent spirits who could be called upon to provide aid and good fortune. Alternatively, the wood might have been presumed to house evil spirits who, if they were to hear about a person's intentions or a run of good luck, would do all that they could to spoil it. Knocking on the wood was ultimately a way of scaring these malevolent spirits away.

4. LEFT AND RIGHT BRINGS GOOD AT NIGHT

The Victorian proverb *left and right brings good at night* is just one example of a host of superstitions concerned with finding meaning in the body's involuntary twitches and movements. The belief here is that while a twitch in your right eye is a sign of good luck and a twitch in your left is a sign of bad luck, both eyes twitching together is said to be a sign that some good will come later in the day. Similarly, another tradition claims that a twitch in your right eye would foretell seeing an old friend, while a twitch in the left would foretell seeing an enemy.

5. MORNING DREAMS COME TRUE

The superstition that *morning dreams come true* is an old English proverb probably derived from nothing more than the fact that the dreams had immediately before waking are the most easily remembered. The proverb itself dates from the sixteenth century, but the idea behind it is considerably older and was even referred to by writers in Ancient Greece and Rome; in his *Satires*, the Roman poet Horace talks of a vision that 'appeared to me . . . when dreams are true'.

6. SEVEN-YEAR ITCH

The phrase *seven-year itch* is typically used to describe a married person's disinterest in their relationship and their temptation to cheat on their partner after a period of seven years. In this context the phrase comes from the title of a 1952 play, *The Seven Year Itch*, written by the American playwright George Axelrod that was famously adapted for cinema in 1955. Far from having connotations of marital infidelity, however, Axelrod's title was taken from a tradition in American folklore that claims anyone affected by poison ivy or 'prairie itch' (an old slang name for scabies) would be destined to suffer the same symptoms at roughly the same time every year for the next seven years.

7. SPEAK OF THE DEVIL

Speak or *talk of the Devil* has been a popular expression, employed when someone who is being talked about makes an unexpected appearance, since the seventeenth century; different versions of the full phrase include *speak of the Devil and he's at your elbows,* and *speak of the Devil and see his horns.* Phrases like these have their origins in the ancient superstition that mentioning the Devil by name would somehow tempt him to appear, thereby bringing about some kind of misfortune or calamity. This idea ultimately gave rise to an array of peculiar euphemisms for the Devil – like *the Old Serpent* (fourteenth century), *the wicked one* (late 1500s), *Old Nick* (mid-1600s) and *Old Scratch* (mid-1700s) – which would be used in its place.

8. THE SWINE HAS RUN THROUGH IT

Weddings are a fertile source of traditions and superstitions, and if they are all to be believed then even something as straightforward as the bride's journey to church can prove a minefield of ill omens. In English folklore it is said to be good luck for a wedding party to pass a policeman, a blind man, a lamb, a spider in its web or a dove, but it is unlucky to pass a crowing cockerel, a funeral or a pig. In fact seeing a herd of pigs cross the path of a wedding party was once considered such a bad sign that saying that *the swine has run through it* became a northern English euphemism for a marriage that had broken down.

9. THERE'S LUCK IN ODD NUMBERS

Odd numbers have long been considered the luckier counterpart to even numbers by peoples and cultures all around the world. Collections like the Christian trinity, the five classical elements (water, earth, air, fire and ether), the 'seven steps' taken by Buddha at his birth and the nine Muses of Ancient Greece have all reinforced this idea over the centuries, to the extent that by Shakespeare's time *there's luck in odd numbers* had become a popular English proverb which he included in *The Merry Wives of Windsor* (V. i).

10. *The* WRONG SIDE OF BED

Waking up on the wrong side of the bed is a common superstitious explanation for a run of bad luck or for someone's uncharacteristically irritable mood. The idea that a bed has a 'right' and 'wrong' side dates back at least to Ancient Rome, where the 'wrong' side was always considered the left – it was once also considered unlucky to put on your left shoe before your right, and to step out your front door with your left foot first (see also OVER THE LEFT SHOULDER).

XLIV

TEN WISE WORDS AND ADVICE

Sayings and proverbs are often intended to offer advice and words of wisdom, and those listed here wisely warn against everything from procrastination and laziness to conceitedness, materialism, timewasting and even pessimism. Whether the advice instilled in these expressions is good or not is a matter of personal opinion, and there will almost always be a contrary voice looking to turn sayings like these on their head or offer an alternative interpretation. As Oscar Wilde once commented, 'People who count their chickens before they are hatched act wisely, because chickens run about so absurdly that it is impossible to count them accurately.'

1. DON'T HALLOO UNTIL YOU'RE OUT OF THE WOODS

Halloo is an old seventeenth-century English exclamation that was once used to draw attention to something or convey surprise. *Don't (shout) halloo until you're out of the woods* is an advisory proverb dating from the late eighteenth century, which can be interpreted either as a warning not to celebrate until you are sure all danger has passed, or else advises against drawing attention to yourself in dangerous areas.

2. THE EARLY BIRD CATCHES THE WORM

Perhaps dating back as far as the fifteenth century, *the early bird catches the worm* wisely advises that those who arrive first or are willing to put in extra effort will be rewarded, while those who are lazy will typically miss opportunities already claimed by others. Equivalent to the equally ancient *first come, first served*, the image of *the early bird* can be easily turned around to contradict its meaning – 'being early didn't help the worm' – while the American comedian Steven Wright once famously quipped 'it's the second mouse that gets the cheese'.

3. FIRST CATCH YOUR HARE

The nineteenth-century saying *first catch your hare* warns against wasting time imagining what you will do with something long before you have attained it. It is often claimed to come from Mrs Glasse's *Art of Cookery*, a famous English cookbook published in 1747 that supposedly featured a recipe for jugged hare that began with the utterly unnecessary instruction 'first catch your hare and kill it'. Sadly Mrs Glasse's cookbook features nothing of the sort, and the true origin of the line remains unknown.

4. A FOOL MAY GIVE A WISE MAN COUNSEL

Fools are common subjects of advisory proverbs and sayings, particularly those showing how something should not be done or advising against doing something unwise, like *fools rush in where angels fear to tread* and *fools and children should never see half-done work*, an eighteenth-century warning against showing something that is incomplete to someone unable to appreciate that it is still a work in progress. Some sayings, however, demonstrate how the ignorance or innocence of an unwise person can have its positives, and *a fool may give a wise man counsel* is a seventeenth-century reminder that good advice can sometimes come from unexpected sources.

5. THE GAME IS NOT WORTH THE CANDLE

If *the game is not worth the candle*, then it is not worth continuing with it as the cost or effort involved appears unlikely to pay off. Adopted into English in the seventeenth century from its French equivalent, *le jeu ne vaut pas la chandelle*, this proverb alludes to someone working on some time-consuming project by candlelight: if the project is worthless, then the candle will have been spent for no return.

6. IF THE SKY FALLS WE SHALL CATCH LARKS

Depending on whether you are an optimist or a pessimist, the fifteenth-century proverb *if the sky falls we shall catch larks* can be interpreted in two very different ways. To the eternal optimist, it advises looking on the bright side even in the face of disaster: 'the sky might be falling, but at least it has brought the skylarks into our reach'. To the pessimist *the sky falling* is simply another example of a proverbial impossibility, and so the saying warns against making arrangements based on some unlikely or impossible event.

7. LEARNING IS BETTER THAN HOUSE AND LAND

Proverbially, learning is said to be better than a number of different things, including *silver and gold*, *earning* and, since the late 1700s at least, *house and land*. The sentiment behind all of these is clear: a person's wealth and possessions are ephemeral, and in case of their loss it is always best to have something else to fall back on. The same idea was even more neatly summed up by the English playwright Samuel Foote in his 1752 comedy *Taste,* which includes the line, 'When house and land are gone and spent, / Then learning is most excellent.'

8. NEVER TOUCH YOUR EYE BUT WITH YOUR ELBOW

The advice that you should *never touch your eye with aught but your elbow* dates from the seventeenth century. It is of course impossible to *touch your eye with your elbow,* so the recommendation here is to not touch your eye at all. The Jacobean writer George Herbert took this advice a step further in his *Jacula Prudentum* ('Wise Darts'), a collection of pithy mottos and sayings published in 1640, in which he further advised that 'Diseases of the eye are to be cured with the elbow.'

9. A RICH MAN'S JOKE IS ALWAYS FUNNY

The couplet 'Money is honey, my little sonny, / And a rich man's joke is always funny' was coined by the nineteenth-century Manx poet and scholar T. E. Brown. The shrewd tagline *a rich man's joke is always funny* soon became a popular maxim in Victorian England, taken both as a warning against associating with sycophantic people and of being jealous of a rich man surrounded by flattering, laughing companions, as all may not be as it seems. A similar sentiment is carried by the older eighteenth-century proverb *he that has a full purse never wanted a friend,* although both sayings can be said to derive from the biblical adage that 'wealth maketh many friends' (Proverbs, 19:4).

10. SEW THE BUTTON ON

The Victorian saying *sew the button on* advises that you

should always immediately make a note of anything that you wish to remember, otherwise it is likely to be forgotten just as easily as a button that has come loose is liable to be lost if it is not reattached immediately. Probably partly inspired by the earlier eighteenth-century expression *a stitch in time saves nine*, proverbs advising against procrastination are common in English, but quips and witticisms turning the notion on its head are just as popular. As Mark Twain famously recommended, 'Never put off till tomorrow what may be done day after tomorrow just as well.'

XLV

TEN NICKNAMES

Long before it came to mean 'to prolong' or 'contrive', the verb *eke* meant simply 'to increase' or 'add to', and in Old English an *eke* was another word for an extra part or supplement added to something larger. An *eke-name* was ultimately an additional name, used alongside (and eventually in place of) an existing one. Over time, the final N of *an* mistakenly joined to *eke*, and by the early fifteenth century these alternative names were being called *neke names*, and eventually *nicknames*.

1. *The* AMERICAN CINCINNATUS

Cincinnatus was an early Roman statesman and general who, in 458 BC, was forced out of retirement and given absolute power over the city. Its chief consul, Minucius, had been kidnapped by invading forces and both his absence and the threat of an impending invasion had thrown Rome into turmoil. Cincinnatus – a former city consul – proved a superb leader and soon the invasion was quashed, Minucius returned to the city and, refusing to abuse the powers that had been granted to him, Cincinnatus immediately rescinded his control over Rome. For this noble decision (which he was remarkably forced to repeat under similar circumstances several years later) Cincinnatus became a legendary model of selflessness and virtuousness. More than 2,000 years later his name was revived as a nickname for George Washington, who became known as the *American Cincinnatus* for his willingness to rescind absolute power in the aftermath of the American Revolution.

2. AMERICA'S SWEETHEART

The Canadian silent-film actress Mary Pickford was known as *America's sweetheart* at the height of her career in the 1910s and 20s. One of the biggest stars of her time, in 1919 Pickford helped to found the film studio United Artists alongside D. W. Griffith, Charlie Chaplin and her husband Douglas Fairbanks, and ultimately established herself not only as a hugely successful actor but also an astute businesswoman and film producer. As Samuel Goldwyn, one of the founders of rival studio MGM, once quipped, 'It took longer to make one of Mary's contracts than it did to make one of Mary's pictures.'

3. *The* ANGEL OF DEATH

The nickname *Angel of Death* has been applied to several monstrous characters from history, but perhaps most infamously Josef Mengele, the chief physician of Auschwitz concentration camp in Poland. Mengele is thought to have been responsible for the deaths of 400,000 people during his twenty-one months in charge of the camp. After it was abandoned in 1945, he escaped an American prisoner of war camp under a false name and eventually fled to Argentina, where he remained in exile until his death in 1979. Incredibly, Mengele was never brought to justice for his crimes.

4. AULD REEKIE

Edinburgh has been nicknamed *Auld Reekie* since the late eighteenth century at least, although the name originally only applied to the city's central Old Town district. The name literally means 'Old Smoky', and refers to Edinburgh's once characteristic smoke-filled atmosphere. Around the same time, Edinburgh also came to be known as *the Athens of the North*, in reference to its world-class academic reputation and its striking neoclassical architecture.

5. *The* BIG APPLE

In American slang in the early 1900s, describing something as a *big apple* implied that it was an object of desire, or the largest or grandest example of its type. It was in this context that New York's horse-racing circuit, regarded as one of the best in the country, was first nicknamed *the Big Apple* in 1921 by the local sports journalist John J. FitzGerald. Writing in the *New York Morning Telegraph*, FitzGerald continued to use the name week after week, and soon it established itself not only as a nickname for the racecourse, but for the city as a whole; the earliest use of *the Big Apple* in clear reference to New York City dates from 1922.

6. DEAD MAN'S HAND

In card games like blackjack and poker, dozens of different hands and combinations of cards have their own nicknames, some more formally recognized than others, and many with surprisingly ingenious or unusual origins. A pair containing an ace and a queen, for instance, is sometimes known as an 'Antony and Cleopatra'; a king and a queen is a 'Ferdinand and Isabella', the rulers of Spain at the time of Christopher Columbus; a king and a nine is known as 'dogs', from a pun on 'K-9'; and an ace, known as a 'bullet', and a two, known as a 'duck', are together nicknamed 'hunting season'. The *dead man's hand* contains a pair of aces and a pair of eights, so-called as it was the hand Wild Bill Hickok was holding when he was shot dead in Deadwood in 1876.

7. *The* FATHER-IN-LAW OF EUROPE

Christian IX, king of Denmark from 1863–1906, earned the nickname *the father-in-law of Europe* in the late nineteenth century in reference to the array of different royal houses into which his six children were wed. From oldest to youngest, his offspring went on to become Frederick VIII of Denmark; Queen Alexandra, wife of Edward VII of the United Kingdom; George I of Greece; Empress Maria Feodorovna, wife of Alexander III of Russia; Thyra, Crown Princess of Hanover; and Prince Valdemar, wife of Princess Marie of Orléans. Indeed Christian's children were so widespread that to this day he remains an ancestor of almost all of the existing royal houses of Europe – Queen Elizabeth II is his great-great-granddaughter.

8. *The* LAST FRONTIER

As part of their regional insignia – which also includes official state songs, mottos, birds, flowers and even fossils – all fifty of the United States have their own state nicknames. Arizona for instance is 'The Grand Canyon State'; South Dakota is 'The Mount Rushmore State'. California is 'The Golden State', a reference both to its fine weather and the California Gold Rush of the mid-1840s, and

Florida is 'The Sunshine State'. As America's northernmost state, Alaska has been known as *The Last Frontier* since it joined the Union in 1959.

9. *The* OLD LADY OF THREADNEEDLE STREET

Since 1734, Threadneedle Street in London has been home to the Bank of England. The bank is nicknamed *The Old Lady of Threadneedle Street*, a personification that originally derived from a speech given in the House of Commons in 1797 by the Whig politician (and renowned playwright) Richard Brinsley Sheridan. In his speech, Sheridan referred to the bank as 'an elderly lady in the City, of great credit and long standing', and the image stuck; just a few weeks later, a satirical cartoon appeared in the London press showing an old lady in a vast Georgian dress made of banknotes, sitting atop a chest of gold, vainly trying to deter the advances of a spindly young man. The caption to the cartoon – 'Political Ravishment, or the Old Lady of Threadneedle Street in danger!' – made it clear that the young man in question was Prime Minister Pitt the Younger, who at the time had just introduced several bold initiatives in an attempt to reduce the national debt.

10. *The* UNION JACK

The current flag of the United Kingdom was officially adopted in 1801, but its design dates back to 1603 when James Stuart rose jointly to the thrones of England and Scotland as King James I and VI. The flags of the two nations combined in 1606 and by royal decree what was then known as the Union Flag was created. The name *Union Jack* first began to appear in the later seventeenth century, with the earliest reference to 'His Majesty's Jack' dating from 1674. Although both are officially recognized names today, *Union Jack* was originally a nickname derived from the fact that in the seventeenth and eighteenth centuries the new Union flag was typically flown on ships in the same position as a naval 'jack' would be.

XLVI

TEN QUESTIONS

The ten expressions listed here are all rhetorical questions. Mostly they comprise English slang phrases that would be used as witty responses or asides, drawing attention to or passing comment on something remarkable – such as someone's incessant chattering (YOU MUST KNOW MRS KELLY?) or their interfering, meddlesome nature (WHO'S ROBBING THIS COACH?).

1. AND DID HE MARRY POOR BLIND NELL?

Poor blind Nell was the heroine of a grim and expletive-strewn nineteenth-century Australian ballad. Introduced to Europe during the First World War, the song is thought to have been a bawdy parody of the melodramatic sagas that were popular at the time. Several different versions of its lyrics exist, but the usual first verse – 'The sun shone on the village green, / It shone on poor blind Nell. / But did she see the sunshine? / Did she fucking hell!' – more than sets the tone for what is to come; the comedian Spike Milligan once commented that Nell eventually becomes involved in 'more perversions' in the song's thirty-two bars of music 'than a victim of Caligula'. Nevertheless, the song proved popular enough in the 1910s to 20s to inspire the British expression *and did he marry poor blind Nell?*, usually used in response to being told something apparently utterly improbable.

2. DIDN'T THAT CHOKE YOU?

The idea that lies can choke you or 'stick in your throat' has been proverbial in English since the seventeenth century, when 'If a lie could choke him, that would have done it' was listed in *A Compleat Collection of English Proverbs* compiled in 1680. *Didn't that choke you?* was a Victorian equivalent used as a witty response to someone who had apparently just told some unbelievable story.

3. DID SHE FALL OR WAS SHE PUSHED?

When it first appeared in the language in the late nineteenth century, *did she fall or was she pushed?* was a gossipy slang expression questioning whether a pregnant woman had planned her child or not. This meaning changed in the early 1900s when the phrase became associated with the scandal of Violet Charlesworth, a twenty-four-year-old Edwardian heiress who swindled thousands of pounds out of stockbrokers, investors and other high-society gentlemen before faking her own death on the cliffs of Penmaenbach, north Wales, in 1908. Police became suspicious when Charlesworth's body could not be found, and it soon emerged that she had 'died' leaving debts of £27,000 (equivalent to more than £2,500,000 today). After a much-publicized manhunt, she was tracked down to Oban in south-west Scotland where she was arrested and eventually sentenced to five years hard labour. In light of Charlesworth's hoax, *did she fall or was she pushed?* soon became a much more general enquiry of someone's guilt or their involvement in some underhand scheme.

4. HOW'S YOUR FATHER?

In British English, *how's your father?* or *how's-yer-father* has been a slang term for sex since the early 1900s. It was originally one of the many catchphrases of an Edwardian music hall comedian named Harry Tate, who became known for suddenly asking 'How's your father?' in improvised sketches when he was stumped for a better comeback or wanted to change the subject. The phrase soon caught on among the soldiers of the First World War, who initially used it with a number of different meanings and in several different contexts. As well as a euphemism for sex, *how's your father?* was also used to mean 'nonsense' or 'balderdash'; to emphasize or intensify expressions, in the same way as *like hell!* or *like billy-o!*; could refer to any great fuss or commotion; and was even used in a similar way to 'whatchamacallit' or 'thingamabob', to refer to anything or anyone whose proper name had been forgotten.

5. IS THE POPE CATHOLIC?

Expressions like *is the Pope Catholic?* – to which the answer is an obvious 'yes' – first began to appear in American slang in the early 1900s as ironic replies to equally obvious questions or suggestions. Among the earliest of all was *does a bear shit in the woods?*, which dates back to the 1910s and 20s, and since then all manner of different versions have cropped up in the language from straightforward examples like *is the sky blue?*, *do birds have wings?* and *do fish swim?* to far more outlandish ones like *is a pig's ass pork?*, *do beavers piss on flat rocks?* and *is a frog's ass watertight?*. More recently, a number of expressions conversely implying an emphatic 'no' have begun to appear, including *does a chicken have lips?*, *does a snake have knees?* and even, combining the two most famous examples of this type, *does the Pope shit in the woods?*.

6. WHAT DID HORACE SAY, WINNIE?

Horace and Winnie were characters created in the 1940s by the English radio and music hall comedian Harry Hemsley. In one of his acts, Hemsley was renowned for playing all the members of a family, each with its own distinctive voice; Horace, the youngest of the family, was utterly intelligible to anyone except his elder sister Winnie, who would be asked to interpret for the others. Hemsley's catchphrase, *what did Horace say, Winnie?*, soon caught on as a quirky response to anything indistinct or illogical.

7. WHAT WILL MRS GRUNDY SAY?

The proverbial stick-in-the-mud *Mrs Grundy* has been the embodiment of dour, overcritical mannerliness since the early 1800s. She comes from *Speed the Plough*, a 1798 comedy by the playwright Thomas Morton, in which an unseen 'Mrs Grundy' is the sneering, judgemental neighbour of Dame Ashfield, who appears constantly concerned with what she might be thinking. Although Mrs Grundy herself never appears on stage, the mere threat of her disapproval became proverbial in English and Dame Ashfield's catchphrase, *what will Mrs Grundy say?*, was soon being used to draw attention to anything that might upset a similarly conservative or pernickety character.

8. WHO BREAKS A BUTTERFLY UPON THE WHEEL?

The 'breaking wheel' was a medieval instrument of torture, to which a victim would be strapped and then their legs and arms broken. The image of *breaking a butterfly on the wheel* ultimately refers to putting great effort into accomplishing something insignificant, and asking *who breaks a butterfly upon the wheel?* – a quote from Alexander Pope's *Epistle to Dr Arbuthnot* written in 1735 – is often used to criticize any unnecessarily severe punishment. The phrase was famously used as a headline in *The Times* in 1967 after it was reported that Mick Jagger and Keith Richards had been given jail sentences following a drugs raid at Richards' home. After a storm of protests prompted by the article, the pair's sentences were overturned.

9. WHO'S ROBBING THIS COACH?

Dating from the mid-1900s, *who's robbing this coach?* is an Australian expression essentially meaning 'mind your own business!' or 'let me get on with it!'. It is said to derive from an old bawdy joke about highway robbery, in which a band of rugged young outlaws hold up a coach and rob all the passengers. Dissatisfied with their haul, the bandits then threaten to rape all the female passengers, prompting one of the men on board to plead, 'Please, have mercy, spare the women!' – to which the sole elderly female passenger replies, 'Who's robbing this coach, anyway?'

10. YOU MUST KNOW MRS KELLY?

Asking someone if they *must know Mrs Kelly?* was a late-nineteenth-century catchphrase used to interrupt or poke fun at an unrelenting chatterer. It derives from a sketch by the English music hall comedian Dan Leno, one of the biggest stars of his day, whose act typically consisted of a series of comic monologues delivered by an array of different characters. Among Leno's creations were a henpecked husband, a gruff sergeant major, a beefeater showing tourists around the Tower of London and, in this case, a gossipy old lady recounting the ludicrous escapades of her friend 'Mrs Kelly'.

XLVII

TEN FOLK ETYMOLOGIES

Often when the origin of a particular word or phrase is unknown, entirely fictitious 'folk etymologies' arise that purport to solve the mystery. Ten examples of these etymological tall tales are listed here, and although none of them is true they prove an intriguing set of stories nonetheless – and in the case of KNOW YOUR ONIONS, provide arguably a better explanation than the truth.

1. BATE ME AN ACE, QUOTH BOLTON

Bate me an ace, quoth Bolton is a long-obsolete Elizabethan expression of surprise or disbelief. *To bate an ace* has meant 'to decrease by a tiny amount' since the 1500s at least, but the mysterious addition of *quoth Bolton* is often credited to Elizabeth I. According to the tale, the compiler of a sixteenth-century collection of proverbs was given an audience with the queen at which to present her with his work. On explaining that the book contained every proverb in the English language, the queen apparently exclaimed, 'Bate me an ace, quoth Bolton!', simultaneously showing her disbelief and using a proverb which the writer had apparently overlooked. As imaginative a story as this is, however, it is widely considered untrue.

2. *To* BURY YOUR HEAD IN THE SAND

To bury your head in the sand has meant 'to refuse to acknowledge something uncomfortable or problematic' since the mid-eighteenth century. It derives from the misconception that ostriches literally bury their heads in the sand in order to avoid danger – or, as the Roman scholar Pliny the Elder explained, 'they imagine, when they have thrust their head and neck into a bush, that the whole of their body is concealed'. Ostriches do have a habit of lowering their heads to the ground to scan their surroundings, and have been known to lie down in an attempt to appear inconspicuous, but they certainly do not bury their heads.

3. *To* COME A CROPPER

In 1867, a Nottinghamshire firm called H. S. Cropper & Company began manufacturing a new design of printing press known as the Minerva. The design proved hugely successful and within just twenty-five years some 14,000 Minerva machines were in use across Britain. The name *Cropper* soon became a byword for any printing press or similar device, while any printer who suffered an accident at work – it was not unheard of for fingers to be lost in the presses' weighty mechanisms – was said to have *come a cropper*. Sadly, while it is true that Cropper's company was one of the most successful of its day, *to come a cropper* is instead thought to derive from an earlier eighteenth-century expression *neck and crop*, which was used in much the same way as 'head over heels' is today.

4. *To* KNOW YOUR ONIONS

There is an interesting and surprisingly apt tale among etymologists that claims that *to know your onions* refers to the nineteenth–twentieth-century grammarian C. T. Onions, who became editor of the *Oxford English Dictionary* in 1895. Over the next six decades, Onions worked on the *OED* alongside several other significant titles including a renowned *Shakespeare Glossary* in 1911 and the first *Oxford Dictionary of English Etymology*, published posthumously in 1966. *Knowing your Onions*, ultimately, could be interpreted as 'being well read' or 'having a good knowledge of the language'. As befitting an explanation as this would be, *to know your onions* is in fact an American invention that first appeared in the 1920s alongside a host of similar and seemingly random phrases like *to know your eggs*, *to know your oil* and *to know your apples*, all of which meant simply 'to know what's what'.

5. *To* PAINT THE TOWN RED

To paint the town red has meant 'to have a boisterously good time' since the late nineteenth century. Numerous different theories of its origin exist, but perhaps the most famous is that it derives from the night of 6 April 1837, when the notorious Henry Beresford, Third Marquis of Waterford, and a group of his drunken friends ran riot around Melton Mowbray in Leicestershire, destroying property, assaulting policemen and literally 'painting the town red'. Historical accounts of the marquis' paint-flinging riot confirm that it certainly took place, but given that the earliest record of the phrase *to paint the town red* dates from 1883 (almost fifty years later) and comes from the *New York Times* (rather than any similar British text), suggests that this might not be its genuine origin.

6. RULE OF THUMB

One popular explanation of the seventeenth-century expression *rule of thumb*, meaning 'a rough guideline', is that it derives from an obsolete English law that legally permitted a husband to strike his wife with any implement no thicker than his thumb. There is, however, no evidence to suggest that any such law existed, and the phrase seems simply to derive from the thumb often being used as an improvised measuring device.

7. SAVED BY THE BELL

Someone who has been *saved by the bell* has escaped an awkward or dangerous situation thanks to some timely interruption. Despite the fact that no record of the phrase dates from before the early 1900s, one popular theory claims it has its roots in the Middle Ages, when medical science was still in its infancy and stories of paralysed or unconscious people being buried alive were apparently common. To avoid a similar fate, some bodies were supposedly buried with a length of twine running up through the soil to a bell suspended above ground. If the person inside were suddenly to awaken, ringing the bell would alert those above and the unfortunate victim – a proverbial *dead ringer* – could be rescued. As intriguing a tale as this is, it is sadly not the true origin of *saved by the bell*, which instead derives from boxing matches brought to a premature end before a weaker fighter is knocked out. It is nonetheless true that designs and patents for so-called 'safety coffins' fitted with bells were produced until as recently as the nineteenth century.

8. SQUARE MEAL

Popular history claims that *square meals* derive from sailors in the Royal Navy being served their heartiest meal of the day on square plates or trays, which could be easily handled and stacked away securely even in rough seas. There is no doubt that square-shaped plates were once used by the Navy, but the fact that all the earliest recorded references to *square meals* come from exclusively American sources suggests this is not its true origin. Instead, in this context *square* means 'solid' or 'substantial', the same sense as found in expressions like *fair and square* and *to call something square.* One of its earliest known uses comes from an 1865 advertisement in *Harper's Magazine* for 'The Howling Wilderness Saloon' in Virginia: for just fifty cents, the Saloon offered a *square meal* which it explained 'is not, as may be supposed, a meal placed upon the table in the form of a solid cubic block, but a substantial repast of pork and beans, onions, cabbage and other articles of sustenance that will serve to fill up the corners of a miner's stomach'.

9. UNDER YOUR HAT

A popular myth claims that keeping something *under your hat* and thereby keeping it secret derives from the Hundred Years War, when British soldiers would apparently keep spare bowstrings and arrowheads under their helmets so as to keep them dry. Whether or not this practice was ever employed is irrelevant, as the phrase did not appear in the language until the late nineteenth century, several hundred years later. Keeping something *under your hat* implies simply 'keeping it in your head' and so not telling anyone.

10. WILD GOOSE CHASE

It is often wrongly presumed that anything referred to as a *wild goose chase* is said to be literally as futile or as difficult as trying to chase after a wild goose. In fact the phrase is not a 'wild-goose chase', but rather a 'wild goose-chase'; its true origin is an old form of horse racing in which a leading rider would set an especially winding and difficult course, which would then be copied as accurately as possible by a second horseman, and then a third and so on, in much the same way as one goose follows immediately behind another in flight. Originally mentioned in Shakespeare's *Romeo and Juliet* (II. iii), soon this kind of follow-my-leader race came to be generally applied to any tricky or erratic course, and eventually any particularly convoluted or time-consuming search.

XLVIII

TEN PHRASES OF UNKNOWN ORIGIN

Sometimes there is simply not enough evidence to be able to present any potential origin of a word or phrase. The ten phrases listed here are perhaps among the most familiar in this entire book, but they are all complete mysteries.

1. APPLE-PIE ORDER

Apple-pie order is an old English expression referring to perfect neatness or absolute organization, while an *apple-pie bed* is one where the sheets have been folded so tightly that it is almost impossible to climb into it. Both terms first appeared in the 1780s, but from where they are derived is a mystery. One theory suggests that *apple pie* might be a corruption of the French *cap-à-pied*, meaning 'head to foot', or *nappes pliées*, meaning 'folded covers' or 'folded cloths', but neither of these ideas seems any more likely than the other.

2. BLACK SHEEP

Quite why an estranged or dishonoured family member should be known as a *black sheep* is unknown. *Black* might simply mean 'adverse' or 'unfavourable' here as it does in *black market* or *black mood*. It might be a more practical term, alluding to the fact that a black sheep's wool would be harder to dye than a white fleece, and so would be of lesser value to a farmer. Or perhaps it comes from an old biblical story in which the shepherd Jacob requested all of the 'black sheep among the lambs' as payment for his many years of loyal service. Which (if any) of these explanations is correct remains unclear.

3. BOB'S YOUR UNCLE

A number of potential origins of *Bob's your uncle* have been proposed over the years, ranging from some kind of reference to the bob at the end of a pendulum to the use of 'bob' to mean 'accomplice' among nineteenth-century criminals, and even to some kind of confusion between 'Bob' and 'God'. A more convincing idea is that the *Bob* in question was Prime Minister Robert Gascoyne-Cecil, Third Marquis of Salisbury, who made his nephew (and future Prime Minister) Arthur Balfour the Chief Secretary of Ireland in 1900. His appointment was widely criticized at the time as Balfour had little diplomatic experience and had seemingly only been given the high-ranking position because, quite literally, Bob was his uncle. However, the fact that the earliest record of *Bob's your uncle* dates from the mid-1920s, more than two decades after Balfour's promotion, suggests that this theory too is far from certain.

4. BREAK A LEG

Actors are a notoriously superstitious group who, alongside avoiding whistling and mentioning Shakespeare's 'Scottish play' by name, have long considered it bad luck to wish 'good luck', and instead tell one another to *break a leg*. The phrase's origin is a mystery, with an array of potential explanations ranging from a performer crouching to pick up flowers thrown onto the stage, to some kind of confusion with an actor having his 'big break' in a particularly successful production. One story even connects it to John Wilkes Booth, the American actor who assassinated Abraham Lincoln in Washington DC's Ford's Theatre in 1865, who apparently broke his leg as he leapt the 3.5 m (12 ft) drop between the president's box and the stage as he made his escape.

5. COCK AND BULL STORY

Describing anything fanciful as *cock and bull* dates from the seventeenth century. A popular explanation claims the phrase refers to the bantering rivalry between two taverns, The Cock and The Bull, in the Buckinghamshire village of Stony Stratford, north of London. While it is certainly true that these two inns exist (and a good-natured rivalry between two neighbouring English pubs is certainly plausible), the fact that an identical expression, *coq-à-l'âne,* has existed in French since around the same time casts doubt on this explanation. Perhaps the original *cock and bull story* was some ancient fable or long-lost folktale, but what that tale was – if indeed it ever existed – remains entirely unknown.

6. As HAPPY AS LARRY

As happy as Larry has been used to describe a state of utter contentment since the mid-1870s, when the phrase first appeared in New Zealand before spreading to Australian and then British English. So who was Larry? A possible contender is Larry Foley, a nineteenth-century champion middleweight boxer born in Bathurst in 1849, who remained undefeated throughout his career and was one of the biggest boxing stars of his day. Alternatively, *Larry* might not be a 'who' but a 'what': a *larrikin* was a yob or a hooligan in nineteenth-century New Zealand slang, while a *larrie* was a gag or a practical joke. Which of these is the proverbially happy *Larry* it is impossible to say.

7. RAINING CATS AND DOGS

The phrase *raining cats and dogs* has been used to describe a heavy rainstorm since the mid-seventeenth century. Several different theories of its origin have been suggested over the years, ranging from straightforward explanations claiming that it is a corruption of the French word for 'waterfall', *catadoupe,* or else a reference to the size or noise made by heavy raindrops, through to ever more outlandish tales of cats and dogs being lifted up into the air by windstorms and even witches' cats and dogs being used to cast spells commanding the weather. Surprisingly for such a light-hearted phrase however, perhaps the most likely explanation is that it alludes to the bodies of dead animals being swept away by floodwaters: in his poem 'A Description of a City Shower' in 1710, Jonathan Swift grimly wrote of 'Drowned puppies, stinking sprats, all drenched in mud, / Dead cats, and turnips-tops' that all 'come tumbling down the flood.'

8. *It's not over* TILL THE FAT LADY SINGS

Implying that there is still time for an outcome to change, *it's not over till the fat lady sings* is often presumed to derive from the stereotypical image of an oversized soprano thundering out the grand climactic aria of an opera. Some explanations even point to Richard Wagner's 1848 opera *Götterdämmerung* for the phrase's specific inspiration, as it famously concludes with the Valkyrie Brünnhilde riding her horse into a funeral pyre and burning to death – but not until after she has completed her exhausting fifteen-minute swansong. The first written evidence of the eponymous *fat lady* dates from no earlier than the 1970s, however, when the phrase initially appeared in a number of sports reports in the southern United States. Almost a century after Wagner's death and about as far removed from Bavarian opera as it is possible to be, all this casts doubt on the traditional image of the operatic *fat lady*, while reports of an earlier similar expression in local southern American slang, *church ain't out till the fat lady sings*, might even suggest that it originally referred to some famously large local choirmistress.

9. *The* WHOLE NINE YARDS

Meaning 'everything' or 'all the way', *the whole nine yards* is one of the most problematic and mysterious expressions in the entire language. Dozens of different explanations of its history have been suggested over the years, among them the idea that the original *whole nine yards* referred to the full untied length of a hangman's noose; the nine cubic yards of earth displaced in digging a communal grave; the nine-yard-long machine-gun belts used on aircraft in the Second World War; the nine cubic yards of concrete or garbage held in a standard truck; the nine yards of material required to make the best suits, veils, kilts, saris, or even nuns' habits; the nine yards of open ground between the wall of a prison and the outer fence; and even the nine yards of intestines supposedly removed in a ritual disembowelment. For many years the phrase was presumed to have been a post-war invention but research carried out as recently as 2013 has since antedated it to 1908, making any explanation referring to fighting aircraft and garbage trucks just as questionable as medieval disembowelment. Either way, its true origin remains unsolved.

10. *The* WHOLE SHEBANG

When it first appeared in American slang in the 1860s, *shebang* referred to some kind of temporary wooden hut or shed. In 1869, Mark Twain used it to mean 'the current topic' or 'the matter at hand'. Three years later he used it again as the name of a type of coach. An 1878 *American Sportsman's Glossary* confused things even more by defining a *shebang* as 'any sort of structure, from a shanty to a hotel', but by the early 1900s it seems to have specifically become another name for an inn or tavern. *The whole shebang,* meaning 'the whole thing', finally emerged in the 1920s. Its origin, and that of the word from which it is derived, remains unknown.

XLIX

TEN PECULIAR EXPRESSIONS

When the English language gets strange, it gets very strange. From a naval title bestowed on a vomiting friend to a cloud formation named after a Turkish martyr, the ten expressions listed here have been selected for nothing more than their peculiarity.

1. ADMIRAL OF THE NARROW SEAS

In the seventeenth and eighteenth centuries, an odd trend appeared in naval slang of bestowing invented titles on certain people or characters. An *admiral of the red*, for instance, was a heavy drinker; an *admiral of the white* was a coward; an *admiral of the blue* was a publican, so-called as he would typically wear a blue apron; and an *admiral of the red, white and blue* was anyone ludicrously overdressed, referring to the ostentatious uniforms of certain public officials at the time. By far the strangest of all of these titles was *admiral of the narrow seas*, defined in one eighteenth-century slang dictionary as 'one who from drunkenness vomits into the lap of the person sitting opposite to him'; a *vice admiral of the narrow seas* was 'a drunken man that pisses under the table into his companions' shoes'.

2. BARBARA AND HER BAIRNS

The old Yorkshire expression *Barbara and her bairns* describes a particular cloud formation comprising a thick bank of cloud in the western sky flanked by two smaller banks, one above and one below, known as its 'children' or 'bairns'. The *Barbara* in question is St Barbara, a third-century Turkish martyr whose name is invoked as protection against thunder and lightning. According to accounts of her life, having discovered that she had converted to Christianity Barbara's father beheaded her, only to be killed himself immediately afterward by a thunderbolt. St Barbara is also the patron saint of artillery, gunpowder and explosions and her feast day, 4 December, is often observed by the Royal Artillery, the US Army and the US Marine Corps Artillery, which awards an Order of Saint Barbara to some of its members.

3. THE BURYING'S GONE BY AND THE CHILD'S CALLED ANTHONY

The burying's gone by and the child's called Anthony is an old Yorkshire and Lancashire expression once used when someone arrives too late for something and has missed the point of their visit. The image is presumably that of someone turning up late for a church funeral, only to discover that *the burying's gone by* and that the church is now full of people celebrating the christening of a *child called Anthony*. First recorded in this form in the late nineteenth century, on its own *the burying's gone by* is an even earlier expression of tardiness dating from the late 1700s.

4. DICK'S HATBAND

In the eighteenth century, *Dick's hatband* became a popular point of reference in English slang, to which anything particularly unusual or out-of-the-ordinary was proverbially compared. To be *as tight* or *as queer as Dick's hatband* meant that something was very peculiar indeed, although an array of different versions of the phrase soon began to appear which variously described *Dick's hatband* as *fine, old, plain, false, crooked* and even *cursed*. By the nineteenth century it had crossed the Atlantic to America, where it also came to refer to anything ramshackle or makeshift, and has remained in infrequent use ever since. Precisely where it comes from, however, is unknown. While some accounts claim *Dick* is really *Old Nick*, the Devil, the most commonly held suggestion is that *Dick* was originally Richard Cromwell (IN THE REIGN OF QUEEN DICK) whose short-lived rule as Lord Protector after the death of his father Oliver Cromwell in 1658 could have come to imply that the crown of England (the *hatband*) was a poor fit for him.

5. *To* DIE THROUGH WANT OF LOBSTER SAUCE

Proverbially, *to die through want of a lobster sauce* is to suffer or torment oneself over a relatively minor issue or irritation. The phrase supposedly alludes to a tale from French history in which Louis de Bourbon, a seventeenth-century *général* of the French Army, decided to throw a lavish banquet for the king, Louis XIV. Bourbon's chef took it upon himself to produce the most extravagant menu he could muster, including among its many dishes a rich lobster sauce. But when the fresh lobsters he required failed to be delivered in time, he was so overcome with shame and disappointment that he threw himself onto his sword.

6. *To* FORGET THAT THE MISSION WAS TO DRAIN THE SWAMP

In its entirety, the Americanism *to forget that the mission was to drain the swamp when you're up to your neck* (or *your ass*) *in alligators* is used to imply that when setting out to do a particular job or task, it is easy to become sidetracked by some other issue and ultimately lose sight of your original goal – when fighting off alligators, the objective of draining their swamp becomes less important. The phrase dates from the 1970s and is thought to have its origins in American politics, where *draining the swamp* was once used as a metaphor for removing corruption and sleaze from the US government.

7. *To* GUANO THE MIND

Guano is a natural manure formed from the accumulated excrement of huge flocks of tropical seabirds. In the eighteenth century, European explorers to South America and the Pacific – notably Alexander von Humboldt – discovered that it was an excellent fertilizer and 'guano mining' soon became big business. By the mid-nineteenth century *guano* had become a byword for anything that nourished or fertilized, and in his 1847 novel *Tancred, or The New Crusade*, the writer (and future British Prime Minister) Benjamin Disraeli wrote of one his characters having 'guanoed her mind by reading French novels'.

8. IF MY AUNT WAS A MAN SHE'D BE MY UNCLE

If my aunt was a man she'd be my uncle has been used in English since the mid-seventeenth century as a sarcastic response to anyone who has stated the obvious, or anyone who has based their argument on some spurious or unrealistic condition: 'if only *x* had happened, then *y* could have happened' / 'Yes, and if my aunt was a man, she'd have been my uncle.' Similarly sarcastic replies include *Queen Anne is dead* and *The Dutch have taken Holland*, both eighteenth-century examples of 'old news' used in response to anyone who excitedly tells a story or piece of gossip that is already widely known.

9. MOLL THOMPSON'S MARK

Wondering who *Moll Thompson* was is irrelevant here, as all that really matters is the fact that her initials MT can be read as 'empty', and so in the 1700s and 1800s saying that your bottle or glass had *Moll Thompson's mark* on it meant that you had finished your drink. The phrase probably originated among sailors' and dockworkers' slang, who would supposedly mark empty packages and crates with the letters 'MT'.

10. PAPER TRUNK AND A TWINE LOCK

English is home to a handful of strange *papery* sayings and phrases, many of which relate to its thinness or flimsiness: as defined in a 1909 dictionary of *Passing English of the Victorian Era*, a *paper trunk and a twine lock* is 'the least possible amount of luggage packed in an old news sheet and stringed'. Similarly, *paper-skull* was a late-seventeenth-century nickname for a fool or simpleton; an eighteenth-century *phrase of paper* was an eighth of a sheet, and hence any small notelet or business card; and a nineteenth-century *paper marriage* was one born out of convenience or financial gain rather than love.

L

TEN GOODBYES

Appropriately enough for the final chapter, here are ten phrases and sayings that either concern escape or departure, or else can be used in place of your run-of-the-mill goodbyes.

1. *To* AMPUTATE THE MAHOGANY

To cut your stick, meaning 'to leave', was a popular Irish expression in the mid-eighteenth century thought to allude to the practice of 'cutting' or fashioning a makeshift walking stick from the fallen branch of a tree. By the mid-nineteenth century it had presumably become such a familiar turn of phrase that it fell victim to a peculiar trend in Victorian slang of substituting the words of a phrase or saying with direct synonyms to create an entirely new expression, and so *cut* became *amputate*, and the *stick* became *mahogany*; in another version, *cut your stick* became *saw your timber*.

2. HASTA LA VISTA

Widely popularized in the 1990s as the catchphrase of Arnold Schwarzenegger's title character in *Terminator 2: Judgment Day*, the Spanish farewell *hasta la vista* literally translates as 'until the (next) sight', or essentially 'until I see you again'. It is one of a number of foreign goodbyes to have been adopted into English over the years, alongside other Spanish expressions like *hasta luego* (literally 'until then') and *hasta mañana* ('until tomorrow'). The Italian *arrivederci* and French *au revoir* both mean 'to the seeing again', while the French *adieu*, first recorded in English in the fourteenth century, derives from the French word for 'God'.

3. MOONLIGHT FLIT

The phrase *moonlight flit* has been used since the early nineteenth century to refer to the practice of leaving a hotel without paying the bill, or absconding from rented accommodation without paying the landlord. Similarly, *to do a moonlight* and *to shoot the moon* both mean 'to leave under cover of darkness', while *to go between the moon and the milkman* means 'to go after dark and before dawn'.

4. MORITURI TE SALUTANT

The Latin address *morituri te salutant* is usually translated into English as 'those who are about to die, we salute you'. Popular history has long associated this phrase with gladiatorial battles in Ancient Rome, and a common misconception is that this would have been an audience's final respectful 'salute' to the gladiators about to begin a fight to the death in a Roman arena. In fact the reverse was true: the 'salute' was given *by* 'those who are about to die' to the emperor, the implication being that should they be killed they would be unable to show their respect after the fighting had ended. That this farewell salute was used before *all* gladiatorial combats is another misconception, as it is only recorded at one event in the entire history of Rome: a great *naumachia*, an enormous staged sea battle, organized by Emperor Claudius in AD 52.

Mock naval battles were a lavish yet relatively common form of entertainment in Ancient Rome and amphitheatres were often intentionally flooded in order to accommodate them. Uniquely, however, Claudius's immense *naumachia* was held on a lake near Avezzano in central Italy, and all those made to take part (the *naumachiarii*) were convicted criminals and murderers who had been sentenced to battle one another to death for the emperor's entertainment in a spectacular 'death by massacre'. It was these *naumachiarii*, the Roman historian Suetonius explains, who saluted the emperor with the words *morituri te salutant*, and apparently the phrase was never used again.

5. MY NAME IS HAINES

Sometime in the early 1800s, the American President Thomas Jefferson was out riding near his home in Virginia when he happened across another man on his horse who joined him for the rest of his journey. Unfortunately, the man failed to recognize the president and in his ignorance began a lengthy conversation in which he continually bad-mouthed the government and criticized Jefferson's leadership. After some time the pair reached Jefferson's home and, unperturbed, he invited the man inside. He accepted, but as he was about to come down from his horse, he finally asked his companion's name. 'Thomas Jefferson,' the president replied. The man paused for a moment before stating bluntly, 'My name is Haines', and galloping away. This anecdote, apparently a personal favourite of Jefferson's during his lifetime, led *my name is Haines* to become a popular expression in mid-nineteenth-century America, used whenever it becomes necessary to leave somewhere abruptly or prematurely.

6. SEE YOU LATER, ALLIGATOR

See you later, alligator apparently owes its familiarity to a song of the same name by Bill Haley and His Comets released in 1956 to promote Haley's musical, *Rock Around The Clock*. The song proved a huge success, selling a million copies in America alone, which undoubtedly helped to firmly establish the phrase in the language. Whether it had been in use beforehand or was coined by its writers, however, is unclear.

7. *To* SLING YOUR HOOK

The earliest known use of *sling your hook* in English dates from the mid-nineteenth century, although it is probable that it was in use long before then. Although its origin is debatable, perhaps the most likely explanation is that the *hook* is a ship's anchor, and so *slinging your hook* meant raising your anchor and sailing away; an earlier similar expression was *to cut* or *slip the painter*, referring to the rope used to secure a boat to a quayside, which dates from the seventeenth century.

8. SO LONG

So long is a fine example of an expression whose simplicity and familiarity hide the fact that, out of context, it really does not make a great deal of sense – why would you wish it to be *so long* until you meet again? This might suggest that it was not originally an English phrase, and in fact there are several foreign farewells of which *so long* is often said to be a corruption, including the Irish *slán*, the Hebrew *shalom* and Arabic *salaam.* The most likely explanation, however, is that *so long* derives from one of the languages of northern Europe, and would originally have been adopted into American English in the eighteenth or nineteenth century via immigrants speaking German (*so lange*), Swedish (*hej så länge*) or Norwegian (*adjø så lenge!*)

9. TAKE A POWDER!

Telling someone *to take a powder* – or specifically *a run-out* or *walk-out powder* – has been used in American English to mean 'get out!' since the early 1900s. Little known outside of the US, this phrase is thought to derive from the taking of medicinal powders to relieve all manner of aches and pains, in which case the powder in question might be a 'headache powder', in the sense that the evicted person is being a nuisance, or else a purgative or laxative powder, hence (for obvious reasons) *run-out powder.*

10. WALK YOUR CHALKS!

In 1638, Marie de' Medici, mother of the reigning King Louis XIII of France, paid a visit to England. The queen had been due to stay at a grand mansion in Colchester but brought with her such a vast entourage that in order to secure enough accommodation for the party a number of local townspeople were temporarily evicted. Those with the most spacious homes would find a chalk mark drawn on their front door, indicating that their house had been chosen for the queen's use. This anecdote is often said to be the origin of the eighteenth–nineteenth-century expression *walk your chalks!,* meaning 'get out!' or 'go away!', but as intriguing a tale as this is it is more likely that the phrase originated among English landlords who would apparently once have drawn chalk marks on the doors of tenants who had outstayed their welcome.

INDEX